RUSSIAN POETRY FOR CHILDREN

# RUSSIAN POETRY
## for CHILDREN

Elena Sokol

THE UNIVERSITY OF TENNESSEE PRESS
KNOXVILLE

**Library of Congress Cataloging in Publication Data**

Sokol, Elena, 1943-
  Russian poetry for children.

  Bibliography: p.
  Includes index.
  1. Children's poetry, Russian—History and criticism.
I. Title.
PG3064.C45S6   1984        891.71′4′099282        83-6703
ISBN 0-87049-406-6

FOR SONJA

# CONTENTS

# ILLUSTRATIONS

IN THE SOVIET UNION the study of children's literature has been a serious endeavor for almost sixty years, producing much scholarship on both Russian and foreign works. In the United States, on the other hand, where the academic respectability of the subject is of more recent origin, little is known of the Russian tradition. The primary difficulty is that few children's books in Russian other than folktales are available in English translation, whereas Winnie-the-Pooh speaks superb Russian. So do Alice, Peter Pan, Doctor Dolittle, and Tom Sawyer, to mention but the best-known examples. English nursery rhymes are an integral part of Russian children's poetry—some children do not even realize they are of foreign provenance. Our lack of familiarity with Russian children's literature is the more regrettable since it has strong historical ties with our own Anglo-American tradition.

More than half a century after English rhymes were first transposed into Russian, we should begin to correct the imbalance. Publishers of children's books must be made aware of the untapped wealth awaiting discovery. More translators should be encouraged to turn to Russian children's literature. In the meantime, it is up to those of us who have access to those riches to share them with others—hence the present work, which introduces an important phenomenon of modern Russian culture: poetry for young children.

The reader is urged to keep in mind that the poetic tradition—both folk and literary—is more palpable in Russia than it is in our culture. Russians know and love their poetry intensely. For them it is part of daily life, rather than an esoteric experience. It is not surprising, then, that children's poetry rivals prose in popularity, especially in the literature for preschool children, for whom most of the poetry is written. (In the Soviet Union children enter school at age seven.) Further, in Russian society, where literature has been traditionally considered a political force, children's literature acquires a much more charged significance than it has in the West and must be evaluated in that context. With these considerations in mind, I hope this study will not only contribute to a greater appreciation of children's poetry as such, but will also shed some new light on larger questions of modern Russian culture.

The transliteration of Russian follows the Library of Congress System.

I wish to express my appreciation to the International Research and Exchanges Board for making possible my ten-month stay in Moscow in 1971–1972, when I originally became fascinated with Russian poetry for children; and to the Graduate Research Fund of the University of Washington for the support of my project in the summer of 1978 and for a travel grant to Moscow in September 1979. There are also the innumerable friends and colleagues without whom this book could not have been written: most importantly, Irina Corten, who first suggested that I read Chukovskii's tales one dismal winter day in Moscow; Elena Chukovskaia, who gave generously of time, material, and encouragement; Penelope Kenez and James L. Rice, who commented on several chapters in draft form; and Solomon Ioffe, who in the course of verifying the verse translations proved to have not only the necessary knowledge of a native speaker but also the understanding of a true philologist. I am especially grateful to Hugh McLean and Barry Scherr, whose very attentive reading of the complete manuscript provided me with incisive commentary. Finally, I am indebted to my husband András Fürész, who worked unstintingly to help me prepare the final manuscript.

28 January 1983

# INTRODUCTION

IN THE EARLY YEARS of this century two young Russian men of letters, as yet unknown to one another, spent over a year in England. Each originally set out for London as a foreign correspondent for periodicals in Russia; each in the course of his stay became far more devoted to English literature and culture than to the pursuit of journalism. The first was Kornei Chukovskii, who in 1903–1904 spent long days in the reading room of the British Museum, fascinated by the poetry of Browning, Rossetti, and Swinburne. The second was Samuil Marshak, who nine years later went on from London to tramp the British countryside, living almost a year in an experimental school in Wales. Among the many discoveries they made during their respective sojourns were the English nursery rhymes. At the time, neither man could have anticipated the effect his acquaintance with English children's folklore was to have on the development of Russian children's literature. After the revolution, Chukovskii and Marshak achieved renown as children's poets; among their popular works are Russian versions of English nursery rhymes. These verses did not merely introduce some new poems into Russian; they were a crucial catalyst in the development of modern Russian poetry for children. By the example of the English rhymes Chukovskii and Marshak were encouraged in their own writing to draw upon the rich tradition of Russian children's folklore.

Before the twentieth century there was little poetry written for children in Russia. Children, who for hundreds of years had been treated as diminutive adults, came into their own more slowly there than did their Western counterparts. Although by the nineteenth century there were many periodicals catering ostensibly to a younger audience, their usual contents betrayed an old-fashioned view of the nature of the child. Most were hardly suitable for children younger than ten or twelve, and poetry was inconspicuous. Not until the age of symbolism, beginning at the very end of the nineteenth century—a time of aesthetic reawakening in Russia—

did some interest in writing poetry for children arise. That era of artistic flowering coincided with the growing appreciation of the nature of children and childhood, as witnessed by new developments in psychology.

This beginning recognition was officially encouraged after the revolution, when, along with political changes, the new Soviet government embarked upon a campaign to eliminate widespread illiteracy. Its broad support of all aspects of mass education included children's literature. Chukovskii emerged early as a writer, translator, and polemicist of children's literature. Soon Marshak joined the effort, eventually becoming head of the children's section at the State Publishing House in Leningrad, where he was an important source of motivation for other writers. Among his protégés in the second half of the 1920s were members of the avant-garde Oberiu group, most notably Daniil Kharms. In this time of ferment even the futurist poet Vladimir Maiakovskii wrote poetry for children, as did Osip Mandel'shtam and Boris Pasternak.

For a decade after the revolution, until the consolidation of Stalinist dogma, the cultural scene in the Soviet Union was marked by the continuation of prerevolutionary modernist trends, contributing to a lively intellectual atmosphere. Thus Chukovskii in his poetry echoed not only children's folklore, but "grown-up" futurism as well. Further, through his dedication to creating works of high artistic integrity, external obstacles notwithstanding, he helped establish the legitimacy of children's literature as an art form in the Soviet Union. Consequently, the field has attracted serious poets, some of whom, in the manner of Chukovskii and Marshak, have also earned reputations as fine translators.

Since the Soviet government first designated children's literature as an area of high priority, many have been attracted to create it. A less than pure but inevitable motivating force has always been that of economic survival. Writing for children is a relatively safe means of producing an income—and possibly the only one for writers who, often for reasons of censorship, are unable to publish for adults. Since the 1920s children's literature has offered some of them a place of remunerative refuge. (This situation is comparable to that of literary translation of works for adults, an occupation which has helped sustain many Soviet writers unable to publish their own work.) Some writers—Kharms is a good example—have found in it an outlet for otherwise thwarted ideas. At times the censor may make more allowances for fantasy, as opposed to realism, in children's books than in those for adults.

In a discussion of children's literature, it is essential to keep in mind the historic Russian assumption of the influence of literature on society as a whole. Not only do writers defend the place of children's literature in the larger literary tradition, the Soviet government shares that view and includes children's literature in its broader policies. Consequently, the vagaries of government control can be traced there as clearly as in adult literature. The history of children's poetry reflects the fanatical "proletarian" pronouncements of the 1920s, the essential demise of creativity under Stalin, and a hopeful rebirth after Stalin's death. That rebirth during the "thaw" of the late 1950s and early 1960s is accompanied by a renewed interest in the first and last vital period in Soviet culture—the 1920s. Of particular significance from the Anglo-American point of view is the revival of the "English tradition" introduced by Chukovskii and Marshak. In the most general terms, that tradition—whether it is nursery rhymes, the works of Lewis Carroll, or the poems and stories of A.A. Milne—represents an acute understanding of children and an ability to communicate with them on their own terms, through fantasy and play. In Russia that understanding and ability to communicate was demonstrated, above all, by Kornei Chukovskii, after his encounter with the "English tradition." Therefore it is with him that the story of Russian children's poetry must begin.

As will be seen, in the ensuing chapters Chukovskii's presence is largest, though by no means exclusive. This is in direct proportion to the overwhelming importance of his place in the history of Russian children's poetry in our century. His role may be said to be tripartite—and any one of the parts alone would be sufficient to assure his significance. First, there is his extensive investigation into early language acquisition and developmental psychology, especially concerned with children's own linguistic creativity, the results of which are to be found in his book *From Two to Five*. The pursuit of these interests, fueled by his closeness to his own children and by his fascination with the language and folklore of children, led him to formulate "commandments" for children's poets. These also constitute a highly useful method for the analysis of all poetry written for children. This method can be used to identify the special characteristics of children's folklore, as well as to reveal the inadequacies of most of the poetry written for Russian children before the early twentieth century. Second, Chukovskii's brilliant poems, the verse tales, remain unparalleled achievements to this day. Although he was not alone in his endeavors—Marshak and

Kharms were also major children's poets in the 1920s—Chukovskii was the outstanding pioneer. Finally, both his poetry and his theoretical work inspired not only his contemporaries in the early Soviet period, but also the younger, post-Stalin generation. For more than half a century his contribution has remained preeminent—and immensely popular.

RUSSIAN POETRY FOR CHILDREN

# 1

## KORNEI CHUKOVSKII AND HIS POETICS

KORNEI CHUKOVSKII (1882–1969) is one of those rare intellectual figures in the twentieth century who truly deserves to be called a literary Renaissance man.[1] During his long life he achieved fame in three related fields. A youthful background in journalism led him first to literary criticism, then to scholarship, and eventually to reminiscences. At a relatively early stage in his career he became a translator and later a theoretician of the art of translation. His third area of interest—the one for which he is best known both at home and abroad—was children's literature, above all poetry. In that field also, he was both a practitioner and a theoretician.

In 1901, at the age of nineteen, Chukovskii began his career by contributing articles—largely reviews of books and art exhibits—to the *Odessa News* (*Odesskie novosti*). Seeking to gain poetic mastery, he translated poetry from English, a language he started teaching himself while in his teens. Later in St. Petersburg, during the political turmoil of 1905, he wrote verse for his short-lived satirical weekly *The Signal* and for other similar periodicals. Before the revolution he also published lyric poems in the popular liberal journal *Plowland* (*Niva*).[2] Although he was not destined to become even a minor adult poet, he was immensely successful as a children's poet, and up to the present his verse tales are favorites not just of children but of their parents as well.

A crucial early experience contributed to Chukovskii's development as a children's writer: his first visit to London in 1903–1904, where he was sent by his Odessa newspaper as a foreign correspondent.[3] After his newspaper assignment fell through, Chukovskii spent his days reading in the British Museum. Despite his material hardship, he welcomed the opportunity to work toward perfecting his English and to become better acquainted with English literature. He discovered English nursery rhymes: "During my sojourn in England I literally fell in love with the ancient folk songs for children, the so-called 'nursery rhymes'. . . . The opulent fantasy of their daring fancifulness entranced me forever, and I studied their poetics and their ancient and modern history assiduously."[4] Later he adapted some of the rhymes for Russian children, as did Marshak, following his stay in England.

Before turning to children's literature, Chukovskii became established as a provocative interpreter of the contemporary literary scene in St. Petersburg. Upon his return from England he wrote for Valerii Briusov's symbolist journal *The Scales* (*Vesy*), joined in the journalistic struggles of the 1905 revolution, and then went on to work for the liberal press. It was at this time that he met the painter Il'ia Repin and the writers Vladimir Korolenko, Leonid Andreev, Aleksei Tolstoi, Aleksandr Kuprin, and Vladimir Maiakovskii, among others. He was an active and well-known participant in the cultural milieu about which he wrote.

Chukovskii first entered the world of children's literature as if through the back door. His original interest was confined to that of a demanding literary critic and a concerned parent.[5] In 1907 he embarked on a series of polemical reviews and articles, decrying the prevailing trends of literature addressed to Russian children.

> Poetry—that's what is abominably provided for in children's magazines. We do not have any children's poets. Instead there are gloomy personalities who, arousing compassion in each of us, give tortured birth to despondent verses about Easter and Christmas, about little brooks and sleds; for whom it is easier to find a needle in a haystack than to avoid the unavoidable "really", "only", "even",

"suddenly", "in a flash" [*uzh, lish', azh, vdrug, vmig*]; for whom meter is a curse and rhyme the mark of Cain.[6]

Chukovskii first tried his own hand at writing what he found so "abominably provided for" in the same year, when he published the poem "Wind" ("Veter") in *The Path* (*Tropinka*), one of the children's magazines he considered of higher quality than most. Addressed to Kolen'ka, his firstborn son, this long-forgotten attempt incorporates stylized elements from the folk tradition, later to be a recurrent motif of his work.

Two years later, in 1909, Chukovskii first addressed himself to questions of children's language, a subject that was to become one of the chief preoccupations of his life. In his initial article he dealt with the amazingly creative, even poetic qualities of small children's utterances, concluding with a request he would frequently reiterate over the years. "I ask all those who are in some way or other close to children to write down for me all the childish words and expressions that strike them for whatever reason, and to send them to me. . . . We might just hit upon something."[7] Little did Chukovskii realize just how much he would "hit upon" with his innocent appeal. From that time on he regularly received great quantities of mail from interested adults, who endlessly provided him with examples of children's speech. In 1911 he collected the articles on children's literature and language that he had published to date in a small book, *To Mothers on Children's Magazines* (*Materiam o detskikh zhurnalakh*). Therein lay the kernel of his later major work on children's langauge, psychology, and literature—*From Two to Five* (*Ot dvukh do piati*).

In the same year the Sweetbriar (Shipovnik) Publishing House announced *The Firebird* (*Zhar-ptitsa*), a forthcoming periodical for children—with Chukovskii and Aleksandr Benois, prominent member of the World of Art group, as chief editors. They conceived *The Firebird* as an alternative to the colorless, moralizing fare available to children. Although *The Firebird* never became the regular publication promised, a one-volume collection did appear in 1912.[8] Its main contributors were Chukovskii, Sasha Chërnyi, Tolstoi, Mariia Moravskaia, and Sergei Sergeev-Tsenskii. To complement these writers the editors attracted excellent artists to do the illustrations, including Sergei Sudeikin, Sergei Chekhonin, and Mstislav Dobuzhinskii.

In the perspective of his eventual career as a children's writer, Chukovskii's contributions to *The Firebird* were modest. "The Dog

Kingdom" ("Sobach'e Tsar'stvo")—a ten-page story based on an admittedly borrowed but unidentified plot—is an undistinguished didactic tale, in which two boys who mistreat their dog are punished by exile to the "dog kingdom" until they promise to behave better in the future. "Little Chick" ("Tsyplënok")—still reprinted from time to time—is a simple, descriptive prose piece for little children, with accompanying drawings by Chekhonin that rival the text in importance. *The Firebird* also contained Chukovskii's second children's poem—"The Doctor" ("Doktor"), which introduced in a playful way the theme of a sick animal, vaguely anticipating the writer's later love of *Doctor Dolittle*.

Chukovskii's generally acknowledged debut as a children's poet came in 1916, when he wrote his first *skazka* (literally, folktale, but in this context, verse tale)—"The Crocodile" ("Krokodil"). Retrospectively the poet attributed the creation of that tale to two events. On a train to Finland in September 1916, Chukovskii became acquainted with his famous older contemporary, the writer Maksim Gor'kii. During the ride they shared their dissatisfaction with the kind of literature generally available to Russian children and agreed on the need for something better. Gor'kii scolded Chukovskii for merely writing polemical articles; he accused him of constantly criticizing others but never trying to write for children himself. Gor'kii urged him "just to try."[9] Chukovskii accepted the challenge but found he could produce nothing worthwhile upon command, at least not upon adult command. Not long after his meeting with Gor'kii, he made another memorable train trip.

> It happened that my little son became ill and I had to tell him a story. He became ill in the city of Helsinki. I took him home on the night train. He was fussy, cried and moaned. To placate him with something I began to recite to the rhythmic din of the racing train:

> Zhil da býl          (Once upon a time there was
> Krokodíl.            a crocodile.
> On po úlitsam khodíl . . .   He strolled the streets . . .)

> The verse came all by itself. I did not trouble about its form at all. And not for a minute did I think it had any relationship whatsoever to art. I had only a single concern—to distract the attention of a sick child from an oncoming illness.[10]

The next day the boy insisted that his father retell the tale. With the help of the child's phenomenal memory Chukovskii recreated the entire epic, this time transcribing it. Later that autumn he offered it to a respectable publishing house that produced luxurious volumes in gold-embossed covers. The editor's reaction, not unusual for that time, was overwhelmingly negative: "This is a book for street urchins!" Then Chukovskii turned to A.F. Marks, the publisher of *Plowland.* As a result of their discussion, Chukovskii became the editor of a new children's supplement that appeared monthly throughout the year 1917. There in twelve installments he published "Vania and the Crocodile" ("Vania i krokodil"), as the tale was originally called. Almost immediatley after the revolution, despite the acute paper shortage, the Petrograd Soviet printed "The Crocodile" in a mass edition with its original, striking cartoon-like illustrations by Re-Mi. For a while the tale was even distributed free of charge as a political leaflet, since there were always some adults anxious to read its fanciful attack against tyrannical despotism as political allegory in support of the Bolshevik regime.[11]

After their meeting in 1916, Gor'kii invited Chukovskii to the Sail (Parus) Publishing House to help start a children's division there. Together they planned a series of literary almanacs; the first one appeared, after much delay, in January 1918. Although the series never materialized, owing largely to the turmoil of those early post-revolutionary days, the single volume that did appear remains a landmark—the first Soviet book for children. Gor'kii and Chukovskii were determined to attract truly professional writers, both old and young, to write for children. Among those reputed to have been invited were the poets Marina Tsvetaeva, Vladislav Khodasevich, Vladimir Maiakovskii, and Sergei Esenin. While Maiakovskii eventually did write poetry for children, neither he nor any of the other poets in fact contributed to the volume. Among those who did were several of the writers who had written for *The Firebird*—Sasha Chërnyi, Aleksei Tolstoi, Mariia Moravskaia—and also Valerii Briusov and Natan Vengrov. As in *The Firebird*, illustrations by such fine artists as Repin, Dobuzhinskii, Chekhonin, Benois, Vladimir Lebedev, A.A. Radakov, and Iurii Annenkov were an important part of the work. Ironically, at the last moment the publisher insisted on changing the title from *Rainbow (Raduga)* to *The Fir Tree (Elka)* and replaced the original cover design with an all-too-familiar picture of little angels lighting candles on a Christmas tree topped by a Christ child. The revolution in children's literature was far from complete.[12]

During the years immediately following the revolution, Chukovskii was involved with several all-consuming literary projects. Gor'kii selected him to head the Anglo-American division of the publishing house World Literature (Vsemirnaia literatura), where he actively participated in a translation workshop. This in turn led him to establish, with Gor'kii's help, the House of the Arts (Dom iskusstv), which for three years (1919–1922) served as a center of physical refuge and intellectual stimulation for writers, artists, and musicians in Petrograd.[13] Thus Chukovskii was easily kept busy lecturing, translating, and editing, and he found little time to think about children's literature. Furthermore, it was no simple matter for him to reactivate the talent for creating poetry for children revealed by his experience with "The Crocodile." He could not conjure up those lively lines at will. As he later described it, the process was excruciatingly difficult, except during special periods of inspiration.

> Suddenly, for no reason at all—under any circumstances—usually in the summertime when I meet with children more often than with adults, I feel the pressure of some unexpected music in a major key, of some joyful rhythms and holiday words, and I become a poet—for three or four hours. Then—stop!—all the music within me comes to an end no matter how I try . . . I can no longer compose even a single line of poetry. A minute earlier I was literally choking on clear, resilient verses, barely succeeding in writing them down, and now I have grown mute and lifeless . . .[14]

Most of Chukovskii's poetry came in such bursts. "The Cockroach" ("Tarakanishche") and "Wash'em Clean" ("Moidodyr") poured forth on successive days in 1921, while he was ostensibly preoccupied with writing an article on Nekrasov's long satirical poem "Contemporaries" ("Sovremenniki"). After entertaining his children with these tales, Chukovskii filed them away in a drawer, feeling no one would be interested in publishing them. Some time later, in a moment of financial distress, he retrieved them and offered them to several publishing houses—with no success. Then the poems were discovered by his friend Lev Kliachko, a former journalist, who responded to them as would a delighted child. Kliachko arranged to have them published with illustrations by Iurii Annenkov and Sergei Chekhonin, artists well acquainted with the poet. (Both had made drawings for *The Fir Tree*.) From this venture emerged Rainbow (Raduga), a small publishing house specializing in children's books. During its existence in the 1920s it printed most of Chukovskii's works and gradually attracted a solid contingent of writers, among them Marshak.[15]

For a while Chukovskii was prolific as a children's poet. "The Cockroach" and "Wash'em Clean" were published in 1923, followed by "Chatterbox Fly" ("Mukha-tsokotukha," 1924), "Barmalei" (1925), and "Fedora's Misfortune" ("Fedorino gore"), "Wonder Tree" ("Chudo-derevo"), "The Telephone," ("Telefon"), and "The Muddle" ("Putanitsa"), all in 1926. Thereafter his tempo diminished rapidly. Over the next decade he created only three more tales—"Ouch-it-hurts" ("Aibolit," 1929—inspired by Lofting's *Dr. Dolittle*), "The Stolen Sun" ("Kradenoe solntse," 1933), "Toptygin and the Fox" ("Toptygin i lisa," 1934)—and several short poems and adaptations of children's folk rhymes. An overtly propagandistic tale, "Let's Overcome Barmalei" ("Odoleem Barmaleia," 1943) appeared during the war but was never reprinted later. At the end of the war came "Bibigon" (1946), a tale in verse and prose—his last major work for children and distinctly inferior to the earlier ones.

Already by the late 1920s Chukovskii's moments of inspiration had largely disappeared. In retrospect, he himself admitted that by the time he was working on "Ouch-it-hurts" he no longer felt that "former musical wave which would carry [him] along". Not all adults greeted his tales with the fervor of his friend Kliachko. In fact, from the mid-1920s, Chukovskii was continually forced to defend the central and legitimate place of imagination in the lives of children. "My tales were received at bayonet point. The 'leftist pedologists' and other 'people in cases' [cheloveki v futliare] who at that time were sheltered at the Commissariat of Education fell on them in a throng. They were shocked by the new, unusual poetic form, by the fantastic subject matter, by the disparity between my ingenious thematics and their dead, bureaucratic formulas."[16] Until the early 1930s, Chukovskii engaged in a bitter polemic, which in the microcosm of children's literature reflected important features of the larger literary debate of that period.

The leftist pedologists supported an educational trend which in many respects paralleled the proletarian movement in literature. Simply stated, their goal was the total politicization of children's literature. At a very early age children were to be introduced to serious topics of real life, not to the unreal gibberish of fairy tales. Vociferously and relentlessly opposed to any manifestation of fantasy, the pedologists expurgated folk and fairy tales from recommended reading lists and library shelves. They were of the opinion that anthropomorphism and verbal play could only confuse the minds of children. Their virtual reign of terror came to an end in 1932, as did that of the Russian Association of Proletarian Writers (RAPP), when Stalin dissolved rival cultural organizations and established centralized government control over the arts.[17]

Chukovskii's tales, full of anthropomorphized beasts and animated objects, were an easy and primary target. His playful approach, labeled "Chukovskiism" (Chukovshchina) by his opponents, became the focus of a heated debate.[18] Among the most infamous of the attacks was a vicious tirade in *Pravda* by Lenin's widow Krupskaia against "The Crocodile."[19] (I have included a translation of it in the Appendix, since it provides excellent insight into the proletarian era.) Despite the strength of his convictions, by the end of 1929 Chukovskii, as so many others, broke down under the steady barrage of vehement criticism. He publicly rejected his children's books as old-fashioned and affirmed the need to write new ones about the future.[20] Fortunately, he turned out to be incapable of carrying out that task.

Although the destructive role of the proletarian movement most obviously hurt Chukovskii's writing for children, it was not the sole factor affecting his work. By the 1930s his immediate source of inspiration, his own children, had left him. Three had already grown up; and his youngest, the beloved Mura, died tragically of bone tuberculosis in 1931.

By 1934, the year socialist realism was proclaimed the official artistic "method" in the Soviet Union, Chukovskii's actively creative phase as a children's poet was over. In the 1930s he wrote two autobiographical novellas for school-age children. *Solnechnaia* (1932), based on his encounters at the children's sanatorium where he used to visit his ailing daughter, apparently dissatisfied him and was not reprinted after 1939. *Gymnasium* (*Gimnaziia*, 1938), inspired by his own boyhood, was later published in an expanded version as *The Silver Crest* (*Serebriannyi gerb*).[21] During this period Chukovskii also devoted much time to translating fiction for children.[22] After World War II, when cultural life in the Soviet Union reached its nadir, Chukovskii was attacked for writing "Bibigon."[23] With that attack his children's poetry fell into official disfavor, which lasted until Stalin's death, when Chukovskii reemerged as a major figure.

During his last years Chukovskii's major contribution to the realm of children's literature was his active role in bringing that world to Russian children. He read his poetry throughout the Soviet Union, entertained, and played with children who visited his house in Peredelkino, the writer's colony outside Moscow where he had settled before the war. Annually he arranged two bonfire festivals for children—"Hello, Summer!" and "Farewell, Summer!"—charging an entrance fee of five or ten pine cones per person. Held in a small outdoor amphitheater behind his house, the programs typically included poetry readings and musical performances by both children and adults. Sometimes the celebrated puppeteer Sergei Obraztsov brought his theater from Moscow. At least once the eminent scholar of medieval literature Nikolai Gudzii narrated the apocryphal tale "The Descent of the Virgin Mary into Hell." Young and old invariably enjoyed themselves—so much so that Chukovskii's family, friends, and spiritual heirs continued the tradition for several years after his death. Chukovskii also established a children's library, originally a small collection of books in his house in Peredelkino. When it grew too large for him to keep at home, he had a separate little house built near his own and transferred the collection there. Eventually he donated it to the local community.[24]

To the end of his life Chukovskii's interest in the Anglo-American tradition for children remained as strong as it had been at the earliest stage of his career. During his last visit to England, in 1962, to receive an honorary degree from Oxford University, he paid a visit to Iona and Peter Opie, the well-known collectors of English children's folklore, whose work he much admired. He also was an enthusiastic follower of the famous American children's writer Dr. Seuss (pseudonym of Theodor Geisel), whose playful verses admirably reflect Chukovskii's own ideas concerning children's poetry. Not only did he acquire as many of Seuss's works as he could, he encouraged young translators to attempt Russian versions of them.[25] One wishes he himself had had time enough for the task.

Chukovskii spent his long life surrounded by children. Although his literary career involved much that was in no way connected with children, it was always to them that he turned in the end. His daughter Lidiia, who has written at length and with great warmth about her father, once characterized his attitude toward children in the following way: "To say that he loved children is to say nothing. We should rather say that they never stopped amazing and delighting him. He loved the saying of Aristotle: 'All good comes from amazement.' Children were the richest material for the application of this amazement. All his life he observed children, considering them creatures who think uniquely."[26] Chukovskii shared with his young friends a naively joyful approach to life. As he grew older people close to him never ceased to marvel at the childlike qualities of the "gray-haired little boy." Frequent eulogies have emphasized his youthful spirit. The dramatist Evgenii Shvarts, who many years earlier had also written some poetry for children, congratulated Chukovskii on his seventy-fifth birthday. "Kornei Ivanovich is blessed with the enviable gift of eternal youth. He never stands still.

It will not be easy for old age to catch him."[27] And Shvarts was right. Chukovskii died in 1969, still vigorous, in his eighty-eighth year.

As one of Russia's pioneering connoisseurs of children, Chukovskii most importantly laid the basis for a modern theory of poetry for children. Although he never consciously set out to formulate a poetics, over the years he did in fact accomplish just that. Many of his observations of and investigations into early language acquisition, developmental psychology, and children's own verbal creativity help answer the fundamental question of how children can best be reached by poetry. His marvelous poems for children, which will be treated in chapter 4, definitively embody his ideas.

Chukovskii's biography reveals two major sources of inspiration for his poetics. First, there was his great love of children and his fascination with their linguistic development, originally manifest when he himself was a young father of several small children. It is hardly a coincidence that soon after he began raising a family he devoted articles to children's literature and early language acquisition.[28] Second, there was his intense annoyance with narrow-minded, insensitive adults who showed no understanding of the special attributes and needs of children. In his 1907 polemical review of children's periodicals, he asserted, "Give the reader less and take more from him—there is the slogan with which a children's magazine should come out."[29] While before the revolution his ire was aroused by blindly patriotic and religious or overbearingly didactic editorial approaches, after the revolution he was forced to contend with the equally dogmatic proletarian mentality. It was above all the strong campaign of the pedologists that prompted him to publish in 1928 his practical treatise *Little Children,* based on both his pre- and early postrevolutionary articles.

Retitled *From Two to Five* in its third edition in 1933, Chukovskii's work went through twenty-one editions by the time of his death in 1969.[30] The first modest volume of three chapters and ninety-five pages eventually grew to six chapters and almost four hundred pages, incorporating much new material and several articles originally published separately. But the general thrust remained unchanged over the decades. Chukovskii merely expanded his material and elaborated his views on children's language, on their own poetic creation, and on their need for nonsense and fantasy, the respective subjects of the three chapters of *Little Children.* The additional chapters of later editions further developed those original themes. A second chapter was devoted to child language, another—entitled "Defense of the Fairy Tale"—incorporated his subsequent articles in the polemic against shortsighted "realists," and a third—"Commandments for Children's Poets"—presented more observations based on children's language and their own poetic activity.

In dealing with questions of early language acquisition and developmental psychology, Chukovskii made no pretense of being a psychologist, a linguist, or even a pedagogue. "I am . . . a writer," he says in his introduction. "I have been observing children exclusively for the sake of my needs as a writer." As a beginning children's poet he turned to his audience for help: "When . . . I first began creating poems for children, I saw that I had no teachers or predecessors in that field. . . . So I decided to learn from children."[31] Since he was an extraordinarily acute observer of children and most gifted in communicating with them, Chukovskii's own point of view is of primary interest.

One of the memories he associates with the origin of this interest reveals his underlying curiosity about the seemingly ineffable nature of the child. The need to recuperate from a serious illness forced him one summer to spend long, leisurely hours on the beach, where he became acquainted with the many children who also frequented that place. "All around me there resounded unceasingly the clear language of children. At first it simply amused me, but gradually I concluded that beautiful in itself, it had great scientific value, since by studying it we reveal the amazing principles of children's thought, of the child psyche" (335). From that time on Chukovskii never parted for long from the company of children. Closer at hand he proceeded to observe the development first of his own four children, then his grandchildren, and finally his numerous great-grandchildren. The depth of his involvement with them heightened his insight into poetry for children. He was able to approach children on their own terms, both in daily life and in his work for and about them. As early as the beginning of this century he studied the spontaneous communicative behavior and verbal play of young children in the context of an intimate relationship with another person (to wit, himself). By natural inclination and pure intuition, he began his inquiries then in areas which professional psychologists and psycholinguists have only recently begun to explore.[32]

For Chukovskii the actual process of writing for children was primarily instinctive. However, his retrospective analysis of that largely unconscious process provides useful insight and guidelines for anyone interested in poetry for children. His familiarity with children's language proved an ideal point of departure for writing children's poetry, since early language acquisition is a crucial phase of a child's cognitive development. The two processes are in fact inseparable.

Chukovskii devoted much attention to two aspects of children's linguistic-cognitive growth: their ordinary speech and their spontaneous poetry (which some may view as part of their ordinary speech). From the very start he was interested in children's typical speech patterns. Their wondrously naive perceptions, due to limited experience and insufficient knowledge, frequently evoke the striking imagery of sensitive poets. They naturally use the literary device *ostranenie* (making strange or defamiliarization), a concept brought into popular usage by the Russian formalist Viktor Shklovskii soon after Chukovskii developed his interest in children. "Children's semantic perception of words is keener than [that of adults]. We have been handling words for so long that our sensitivity to words has been dulled. Our language is mechanical; we use it without noticing it. But because of the freshness of his perceptions, a child is a more pedantic and demanding controller of our speech."[33] From his observations of the creative nature of children's language came Chukovskii's related interest in their poetic utterances. It should be made clear that the "poetry" he studied was that which young children produce spontaneously, in no way prompted or tutored by adults. The poetry Chukovskii treated is often poetry within prose—poetic outbursts or interpolations in an otherwise prosaic context. From his study of their spontaneous verse, Chukovskii concluded that children typically create it while jumping or dancing and that it is permeated by joy.[34] He indicated two fundamental qualities of normal childhood. Children spend much of their time in motion—running, jumping, hopping, dancing, and rolling about. The psychologist Susanna Millar has provided a useful summary of this phenomenon.

> The "need" to move, jump, shout and "let off steam" generally recognized in the young is not . . . merely a reaction to exciting stimulation although the latter may be an occasion for it. The fact that children find it less easy than adults to sit still for long periods, not to bang their heels against the chair, not to jump up, or move their arms, or touch objects, to execute fine movements with their fingers and modulate their voices, is not a question of having more energy to spill, but of comparative lack of integration and control of the movement systems.[35]

Along with seemingly incessant movement, happy children usually are at least smiling and more likely laughing, expressing some degree of contentment or pleasure. From this comes the joyful quality of the verse they create. As Chukovskii put it, "When the jumping stops, so does the creation. . . . A sad, sickly, or sleepy child will not create a single line of verse."[36]

In children's verses, as in all of their behavior, both verbal and nonverbal, repetition is an important characteristic. Having created a line or two, they recite it, or more likely shout it, over and over.[37] In the course of this repetition rhyme often emerges. Chukovskii interpreted this method of producing rhyme as an efficient means of practicing sounds the child has not yet mastered. That is, children exploit opportunities to articulate a variety of words with only a minimal change in initial sounds.[38] A more sophisticated type of rhyme Chukovskii observed in children's verse involves not just random sound pairs but more carefully selected semantic pairs. From many examples he identified "the child's striving to rhyme words belonging to a single semantic category, systematizing them in this way according either to contrast or to similarity."

| | |
|---|---|
| Niánia ego niánchila, | (Nursemaid nursed him, |
| máma ego mámchila. | Mama "mommed" him.) |
| (623) | |

Such verses are necessarily short, usually consisting of just two lines. But then, of course, those two lines can be, and often are, repeated endlessly. I recall my daughter's first such verse at the age of twenty-one months:

Mama in the car!
Sonja in the car!

The first time that she pronounced these lines she repeated them several times. A few months later she still recalled them periodically while riding in the car, always chanting them with a giggle. Although unrhymed, they do have a distinct rhythmic pattern. In fact, their trochaic meter is the very rhythm Chukovskii identified as the most frequent in children's verses. Why trochees should predominate remains a matter for speculation. Chukovskii himself readily admits:

I do not know why it is so. Perhaps it is because all children of the world hop and dance to a trochee beat, perhaps it is because trochees give a rhythm in the most major key possible; perhaps it is because all mothers instill this rhythm in their speechless suckling infants when they rock and dandle them, when they play "patty-cake", and even when they sing lullabies ("baiu baiushki baiu" [a traditional Russian lullaby refrain] is a most pure trochaic line).[39]

With rhyme and rhythm as primary features of this poetry, there is a certain tendency for the original meaning of the lines to disappear as the child unconsciously shifts sounds in the course of his excited recitation. Chukovskii's classic example came to him in the following manner. Once under the balcony of his summer house he heard a little boy shouting to him, waving a stick: "Èku piku diadia dal!" (What a lance uncle gave!) In the course of several gleeful repetitions the line became "Èku kiki didi da!"[40] Sense gave way to euphony. And so apparently has it done over the ages in much of children's folklore. Not all nonsense lines can be dismissed simply as ancient number systems, as they have been identified in counting-out rhymes.[41] Instead, in some cases nonsense lines come where rhythmic flow has gained precedence over meaning. Moreover, this phenomenon is hardly restricted to children and folklore. Modern poetry, especially in the early decades of this century, experimented widely with the nonrational. Dada, futurism, and surrealism come to mind immediately. In a discussion of the trans-sense element of Russian futurist poetry, Shklovskii made an important point, bringing one back to children. "People do not need words merely to express a thought, nor even to replace one word with another, or to make it a name, attaching it to an object: people also need words outside sense. . . . One need not be a poet to revel in words outside sense and even to get drunk from them."[42] Shklovskii went on to remind one of children and their folklore. He would have appreciated an observation by John Holt in *How Children Learn:* "How a sound feels seems to be as important as the sound itself."[43]

In striking contrast to the *èkikiki* described (Chukovskii used the term to designate all short, repetitive verses arising during what he called "shaman-like" movement), some children in intense solitary play create long poetic monologues. Chukovskii reported instances of such activity that were said to have lasted for as long as an hour and a half.[44] Although such extended poems are far rarer than *èkikiki,* their existence better enables one to understand children's interest in and ability to concentrate during an adult's reading of relatively long narrative poems. One outstanding feature of such long poems is their "amazingly distinct graphic quality." Chukovskii further described them as "pictures in verse," an unbroken chain of very clear verbal pictures.[45] Here meaning is far less subordinate to rhyme and rhythm than in *èkikiki.*

At first it might strike one as strange that nowhere in his theoretical writings did Chukovskii devote any attention to the typical or most popular thematics of children's verse. Only once in passing did he mention that food and eating appear as major themes in their verbal creativity.[46] This omission, however, seems less odd when one realizes that the thematic range is endless. Anything, everything in a child's life may serve him as a thematic source. And so it can also be with poetry written for him by adults.

Although Chukovskii was originally considering only children's own verbal creativity, occasional comments in *Little Children* reveal that he was already thinking also of how adults might be guided to write appropriately for a child audience. And indeed, early in 1929, the year after the publication of *Little Children,* there appeared his "Thirteen Commandments for Children's Poets," later incorporated into *From Two to Five.* "Of course, commandments is too strong a word for these unassuming rules. They are simply signposts, placed for himself by a beginning children's writer who strove to approach the psychology of small children in order to influence it as much as possible" (723). What Chukovskii modestly called a set of rules is actually the basis for a serious new poetics of Russian children's poetry, whose foundation he laid when he first turned his attention to children's language and challenged much of the traditional literature available to them in prerevolutionary Russia.

In his typically spontaneous, intuitive manner, Chukovskii isolated the most crucial intrinsic and extrinsic aspects of poetry for children, most of which he derived from his study of early language acquisition. In summary he recommended that poetry for children should be graphic, with quickly changing images, lyric, rhythmically varied, and musical; rhymes should be close to one another and rhymed words should carry the main semantic burden; lines should be syntactically independent, with few adjectives, and in trochaic rhythm; the concept of play should be central; it should be poetry for adults too, and educational (696–725). Most of these elements are related, referring either to rhythm and metrics or to sound organization—and common, of course, to all poetry. However, in this study of poetry for children, the uncommon aspects stand out.

A major structural feature of all literature for small children is the interrelationship of text and illustration. Children's books without pictures are simply inconceivable. In works directed toward children from two to eight years, there is necessarily a close connection between verbal and visual content. It is no accident that Chukovskii's very first commandment requires graphic quality of children's poetry. His own interpretation of "graphic" was that "in every stanza and at times in every couplet, there should be material for an artist, because the thought process of young children is uniquely characterized by absolute representation" (704). Chukovskii advocated vivid, concrete poetry that easily conjures up accompanying visual imagery and cries out for illustration. "Poetry printed without drawings loses almost half its effectiveness" (705). While listening to a narrated text, children invariably insist upon seeing what is being described. Especially the youngest ones are often more intrigued by the pictures than by the verbal text.

In children's literature the relationship between text and illustration differs radically from that in adult literature, where in fact illustration is rare. In the article "Illustrations," the Russian formalist Iurii Tynianov explored the question of illustration for adults. He rejected graphic illustration of adult literature, calling it an impossible attempt to link a writer's verbal concreteness with an artist's visual concreteness. However, he admitted two instances when drawings may legitimately coexist with verbal art. In the first, they do not serve as specific illustrations to the text but merely as compatible graphic design. The second case is relevant to Chukovskii's conception of illustration in children's literature, "when a drawing plays a more independent role, already on the *plane of a word*—that is using graphics as an expressive element in verbal art. Poetry operates not only and not strictly as a *word*, but as an expression. All equivalents of a word are subsumed in the concept 'expression.' "[47] It is precisely as word equivalents that Chukovskii understood the role of illustrations. Children's minds operate on a very literal level, demanding concrete visual imagery to satisfy their expectations. Illustrations serve, therefore, to bridge the gap between children's demands and their capabilities of absorbing verbal information.

Just as children's needs and expectations necessitate the use of abundant illustrations to accompany the poetic text, so they help determine its intrinsic structural qualities. The tendency in children toward perpetual motion, in conjunction with their limited attention span, suggests their poetry should have compatible qualities. Chukovskii found the overall structure of successful children's poetry characterized by "the fastest possible shifting of images." "Since children's vision at the beginning perceives less the quality of things, than their movement, their actions, the subject of a long poem for small children should be varied, in motion, changeable; each five or six lines should demand a new drawing. Where this is not the case, children's poetry . . . does not work" (705). Originally Chukovskii referred to this quality as "cinematic"—not an uncommon epithet during the 1920s, when vanguard Soviet filmmakers, including Eisenstein, Pudovkin, and Dovzhenko, were exploring the structural possibilities of the newest artistic medium, above all, montage. Changing imagery does not imply the frequent introduction of totally new ideas, but simply new positioning, new interrelationships. In that way children are neither bored nor overwhelmed.

Movement in poetry comes not only from shifting imagery, but also, and very importantly, from underlying structural rhythms. Chukovskii's point of view seems paradoxical at first. On the one hand, he spoke of the need for metrical variation in order to convey different emotional tones. This is best exemplified by "The Crocodile," in which he "went from trochees to dactyls, from two-foot lines to six-foot ones" (706). At the same time he maintained that the dominant rhythm should be trochaic, which he identified as the rhythm underlying children's jumping and dancing. In fact there is no irreconcilable contradiction between the two statements. Trochaic meter may be used extensively, yet not necessarily exclusively. As it happens, much Russian poetry for children is written in trochaic meter.

Theodore Roethke once observed, "Repetition in word and phrase and in idea is the very essence of poetry . . . ."[48] In children's poetry repetition, due to its central role in language acquisition, takes on additional, extra-aesthetic significance. The process of language learning and cognitive growth in general gives repetition a natural place and a highly important function. The repetition of individual sounds, words, phrases, whole sentences is as essential to children's poetry as it is natural to their speech, since patterned repetition is a fundamental feature of early cognitive development in general.

One major manifestation of sound repetition is rhyme. In the early stages of language acquisition, Chukovskii noted, there is a marked tendency toward the use of rhymed word pairs. "At first . . . rhyme comes to children willy-nilly; such is the structure of their babbling. They cannot get along without consonance" (643). In accordance with this tendency he advocated that children's poets exploit this childish proclivity for close rhymes by frequently using paired rhyme schemes. For children to keep more distant rhymes in mind is difficult, if not impossible. Furthermore, asserted Chukovskii, the rhymed word should carry the main semantic burden of each line. "Often I experiment with my own and others' poetry: I cover the left half of the page with the palm of my hand and try to guess the contents from the right side alone; that is, from the side where the rhymes are concentrated. If I do not succeed, then the poetry must be redone, since it will not reach children in that form" (709–10). Maiakovskii shared this principle of structuring verse. In "How to Make Poetry" he wrote, "I always put the most characteristic word at the end of the line and find a rhyme for it at any cost."[49] Observing the process of language acquisition, adults have noted children's emphasis on the final position. Holt, for example, reported of a twenty-nine-month-old child: "He talks a great deal. . . . when we say something to him, he will often repeat the last word or two, as if for practice."[50]

According to Chukovskii, the verbal texture of children's poetry must be highly "musical," the sounds should be characterized by their "smoothness" and "fluidity" (710), all qualities derived from trends in children's own creativity. Chukovskii learned that small children tend to transform harsh sounds into more mellifluous ones, which at the same time are usually easier to pronounce; recall the phenomenon he labeled *èkikiki*. A great part of childish nonsense talk or trans-sense language (*zaum*), as distinct from adult *zaum*, is not intentional nonsense but simple sound reorganization with no semantic distortion intended. This is not to imply that meaningful content is invariably essential in children's poetry. Sometimes just the opposite is true. Pure sound can play an important role. "The English nursery rhymes are often only music, singing vowels, repetitions of sound, simple candences stressed, full and sonorous rhymes. They are not unconscious of the fact that by placing rhythm at the beginning of life they are conforming to the general order of the universe. They have a harmony all their own that is strange, mocking, and tender. The sense is of less importance than the sound."[51]

In children's poetry underlying simplicity is only natural; complicated ideas and forms could hardly communicate to them on their own level. Accordingly, Chukovskii observed that to support quickly moving thematics, verse lines should be syntactically independent units, "living their own lives and forming separate organisms. This principle is supported by children's own verbal creativity, where most often a thought pulses in concert with a single line of verse" (710). Thus the use of enjambment is most unusual, and sentences are simple or compound, rarely complex.

In further support of simplicity, diction is largely colloquial and unembellished. The concrete simile stands out as the most accessible figure of speech. Even the metaphor, with no word of comparison, tends to be out of the reach of children, determined literalists by nature. In the area of lexicon, Chukovskii pointed out that scholars have long been aware of a bias in children's speech toward verbs and verb-associated nouns (713), a fact which easily follows from children's propensity for movement.[52] Although this by no means excludes the use of adjectives, Chukovskii cautioned children's poets to use them with discretion. Concrete description is essential for young children, since they are not yet capable of abstraction.

At first glance Chukovskii's criteria might sound limiting, even stifling of creativity. Yet who, after listening for only a short time to small children talking, would describe their language as unimaginative or their point of view as constricted? To the contrary, most adults are delighted, fascinated, often astounded by children's perceptions of the world. After his experience teaching children to write poetry, the New York poet Kenneth Koch revealed: "one thing that encouraged me was how playful and inventive children's talk sometimes was. They said true things in fresh and surprising ways."[53] (Recall the literary device of "making strange.") In some ways, it is true, the children's poet makes conscious adjustments for a select audience. But fundamentally, the truly good poet calls forth all creative powers, as in any other artistic situation. The poet's gift—an ability to see the world in new ways—is just as vital to children's poetry as it is to that for adults. "It is as if the original freshness of impressions returns to him. All over again, in a childlike way, he listens attentively to words, which for us [adults] long ago became ordinary. As if participating in an ingenious children's game, he himself becomes the same kind of dreamer, visionary, even mischievous child, as are his little readers."[54] For this reason, Chukovskii could say that "the purely literary merit of children's poetry should be measured by the same criteria used for [measuring] the literary merit of all other poetry" (721). Until the end of his life he reiterated this principle, which for him lay at the base of all aesthetically valid poetry for children. "Even while renouncing adulthood the children's poet must retain all his cultural values. . . . I will never cease repeating that where literary merit is concerned, poetry for children must stand on the same level as poetry for adults."[55] Poetry based on such a premise is clearly a legitimate branch of the literary culture contemporary with it. Although from one point of view children's poetry reflects special principles for a special audience, nonetheless it emerges indisputably from the larger poetic tradition. Its poets themselves come from that tradition, and their young listeners and readers are developing within it.

Chukovskii by no means stands alone in his insistence upon the literary merit of children's poetry. In his own country that position is shared and perhaps better demonstrated by poets like Marshak and Maiakovskii, who wrote both for children and adults. Marshak himself once commented that "children's literature must be a work of art."[56] The critic Stanislav Rassadin went so far as to insist that Marshak's poetry for children is the best and chief part of his entire poetic oeuvre, that he would be recognized as a lyric poet if none but his children's poems existed.[57]

Just as literature is traditionally recognized as having three general functions in the life of an individual or of society—aesthetic, cognitive, and didactic,[58] so children's literature may be viewed in terms of those functions in the life of the child. From these functions comes the overall "educational" quality Chukovskii included among his commandments.

One of the most prevalent orientations of children's poetry has been—and continues to be—didactic. Adults insist on overtly teaching children how to live. Typically the didacticism is moral. Works such as Heinrich Hoffmann's *Struwwelpeter*, Wilhelm Busch's *Max und Moritz*, and Hilaire Belloc's *Bad Book of Beasts* set antimodels for children's behavior. In the Soviet Union there is the additional tendency for politically conscious adults to orient didactic poetry ideologically. A poet like Maiakovskii urges children to be good little pioneers—a stage on the road toward being grown-up communists. He blends moral with ideological didacticism, encouraging children not only to be good pioneers but clean ones too.

While children's poets do not always preach, many of them are inclined at least to teach. The word "teach" is used here in the sense of consciously aiding cognition—acquainting children in specific ways with the world around them. With the ever-increasing complexity of life in the modern world, emphasis on this informational function of children's literature is especially strong. There are of course the traditional books about animals, zoos, and circuses, which children love. The complex wonders of technology are also given attention—more so in the Soviet Union, where that stage arrived later than in the West.

Many poems can be classified under the purely aesthetic function—poems that do not preach, nor ostensibly teach, but exist for pure, simple pleasure. Into this category fall numerous rhymes of folk origin and the more recent nonsense verse of Edward Lear, Lewis Carroll, T.S. Eliot, Dr. Seuss, and of course Chukovskii, to name just a few of the most outstanding examples. From such works it is clear that the concept of play is central to the aesthetic function in children's literature.

Play in children's poetry has two dimensions—one is linguistic, the other emotional. Playing with words is an integral part of language learning. When a child is confronted with linguistically imaginative verse, he is reinforced in a process essential to his intellectual development. Frank Caplan, a specialist in the field of toy design and manufacture, has summed it up. "[A child] plays with word patterns as he does with his designs in painting or parquetry blocks. Patterns in words offer great satisfaction to [him]; he will repeat them endlessly to his own delight. If encouraged to listen to their own play with words or to the poetry of playful adults, children will have the confidence to continue playing and experimenting with language forms."[59] Even the venerable Maksim Gor'kii, who showed great concern about the quality of literature for children and first encouraged Chukovskii to write for them, had an enlightened attitude on this subject. As part of his contribution to the polemic with the pedologists, he wrote: "Up to ten years of age a child demands play, and this demand is biologically lawful. He wants to play; he plays with everything and experiences the surrounding world first of all and most easily in play, through play. He even plays with words. It is in word play that the child learns the nuances of his native tongue, assimilates the music and ... 'spirit of the language.' "[60] Fortunately for future generations of Russians, Chukovskii succeeded in establishing wide-ranging play as vital to children's poetry—from the smallest verbal elements to the largest conceptual ones. His "sensical nonsense" ultimately triumphed over the taunts of its detractors, although one occasionally encounters uncomprehending adults even today.

Children's poetry has the additional potential of arousing in its audience a wide variety of emotional responses, offering opportunities for the expression of feelings—fear, anger, love, joy, compassion. One of the most frequently evoked emotions in this poetry is joy, delight, signaled by children's laughter. Marc Soriano's observations of children's folklore are also applicable to much written poetry. "Most of the products of the oral tradition make every effort *to teach children to laugh*. They admit frankly that humor, irony and gaiety are indispensable acquisitions for a child, because they permit him to dominate his problems and have faith in life. These are natural functions in each of us, but they need to be developed. Laughter is not only "in the nature of man," it is also a fundamental part of our adaptation to the world."[61] And how very aptly Nikolai

Chekhov phrased it, when in defense of humorous literature for children in 1909, he insisted that "a child who never laughs is a psychological freak." "The age of childhood is especially marked by the striving for joy, for merriment in life; it is just as legitimate a need as the young growing organism's striving for fast movement. To deprive children of merry, joyful impressions is to give their development a false direction, inappropriate to their nature."[62] In the broad spectrum of children's poetry, from folk rhymes to contemporary verse, humor prevails—conveyed through both thematics and structure. In this way, too, children experience aesthetic pleasure.

Fortunately, the twentieth century, with its serious interest in all aspects of child development, has made it possible to begin describing a theory of poetry for children, one that considers with sensitivity the special qualities of childhood. Toward this end the extensive work of Kornei Chukovskii has been most valuable in establishing guidelines for children's poets. Keeping this poetics in mind, one is prepared to turn to the poetry itself, first to folklore and the prerevolutionary tradition, and then to the postrevolutionary one, to which Chukovskii himself was an outstanding contributor.

**2**

# CHILDREN'S FOLKLORE

MOST RUSSIAN POETRY for children is directly or indirectly linked with the oral tradition. First, the authentic folk genres continue to be transmitted in oral and written form. Second, from the nineteenth century come the stylized folktales of Aleksandr Pushkin and Pëtr Ershov, works that were never the sole property of the adult audience for whom they were intended. And third, of more recent origin is the large body of poetry conceived specifically for children; from Chukovskii, Marshak, and Kharms in the 1920s to the post-Stalin generation, children's poets in Russia have drawn significantly upon the oral tradition. While these links are recognized in Soviet scholarship and criticism, in the West the folklore of Russian children, as well as its modern literary heirs, remains all but unknown. To understand the development of twentieth-century children's poetry in Russia, it is essential to know of its connections with folklore, both historically and stylistically.

Children's folklore is typically divided into two categories: works created for and recited to children by adults; and works transmitted by children themselves, some created in their own milieu and others assimilated from adults.[1] The earliest moments of any child's life are hard to imagine without lullabies and other entertaining rhymes—the poetic forms mothers and nursemaids traditionally introduce to their babies. Then as those babies develop and begin talking sometime in the second year of life, they themselves gradually learn different songs and rhymes and at times create their own. And so the process continues throughout the early years of childhood, when much of children's daily play is accompanied by singing and chanting. Finally, there are longer tales, some in verse, many in prose, which although they may be shared with little children, are complex enough to hold the interest of school-age children.

While an occasional "folk song" was included in eighteenth-century anthologies for Russian children, and stylized folktales began to be published in the latter part of the same century, some in editions for children,[2] the folklore emanating from their own milieu—both that of their elders and their own creation—was not transcribed until the second half of the nineteenth century. During the 1850s and 1860s, decades of burgeoning "democratic" attitudes, when interest in preserving the native oral tradition was well established and emphasis began to be placed on its instructive value, Russian ethnographers, pedagogues, and writers turned their attention to the lore of children. Genres from the oral tradition—tales, songs, riddles—became a regular feature of children's magazines. Folk material also appeared in the pedagogical journal *The Teacher* (*Uchitel'*), some of it sent in by readers upon request of the editors.[3]

In this period folklore served as an important source for much of the pedagogical work of Tolstoi and Ushinskii. When Lev Tolstoi opened his first school for peasant children on his estate Iasnaia Poliana in 1859, only to find no suitable primers, he turned to the oral tradition. "The only books comprehensible to the people and to their taste are not those written for the people, but those which have their origin in the people: folktales, proverbs, collections of songs, legends, riddles."[4] In *Iasnaia Poliana*, the pedagogical journal he published in 1862–1863, he included folktales, anecdotes, riddles, and proverbs. Later, in his second phase of educational activity, he compiled his famous *Alphabet* (*Azbuka*, 1872) and *New Alphabet* (*Novaia azbuka*, 1875), with his versions of Russian and foreign folklore. Konstantin Ushinskii is also remembered for his inclusion of folk-inspired material in textbooks—*Children's World* (*Detskii mir*, 1861) and *Native Word* (*Rodnoe slovo*, 1864). In the teacher's manual to the latter he commented, "I definitely place the folktale above all the stories educated literature has written specifically for children."[5]

It was also at this time that special collections of folklore, varying in degree of authenticity, were first published for children's own reading. The prominent philologist Vladimir Dal' included children's tongue-twisters and counting-out rhymes in his *Proverbs of the Russian People* (*Poslovitsy russkogo naroda*, 1861–1862). A decade later he reworked folktales for his young grandchildren, contributing to a genre that quickly became well established as an important part of Russian children's literature.[6] The work of this period most directly relevant to later developments in written poetry for children is *Children's Songs* (*Detskie pesni*, 1868) by Pëtr Bessonov, who transcribed oral lore as he remembered it from his own childhood. He selected lullabies, infant amusements, animal songs, carols, tales, games, and riddles for the first volume of a projected three-volume work. The first was for very young children; the second and third, which never materialized, were to be for older ones. While some folklorists understandably fault the lack of authenticity of Bessonov's texts, his collection is generally regarded as pioneering in the realm of Russian children's folklore and has been an important source for postrevolutionary children's poets.[7]

The person credited with having produced the first scholarly collection of children's folklore in Russia is Pavel Shein (1826–1900), who began gathering folk songs in the 1850s. Inspired by earlier Russian folklorists and especially indebted to the ideas of Ivan Sakharov, Shein undertook the monumental task of documenting in song the peasants' life from cradle to grave.[8] Although he did not attain his goal before his death, Shein did succeed in collecting and publishing an impressive quantity of material. And most importantly for the present study, his work in the area of children's folklore can be considered complete, since "children's songs" (*detskie pesni*) were his point of departure. Shein's first publication of children's folklore in 1868 had a dedication to Dal' and 122 texts. His definitive edition appeared three decades later with more than twice as many texts. In the 1868 edition Shein made no attempt to classify texts beyond the beginning lullabies. But by 1898 he used broad categories, which in the twentieth century have served as a basis for classifying genres of Russian children's folklore. First come works preserved by adults (lullabies and infant amusements); then those preserved by children, both separately from games (witty rhymes, taunts, ritual calendar songs) and in connection with games (counting-out rhymes and verses directly accompanying games). While Soviet folklorists have expanded and clarified Shein's approach, they have not fundamentally changed it.[9]

By the end of the nineteenth century, much attention in Russia was turned to the collection and study of children's folklore. However, following the broad and fundamental work of Shein, that of other prerevolutionary folklorists was more specific and more narrowly focused. This was the case both in the collection of texts and in scholarship. Some people recorded local material; others collected particular genres.[10] Most commonly, textual transcriptions were scattered in a wide variety of ethnographic journals and publications of provincial archival commissions.[11] Only after the revolution was a concerted effort made toward consolidating materials and improving scholarship.

That effort in the early Soviet period is linked above all with two names, Georgii Vinogradov (1886–1940), a professor at Irkutsk University, and Ol'ga Kapitsa (1866–1939), a professor at the Institute of Preschool Education (later the Herzen Pedagogical Institute) in Leningrad. Decades later their work on Russian children's folklore remains the most comprehensive treatment of the subject to date.

Vinogradov was clearly the more scholarly of the two, at times even pedantically so. Challenging the usual definition of children's folklore as works created for and by children, he recognized only those genres preserved by children themselves. In his attempt to strengthen scholarship in this area, he planned a comprehensive study of all the genres of Russian children's folklore, only a fraction of which he was able to complete. The first and only volume of a proposed series actually to come into being was devoted to counting-out rhymes—*Russian Children's Folklore (Russkii detskii fol'klor,* 1930).[12]

Kapitsa was an equally indefatigable worker. From an interest that originally appeared as she was rearing her children, Kapitsa went on to become an expert in both the written and oral traditions.[13] In 1922 she organized a workshop devoted to children's literature at her institute, attracting, among others, Marshak, who had just come to Petrograd to work in children's theater. Through the workshop Kapitsa passed on her own appreciation of the role of folklore in the lives of children. And with her own pedagogical students she pursued a broad program of study in the same area. Her major work, Children's Folklore (Detskii fol'lkor, 1928), provides a good introduction to the study of Russian children's folklore, including a survey of major genres and the most complete bibliography published until then. Even Vinogradov, who found the book lacking in academic rigor, admitted it was a commendable beginning.[14] Kapitsa became an important organizer in the field, actively participating in the Commission of Children's Daily Environment, Folklore, and Language—a subbranch of the Ethnographic Division of the Russian State Geographic Society. In 1930 she edited the commission's first publication, Children's Daily Environment and Folklore (Detskii byt i fol'klor). Upon the publication of one of her numerous small folk collections Kapitsa wrote: "I am happy that folklore is made available to children. Not a single children's poet has achieved the heights of folk rhymes and songs. It is impossible to delete a single word from them, because they contain nothing superfluous."[15] In all its variety Kapitsa's work confirms the significance of the folk tradition for children's poetry.

Although Chukovskii was not a professional folklorist as was Kapitsa or Vinogradov, he also must be recognized as an important promoter of children's folklore, not only through his adaptations of Russian and English folk rhymes, but through his observations of language acquisition in From Two to Five.[16] Since their deaths the work of Kapitsa and Vinogradov has been known only to experts, but that of Chukovskii is broadly accessible.[17]

In keeping with his observations, Chukovskii strongly recommended that folklore be made available to young children. "All possible folk songs, tales, proverbs, sayings, riddles that constitute the favorite mental food of preschoolers best communicate to a child the fundamentals of his native tongue." Folklore in turn can provide important guidance to modern children's writers. As Chukovskii admitted, "I came to the conclusion that folk poetry is the single reliable compass for a children's writer." While he never advocated imitation, he suggested, "One must not ignore the fact that over many years, in their songs, tales, epics, [and] verses, the people have worked out ideal methods for an artistic and pedagogical approach to the child."[18] Of course children themselves have shaped the folk tradition they so love. This becomes very clear when it is compared with the typical characteristics of children's spontaneous verbal activity.

In the larger context of Russian poetry for children, folklore is of

interest above all as an aesthetic phenomenon. Central here are
its intrinsic characteristics and their relationship to the lives of
young children. While historical, anthropological, sociological, and
ideological aspects are not irrelevant, they are necessarily of secondary importance. The genres under consideration include not only
works created by children, as Georgii Vinogradov would have it, but
also those produced by adults, since there are points of comparison
between the works adults created for children orally and those they
eventually come to write for them. The quantity of original examples provided here is intended both as an introduction to the abundant world of Russian children's folklore, fascinating in itself, and as
a source of reference for the written poetry that will be treated in the
remaining chapters of this book. To the latter end, it is important
that typical devices should stand out sufficiently, in order that their
echoes in later written poetry will be more easily recognized. Thus,
the remainder of this chapter might be viewed as a concise critical
anthology with ulterior motives. Along with the Russian texts and
their translations there are some references to English equivalents
for those readers whose childhood memories are exclusively of English nursery rhymes.

The traditional forms produced by adults are the lullabies
(kolybel'nye pesni), sung from the earliest days to soothe and lull
the baby to sleep; and then the many different ditties known as
"infant amusements" (pestushki, poteshki, pesenki, pribautki)
brought out from the time the baby is a few months old to entertain
and to teach. These are typically sung or recited during the first two
to three years of life, before a child has mastered his or her native
tongue.

Lullabies are many and varied. Their tone, with its corresponding
rhythms and imagery, ranges from religiously solemn to lightheartedly playful. The length may vary from a single short stanza of
four to six lines to more than forty lines.

> Liúli, liúli, liúlin'ki!
> Priletéli gúlin'ki
> Na Volódinu liúlen'ku;
> Stáli Volódiu uteshát'
> Spát' ukládyvat'.
> Iz-za kústochku, iz-za él'nichku
> Bezhít séren'kii volchók,
> Berët Volódiu za bochók
> I nesët na kraék.
> A na tóm-to na kraikú
> Zhivët bédnyi muzhichók

On ni béden, ni bogát,—
Tól'ko sémero rebiát:
Vsé na sólnyshke lezhát.
Prigovárivat' veliát.[19]

(Lullaby, lullaby! / The doves flew up / at Volodya's bedtime; / They began to make him happy, to put him to bed. / From behind a little bush, from behind / a little fir / runs a little gray wolf, / takes Volodya by the side / and carries him to the edge. / And on that, on that edge / lives a poor little peasant, / He is neither poor nor rich, / but has seven children: / All are lying in the sun. / They demand another refrain.)

The thematic possibilities are broad, ranging from almost pure song to more involved narratives (as in the above example), with at least a line or two alluding to the task at hand. "Little gray wolf" (seren'kii volchok)—the child equivalent of "gray wolf" (seryi volk)—is among the most popular characters in this folklore.

In contrast to the obvious tranquilizing aim of lullabies, the object of the infant amusements is to engage directly the baby's attention and emotions. The distinction among the various Russian terms, which Kapitsa made rather impressionistically in Russian Children's Folklore, is derived not surprisingly from the intent of the rhymes. Pestushki (from pestovat', an archaic verb meaning to nurse, to raise and care for) are above all the rhymes accompanying a child's major motor developments, such as sitting, crawling, standing, walking, and running.

"Nózhki, nózhki
"Kudá vy bezhíte?"
—V lesók po moshók:
—Izbúshku mshít'
—Chtóby ne khólodno zhít'.
                                          (1895, 13)

("Little legs, little legs, / where are you running?" / "To the woods for moss / to put on the hut / so it won't be cold.")

Also included here are leg- and lap-riding games.

Tra ta-tá, tra-ta tá
Výshla kóshka za kotá!
Kra-ka, ká, kra, ka-ká!
Poprosíla moloká;
Dla, la, lá, dla, la, lá!
Kóshka-to i ne dalá.
                                          (1895, 14)

(Tra la la, tra la la / the cat married the tom! / Ha ha ha, ha ha ha! / She asked for milk; / Fa la la, fa la la! / But then she didn't give any.)

Good English examples of such riding rhymes are "This is the Way the Ladies Ride" and "Ride a Cock-horse to Banbury Cross."

*Poteshki* (from the verb *teshit'*, to amuse or entertain) are generally verses accompanied by elementary hand, finger, and sometimes toe play. Both of the following popular rhymes are about food, a common motif in children's folklore. Besides porridge, there is no dearth of gingerbread (*prianik*),[20] fancy bread (*kalach*), pancakes (*bliny*), and meat pies (*pirogi*).

> Ládushki, ládushki,
> Gdé byli? U bábushki.
> Chtó eli? Káshku.
> Chtó pili? Brázhku.
> Káshka sláden'ka,
> Brázhka p'iánen'ka.
> Shú! poletéli.
> (1868, 21)

(Clap hands, clap hands, / Where were we? At grandma's. / What did we eat? Porridge. / What did we drink? Home-brew. / The porridge is sweet, / the home-brew makes you drunk. / Shoo! we flew away.)

> —Soróka, soróka!
> Gde bylá?
> —Dalëko!
> Péchka topíla,
> Káshku varíla,
> Na poróg skakála—
> Gostéi sozyvála.
> Gósti priletéli,
> Na kryléchko séli.
> Ètomu dalá,
> Ètomu dalá,
> Ètomu dalá,
> Ètomu dalá,
> A ètomu ne dalá;
> On pó vodu ne khodíl,
> Drová ne rubíl,
> Péchku ne topíl,
> Káshku ne varíl . . . .[21]

("Magpie, magpie! / Where were you?" / "Far away. / I heated the oven, / cooked the porridge, / hopped to the threshold, / invited guests. / The guests arrived, / they sat down on the porch. / I served this one, / I served this one, / I served this one, / I served this one, / but this one I didn't serve; / he didn't go for water, / or chop wood, / or heat the oven, / or cook porridge.")

The didactic implication of "Magpie, magpie" helps identify its adult origin. Undoubtedly the best-known English equivalents of *poteshki* are "Patty-cake," "Pease Porridge Hot," and "This Little Pig Went to Market."

The categories of *pesenka* (little song) and *pribautka* (an especially witty song) are more problematic, for it is difficult to draw the line between those sung to the youngest children and those sung by slightly older ones. Ultimately, as with many if not most English nursery rhymes, no clear distinction can in fact be made. *Pesenki* and *pribautki* are first sung to children too young to speak, but gradually, by two years of age or so, those same children begin reciting them themselves.

> Dón, dón, dón!
> Zagorélsia kóshkin dóm:
> Bezhít kúritsa s vedróm
> Zalivát' kóshkin dóm.
> (1868, 14)

(Dong, dong, dong! / Cat's house has caught on fire. / Hen is running with a bucket / to pour on Cat's house.)

There are two kinds of verses children recite while at play. The first includes verses that either accompany or directly organize games: counting-out rhymes (*schitalki*) and the actual games (*igry*). The second category is a large and diverse one including verses that arise in play situations but that are not attached to specific games. The latter are too numerous to list separately and therefore will simply be named as they are described. In the first group the counting-out rhymes are of primary interest, for they are among the most popular and thus most widespread of children's folk rhymes.

> Odín, dvá,—
> Golová,
> Trí, chetýre,—
> Pritsepíli,
> Piát', shést',—
> Séno vézt';
> Sém', vósem',
> Séno kósim;
> Déviat', désiat',—
> Dén'gi vésit';

Odínnadtsat', dvenádtsat',—
Na ulítse braniátsia.
(1895, 37)

One,   two— / head, / Three,   four— / they   hooked   it   on, / five,
six— / to   carry   hay, / seven,   eight— / we   are   mowing   hay, / nine,
ten— / they  are  weighing  money, / eleven,  twelve— / they  are  quar-
reling in the street.)

This genre is typified by frequent appearance of nonsense.

Pervénchiki,
Druzhénchiki,
Berebénchiki,
Trýntsy, volyńtsy,
Popóvy ladántsy
Tsýken', výken'!
(1868, 64)

Although some of the roots are identifiable, the words as such are
nonexistent and untranslatable. Their effect is best conveyed in
English by a rhyme such as "One-erum, two-erum, cockerum, shu-
erum." More popular and comprehensible are "One, two, buckle my
shoe" and "Eeny, meeny, miney, mo." To the second group belong
the childish incantations (*zaklichki*), usually considered remnants
of pagan beliefs, addressed to natural phenomena and sometimes to
animals. Compare the English "Rain, Rain, Go Away" with the
Russian

Dózhdik, dózhdik, perestán'!
Iá poédu vo Riazán'
Bógu molít'sia,
Khrístu poklonít'sia,
Iá, ubógii sirotá.
(1868, 5)

(Rain, rain, stop! / I am going to Riazan to pray to God, / to bow down
to Christ, / poor orphan I.)

A more common one in these atheistic times is

Ráduga-dugá
Ne davái dozhdía
Davái sólynshka
Kolokólnyshka.
(*Raduga*, 106)

(Rainbow-bow / do not give rain / give sunshine / little bluebell.)

Here Soviet folklorists also place ritual songs (*obriadovye pesni*) and rhymes connected with the calendar (*detskii narodnyi kalendar'*), all stemming originally from the adult folk tradition. The popular seasonal activity of mushroom gathering, for example, has rhymes connected with it.

> Uzh ty gríb gribovói,
> Dovedí meniá domói,—
> Libo sám, libo sýn,
> Libo pásynochek,
> Libo bárchenochek.
>
> (1895, 37)

(Oh you mushroomy mushroom / lead me home, / either you, or your son, / or your stepson, / or a master's son.)

There are the many humorous verses recited to amuse the listener—or in some cases the teller. These include nonsense rhymes and "tangle talk," which confuse the action and destroy the actual relationship between subject and object (*nebylitsy*). Chukovskii coined the term *perevërtysh* for the latter concept, basing the Russian on the English expression "topsy-turvy."

> Dolgonógii zhurável'
> Na mél'nitsu ézdil,
> Dikóvinku vídel:
> Kozá múku mélet,
> Kozél zasypáet,
> A málen'ki kozlënochki
> Múku vygrebáiut,
> A baráshki krúty rózhki
> V dúdochku igráiut,
> A soróki-belobóki
> Poshlí tantsováti,
> A vórony sterezhëny
> Poshlí primecháti.
> Sová iz-za uglá smótrit.
> Nogámi tópchit,
> Golovói vértit.
>
> (1895, 17)

(A long-legged crane / was riding to the mill, / and saw a strange sight: / The nanny goat was grinding flour, / the billy goat was pouring the grain, / and the little kids were scooping out the flour, / and the sharp-horned lambs / were playing a little pipe, / and the white-bellied magpies / went to dance, / and the cautious ravens / went to watch. / From his corner the owl was gazing. / It tapped its legs, / and twirled its head.)

Rhymes such as this, with anthropomorphized animals, especially upset detractors of fantasy.

Finally there are the ever-popular tongue-twisters, (*skorogovorki*), riddles (*zagadki*), taunts and jeers (*draznilki, izdëvki*). Tongue-twisters are, of course, verbal play par excellence.

> Prishél Prokóp, kipit ukróp,
> I pri Prokópe kipít ukróp.
> I ushél Prokóp, kipít ukróp,
> I bez Prokópa kipít ukróp.[22]

(Prokop came, dill is boiling, / Even with Prokop here dill is boiling. / And Prokop left, dill is boiling, / Even without Prokop dill is boiling.)

The linguistic test embodied in this genre is hardly invalidated with the passing of childhood! Riddles combine play with cognition, giving children an opportunity to prove themselves.

> Krasná, sladká, dushísta,
> Rastét nízko,
> K zemlé blízko. (Iagoda)[23]

(Red, sweet, fragrant, / it grows low, / close to the ground. [A berry])

As soon as children are old enough to play together and therefore must share their toys and territory, taunting behavior begins. To an adult it may be astonishing to see how cruel even the youngest people can be to one another, how intent they are on establishing their own worth and even superiority. Taunting rhymes are numerous and suited to many different situations. One eternal butt of jeers is the glutton or "fatty."

> Nikoláshka trébushka
> S'él koróvu da byká
> Sem'sót porosiát—
> Odní lápochki visiát.
>                     (1895, 33)

(Big-bellied Nickie / ate a cow and a bull, / seven hundred piglets— / only their paws are hanging out.)

Both Chukovskii and Marshak rendered in Russian the English equivalent—"Robbin the Bobbin, the big-bellied Ben."

Despite the diversity of genres in children's folklore, its underlying structural unity makes it possible to treat characteristic elements as a whole rather than separately for each genre. Taken thus, the oral tradition provides further excellent evidence of children's needs, adding another dimension to the discussion of poetics begun in the preceding chapter. Over the ages children, along with their mothers and other caretakers, have preserved a relatively stable body of works—works that are, In Kapitsa's words, "especially pleasing, entertaining, and easily memorized."[24] And as one would expect, the typical elements of children's folklore are quite in accordance with Chukovskii's observations of children's language acquisition, which he used as the basis of his recommendations to children's poets. After all, children's spontaneous poetry and their traditional folklore are separate in time of origin rather than in essence.

On the whole, the length of children's folk rhymes is not great, averaging from four to twelve lines.[25] This is especially true of those created to amuse the very youngest, although lullabies, as we have seen, are frequently longer—some babies are loath to fall asleep! Exceptions to the rule are also found among the works children recite themselves. Some of their playful narrative songs contain as many as forty lines. According to Kapitsa, in the repertory of older children there are some exceptionally long works of over one hundred lines.[26] Exceptions notwithstanding, in the main the rhymes tend to be short, as do the individual lines. In most instances the number of syllables per line ranges from three to nine, with the majority being from four to six.[27] Counting-out rhymes have the shortest lines, due to the nature of the process they accompany. While most rhymes are short, they are invariably expanded by repetition. In reciting them children tend to repeat them several times in a row. This situation is best and most easily verified in daily contact with any normal small child, whose urge to recite and repeat is seemingly boundless. Ostensibly short forms acquire new dimensions in actual use.

Turning to the area of rhythm and metrics, one must keep in mind the central place of motion in children's lives. Babies are rocked to sleep or jostled about in lap and leg games; older children run, jump, hop, and skip during play of all kinds. Accordingly, the rhythms of their folklore have developed as appropriate accompaniment to their physical behavior. The meter of the Russian rhymes, which tends not to scan in regular literary, syllabo-tonic fashion, is best described as tonic, and is typical also of adult folk songs. Nonetheless, scansion of separate lines does reveal an underlying binary meter, with individual lines often falling into regular iambic or trochaic patterns. Vinogradov asserts that the melody changes, depending upon whether the meter is trochaic or iambic. "Trochaic meter gives it a lively, enthusiastic coloration; iambic structure slows down the tempo somewhat."[28] Such interpretation of meter remains a highly individual matter, however. In some genres, including lullabies, infant amusements ,and counting-out rhymes, a quite rigid rhythmic pattern is naturally observed. The following one, for example, is in regular trochaic meter:

> Vánia, bánia,
> Chtó pod vámi,
> Pod zheléznymi stolbámi?
> Stúl'chik,
> Mál'chik,
> Sam koról'chik.
>> (1868, 65)

(Bonny Johnny, / what is under you, / under the iron posts? / Little chair, / little boy, / himself a little king.)

In others there may be breaks or shifts in rhythm (pereboi), making it impossible to identify any single meter.

> Tri-ta-tá, tri-ta-tá!
> Výshla kóshka za kotá,
> U kóshki lepéshki,
> U kotá pirozhkí.
> Khódit kót po lávochke,
> Vedët kísku za lápochku.
>> (1868, 18)

(Tra la la, tra la la! / the cat went out after the tom, / The cat had cookies, / The tom had pies. / He walked about the shop did tom, / Leading kitty by the paw.)

As in the metrical innovations in the twentieth-century poetry of Aleksandr Blok, Anna Akhmatova, and Maiakovskii, it is not the regular alternation of stressed and unstressed syllables that is important here. The metrical order comes, rather, from the relationship of stressed syllables, regardless of the number of unstressed syllables between them.

One of the most intriguing aspects of children's folklore is its intricate sound texture, which makes these rhymes in any language a melodic delight. Vinogradov's explanation of why they should be so is that "children come into contact with the world around them through sound."[29] Although a psychologist might approach the subject from a broader perspective, there certainly can be no doubt of the crucial place of sound in a child's overall development. As in all poetry, the acoustic elements in children's folk poetry are many and complex. Yet some of these elements fit into regular patterns and can be described as typical features.

Undoubtedly the most fundamental such pattern is rhyme, a phenomenon children find extremely appealing. Unlike adult folk poetry where end rhyme is often absent, children's oral verse almost invariably has rhyme or close approximations of it, in clear response to children's own linguistic tendencies. Normally the rhymes are paired or adjacent. Often they occur in triplets. Nor by any means is rhyme restricted to the end of the line. Internal rhyme is abundant, as is assonance, alliteration, and every manner of sound imitation. (Recall that animal sounds appear prominently among most children's first words.) In fact, in this poetry sound orchestration in general plays an absolutely vital role. The verbal texture is the single most outstanding feature of these works, especially those texts which contain elements of nonsense or trans-sense language, where meaningful content may be minimal or even nonexistent. Counting-out rhymes provide the best examples of this.

> Péria, éria,
> Súkha, riúkha,
> Piáta, sáta,
> Dúba, kliáka,
>   Klést!
>         (1868, 59)

A larger structural element which contributes importantly to the acoustic organization, as well as to the rhythm and overall composition, is syntactic parallelism. While almost any verse serves to illustrate this phenomenon, the longer narratives are extraordinarily rich in it. The following is a relatively short example.

> Kak u nás-to kozél,
> Chto-to úmnyi býl,
> Sam i pó vodu khodíl,
> Sam i káshu varíl,
> Deda s bábkoiu kormíl.
> Kak poshél nash kozél
> On vo témnyi lés,
> Kak navstréchu kozlú
> Da sém' volkóv,
> Kak odín-to vólk,
> On golódnyi býl,
> On tri góda khodíl,
> Vse kozliátiny prosíl.
>         (1868, 50–51)

(Once we had a goat, / who was rather smart, / he even went for water by himself, / he even cooked porridge by himself, / and fed the old man and old woman. / Once our goat went / into the dark woods, / and he met / seven wolves, / and one of the wolves, / was very hungry, / he wandered three years, / and kept asking for goat meat.)

Even greater repetition is found among the infant amusements.

> A tári, tári, tári!
> Kupliú Líde iantári;
> Ostánutsia dén'gi,
> Kupliú Líde sér'gi;
> Ostánutsia piatakí,
> Kupliú Líde bashmakí;
> Ostánutsia gróshiki,
> Kupliú Líde lózhki;
> Ostánutsia polúshki,
> Kupliú Líde podúshki.
>
> (1868, 9)

(Oh, tra la, tra la, tra la! / I'll buy Lida amber beads; / if money remains, / I'll buy Lida earrings; / if nickels remain, / I'll buy Lida shoes; / if pennies remain, / I'll buy Lida spoons; / if half-pennies remain, / I'll buy Lida pillows.)

One of the interesting phenomena of children's folklore exemplified by this verse is the counterbalancing of syntactic repetition by rhythmic variation. Thus repetition by no means leads to monotony.

As might well be expected, the diction of children's folklore is relatively simple. Especially in the genres created for the youngest children, but not exclusively in them, one finds many childish words—baby-talk diminutives. Concrete nouns predominate on the whole, often in the form of proper names. Verbs are frequent too. Adjectives and other parts of speech are fewer. When adjectives occur, they tend to be concrete and comprehensible to children, often attached to a noun as a fixed epithet, as in "little gray wolf."

If one turns to the question of thematics rather than merely recurrent imagery, it becomes difficult to be precise. The fact is that children's folk rhymes derive their significance more from their manner than from their matter. Except in some longer narrative poems, it is impossible to isolate developed themes. Instead, the meaning of these rhymes must be seen first of all in their function. Different genres accompany different aspects of a child's life. And whether they are purely entertaining or have didactic overtones, their primary mode of communication is verbal play. They embody a way of approaching the world to which children respond with great enthusiasm. On the most basic level they provide extensive linguistic practice. Frequent repetition helps children master the intricacies of their native language. At a step above that the poems offer broad cognitive material. Through them children come into contact with people, animals, objects, and, at times, abstract concepts. All this occurs in a manner compatible with the playful routines of childhood. Furthermore, the process of learning such rhymes helps children develop self-confidence. A child who has just committed another verse to memory is justifiably proud. And, most importantly, they are fun to hear and to recite; such pleasurable activity contributes a crucial ingredient to a child's basic emotional well-being.[30]

While clearly the poetic folk genres serve as the most direct source of inspiration for much modern Russian poetry written for children, the folktale in prose (*skazka*) also deserves attention. Not only has the *skazka* become accepted as a legitimate part of Russian children's literature, it has also left its mark on the development of postrevolutionary Russian poetry for children. The poems of Chukovskii, who did not hesitate to call them *skazki,* owe much to this genre.

Over the course of time Russian children have become the primary audience for many traditional folktales that originally arose in an adult milieu. *Skazki* in which animals and children play a central role are naturally especial favorites. Despite the disapproval of conservative minds, by the turn of the century the publication of *skazki* for children was a rather flourishing business, comprising the best native literature then available to the youngest Russians.[31] After the revolution *skazki* continued to be offered to children in abundance, until the tales came under heavy attack by the proletarian critics during the 1920s. Fortunately, since the death of Stalin, and most notably at present, *skazki* have been appearing in frequent and plentiful editions for young children.

If one isolates only those characteristics of *skazki* that have most obviously affected the written poetic tradition for children, several appear outstanding. Most striking is the frequent repetition, which facilitates memorization and enhances the appeal of these tales. While repetition is a common feature of all folklore, a special type of accumulative, chain composition is found in several of the *skazki* most popular with children, including "House-tower" ("Teremok"), "The Turnip" ("Repka"), and "Johnnycake" ("Kolobok").[32] In a quite simple version of "House-tower" the final accumulative section is the result of seven previous additions.

> —Któ, któ v teremú? Któ, któ v vysókom?
> —Iá, múkha-goriúkha.
> —Iá, blokhá-poprygúkha.
> —Iá, komár-piskún.
> —Iá, mýshka-norúshka.
> —Iá, liagúshka-kvakúshka,
> —Iá, zaíchik-pobegáichik.
> —Iá, lisíchka-sestríchka.
> —Iá, volchíshche—séryi khvostíshche.

("Who, who is in the house-tower? Who who is up high?" / "I, woeful little fly." / "I, hoppy little flea." / "I, squeaky little mosquito." / "I, burrowy mousie." / "I, croaky froggie." / "I, runaway bunny." / "I, little sister foxie." / "I big gray-tailed wolf.")

"House-tower" also provides excellent examples of the Russian folk device of compound names, a construction that usually combines a simple name (here, of course, all animals) with a descriptive noun, often derived from a verb.

Although none of the Russian accumulative tales is quite equal in rhythmic intensity to the well-known English nursery rhyme "This is the House that Jack Built," "The Turnip" comes very close.

> Pozvalá kóshka mýshku:
>   mýshka za kóshku,
>   kóshka za Zhúchku,
>   Zhúchka za vnúckhu,
>   vnúchka za bábku,
>   bábka za dédku,
>   dédka za répku—
> tiánut-potiánut,—výtianuli répku!

(The cat called the mouse / the mouse grabbed the cat, / the cat grabbed the dog, / the dog grabbed the granddauther, / the granddaughter grabbed the old woman, / the old woman grabbed the old man, / the old man grabbed the turnip— / they pulled and pulled again—and they pulled out the turnip!)

In its sequence of characters it is reminiscent also of the English children's game "Farmer in the Dell."

"Johnnycake" (which parallels the English "Gingerbread Man") is not only another instance of accumulative structure, it also illustrates the occurrence of verse within a prose text, a phenomenon found frequently in *skazki*. What in other tales may be no more than a strong tendency toward rhythmic language here is organized as a song.

> Kátitsia-kátitsia kolobók, a navstréchu emú lisá:
> —Zdrávstvui, kolobók! Kakói ty khoróshen'kii!
> A kolobók zapél:
> Po ambáru metĕn,
> Po suséchkam skrebĕn,
> Na smetáne méshan,
> V péchku sazhĕn,
> Na okóshke stuzhĕn.
> Ia ot dédushki ushĕl,
> Ia ot bábushki ushĕl,
> Ia ot zaítsa ushĕl,
> Ia ot vólka ushĕl,
> Ia ot medvédia ushĕl,
> Ot tebiá, lisá, ne khitró uití.

(Johnnycake rolled-rolled along and met a fox: / "Hello, johnnycake! What a fine one you are!" / And johnnycake sang out: / "I am johnnycake, johnnycake, / I was swept from the barn, / scraped from the flour bin, / kneaded with sour cream, / put in the oven, / cooled on the window sill; / I got away from the old man, / I got away from the old woman, / I got away from the hare, / I got away from the wolf, / I got away from the bear, / and I will certainly get away from you, fox!")

Additionally, this verse is an excellent example of acoustic and syntactic repetition.

In *skazki* that exhibit more developed narrative lines, thematics focus upon dramatic and emotional adventures, usually culminating in the triumph of good over evil. Among the most popular are "Goose-swans" ("Gusi-lebedi") and "The Wolf and the Kids" ("Volk i kozliata"). Enthralled by the exciting events of these tales, children have an opportunity to assimilate the traditional moral code without heavy-handed didacticism. But the *skazki* can hardly be dismissed as mere morality lessons. More importantly, they are central to children's psychic growth.

In his defense of the essential place of fantasy in children's literature, Chukovskii correctly insisted that "until seven or eight years of age, for every normal child the fairy tale is the healthiest food—not a delicacy but essential and very nutritious bread; and no one has the right to deprive him of this food which nothing else can replace."[33] In a similar spirit, Bruno Bettelheim recently devoted an entire book to the integrative function of the fairy tale in the psychological development of the child.

For a story truly to hold the child's attention, it must entertain him and arouse his curiosity. But to enrich his life, it must stimulate his imagination; help him to develop his intellect and to clarify his emotions; be attuned to his anxieties and aspirations; give full recognition to his difficulties, while at the same time suggesting solutions to the problems which perturb him. In short, it must at one and the same time relate to all aspects of his personality—and this without ever belittling but, on the contrary, giving full credence to the seriousness of the child's predicaments, while simultaneously promoting confidence in himself and in his future.[34]

Together with the rhymes, these folktales play an indisputably vital role in the lives of young children. In addition, whatever inspiration they may offer children's writers enhances the written tradition. Such is the case generally with Russian children's folklore—it is important both in and of itself and as the time-proven example it offers children's poets.

**3**

# PREREVOLUTIONARY POETRY

$A$GAINST THE BACKGROUND of folklore, there gradually developed in Russia a body of literature self-consciously aware of the child. It was a slow process, related to the discovery of childhood, itself long in coming, as Philippe Ariès has shown.[1] One cannot begin to speak of children's literature in Russia until the late eighteenth century, and the history of their poetry does not begin until the middle of the nineteenth century.

The person generally considered as the father of Russian children's literature is the famous publicist and journalist Nikolai Novikov (1744–1818), who in the 1770s turned his attention to questions of child education in occasional supplements to his newspaper the *Moscow Gazette (Moskovskie vedomosti)*. Between 1779 and 1789 he printed more than forty books for children on a press rented from Moscow University. In the spirit of the age, the nature of these works was primarily scientific and morally instructive.[2] Although he did not directly address children's aesthetic needs, Novikov's recognition of children as a separate audience was an important step. A broader range of material is found in his magazine *Children's*

*Reading for the Heart and Mind* (*Detskoe chtenie dlia serdtsa i razuma*), which appeared for four years (1785–1789) as a regular free supplement to the *Moscow Gazette*. Besides instructive articles and occasional contemporary literature (including works by the sentimentalist Nikolai Karamzin, who also served as editor), *Children's Reading* had material adapted from traditional fables, proverbs, and folktales. In retrospect, it is clear that Novikov's enlightened efforts contain the essential elements of what would become a healthy children's literature over one hundred years later.

By the beginning of the nineteenth century, Russian children were more or less established as a separate literary audience, although hardly in a modern sense. While an ever-increasing number of children's magazines were appearing, their contents amounted to little more than republications of works originally written for adults. Examining assorted volumes, one is struck above all by the tedious, colorless, unimaginative tone and physical layout of these periodicals.[3] Type was small and dense; illustrations, few in number and limited by the technology of the day to black-and-white wood cuts and engravings. Most works were addressed to an older school-age audience. Children may have been nominally recognized as different from adults, but it would be a long time before their elders would learn to address that difference with understanding.

In the first half of the century, there was virtually no poetry written for children. In compensation for this, works for adults gradually crossed over into the children's realm, just as the *skazka* came to enrich children's folklore. To this category belong Ivan Krylov's fables and the *skazki* of Vasilii Zhukovskii, Pushkin, and Ershov, all to some extent indebted to folklore. Children's fondness for these nineteenth-century works once prompted Chukovskii to remark that "the Russian people dictated to our writers the very best children's books," from Krylov and Pushkin at the beginning of the century, to Nikolai Nekrasov, Tolstoi, and Ushinskii later on. Technically the works of Krylov, Pushkin, Zhukovskii, and Ershov fall outside the scope of this study, since their authors did not intend them for children. Yet the fables, and even more the tales, came to occupy such an important place in Russian children's literary upbringing that it is not only enlightening but also essential to isolate the characteristics that make them so attractive to children.

Long considered suitable literary fare for the nursery and early classroom, animal fables have achieved great popularity with both children and their elders. Their didacticism is appropriate to adults' traditional manner of communication with children. Moreover, offering fine material for illustration, they are among the oldest picture books. In Russia fables became available in editions for children by the middle of the eighteenth century.[4] The most popular are those of Ivan Krylov (1769–1844), which first appeared in 1809. Although there was no children's edition until after Krylov's death, his fables did appear from time to time in children's magazines and anthologies.[5] Together with anthropomorphized animals, the rhythmic verse, predominantly short stanzas, abundant rhyme, and colorful colloquial language all help make Krylov's fables accessible to children.

Very high on the list of Russian children's perennial favorites are the verse tales of Aleksandr Pushkin (1799–1837): "The Tale of Tsar Saltan" ("Skazka o tsare Saltane," 1831), "The Tale of the Fisherman and the Fish" ("Skazka o rybake i rybke," 1833), "The Tale of the Dead Princess and the Seven Knights" ("Skazka o mërtvoi tsarevne i o semi bogatyriakh," 1833), and "The Tale of the Golden Cockerel" ("Skazka o zolotom petushke," 1834). Today these *skazki* are frequently reprinted in attractive illustrated editions; versions in English and other languages appear as well.[6]

In view of the already long-standing popularity of Pushkin's tales, it is not surprising that both Chukovskii and Marshak carefully studied them, both singling out "The Tale of Tsar Saltan" as the one most accessible to small children. Written almost a century before the revolution, Pushkin's *skazki* provided much of the basis for the best of children's poetry of the early Soviet period.[7]

Pushkin's interest in folktales was shared by his contemporary Vasilii Zhukovskii (1783–1852), who as early as 1826 published a prose translation of a Grimm fairy tale in *Child's Compaion* (*Detskii sobesednik*). Altogether Zhukovskii wrote six of his own tales. There is some debate about the audience he intended for his *skazki*. While some scholars label them tales for children, they all first appeared in adult periodicals.[8] Zhukovskii's tales may have found a child audience in the 1830s and 1840s, but their heavier style did not assure them the lasting popularity of Pushkin's.

More obviously aimed toward little children are the few short poems Zhukovskii wrote in 1845 to introduce his German-speaking children to the Russian language.[9] They still occasionally appear in modern anthologies of children's poetry.[10] As the titles indicate —"The Little Bird" ("Ptichka"), "Kitten and Kid" ("Kotik i kozlik"), "Skylark" ("Zhavoronok"), "Tom Thumb" ("Mal'chik s pal'chik")—these poems are extremely simple and largely satisfy Chukovskii's stylistic expectations. Concrete visual images are dynamically conveyed through frequent verbs; repetitive syntactic structures set up opportunities for sound play. These and other characteristics, such as recurring diminutives and animal characters, are all familiar from the oral tradition.

A decade earlier, in 1834, Pëtr Ershov (1815–1869), then a nineteen-year-old student at St. Petersburg University, published the first part of his folk-inspired *skazka* "The Little Humpbacked Horse" ("Konëk-gorbunok") in *Library for Reading* (*Biblioteka dlia chteniia*). At the time apparently no one, the author included, realized that the work was ideal for children. Since Pushkin's *skazki* became popular with children, it is no surprise that the work of his closest imitator would follow suit. This popularity, however, did not come until the 1860s, for "The Little Humpbacked Horse" was not republished until after the reign of Nicholas I.[11]

In the late 1860s five children's poems by the prominent poet and publisher Nikolai Nekrasov (1821–1878) appeared in *Notes of the Fatherland* (*Otechestvennye zapiski*), the liberal journal he was editing at the time. The sixth and least remarkable was published in 1873 in an illustrated collection entitled *To Our Children* (*Nashim detiam*). As early as 1868 Nekrasov is said to have planned a separate edition of this poetry, but such a volume never materialized during his lifetime.[12]

All six of Nekrasov's poems are moderately long moralistic narratives, told to children from the point of view of a benevolent adult "storyteller." The themes are typical of the age, depicting the oppressed peasants of poverty-stricken rural Russia. "General Toptygin" (1867), which has survived the test of time, caricatures—in the manner of Nikolai Gogol'—servile behavior in the face of authority. The stationmaster cowers in fright before a tame bear, mistaking it for a general! This amusing story is enhanced by a fast-paced style: syntactic units are short, close rhyme is constant, the vocabulary is concrete and animated.

Least tendentious and most structurally playful is "Uncle Jacob" ("Diadiushka Iakov," 1867), the earliest of these poems. Its structural pattern is varied, built on contrast and juxtaposition. The sound texture is extremely rich, with diction in places clearly echoing children's folk rhymes. After "Uncle Jacob," Nekrasov turned to more tendentious stories, gradually transforming his "folk verse" into a lyric depiction of the languishing masses. While his work for children, considered as a whole, does not deserve the acclaim accorded it by Soviet critics, the best poems have won a permanent place in children's poetic repertory.

If one considers the excellence of poetry in nineteenth-century Russia, from Zhukovskii and Konstantin Batiushkov, forerunners of Pushkin, to Fëdor Tiutchev and Afanasii Fet later in the century, the little that was written for children seems even more paltry.[13] No doubt the most reasonable explanation for this discrepancy is that children were still a largely undiscovered audience, whose needs were improperly appreciated if not totally ignored. At least peasant children had their vital oral tradition, and the ones more fortunate in other respects could borrow "The Tale of Tsar Saltan" and "The Little Humpbacked Horse" from their parents' libraries.

In contrast, how much richer was the poetry dedicated to English children. By the middle of the Victorian era, in addition to many less distinguished books of poetry and myriad collections of nursery rhymes, two most inimitable works of fantasy had appeared in England—Edward Lear's *Book of Nonsense* (1856) and Lewis Carroll's *Alice's Adventures in Wonderland* (1865). Not until many years later would Russian children have access to these works in good translation.[14]

Several Russian writers whose childhoods coincided with the turn of the last century later recalled the noticeable dearth of memorable children's books. The first book Viktor Shklovskii (b. 1893) could remember, for example, was entitled *Naughty Boys and Mischief Makers* (*Shaluny i shalunishki*).

> Na bol'shóm velosipéde
> Bystro ézdit' tak opásno,—
> Govoríl Papásha Féde,
> Govoríl—no vsë naprásno.

(On a big bicycle / it's so dangerous to ride fast, / Papa said to Ted, / he said it—but all in vain.)

The accompanying illustration, as well as the text itself, aroused Shklovskii's ire. "It depicted a bicycle with a gigantic front wheel and a small back one. Such bicycles had not existed for ages. Already for several decades there had been bicycles with two identical wheels and a chain; but in a children's book, children were still being persuaded not to ride on the kind of bicycle that was preserved only in museums."[15] Whether or not his memory served him well, Shklovskii was by no means alone in his criticism of the books available to his childhood generation. Similar opinions were voiced by several of his literary peers, including Chukovskii, Marshak, and Tynianov.[16]

Often the Soviet criticism of turn-of-the-century children's literature reduces the arguments to purely economic issues. It is true that in an era of growing industrialization, as the production of children's books became a more and more profitable commercial enterprise, it attracted business-oriented publishers such as M.O. Vol'f, A. Devrien, and I. Knebel', who were known both for their expensive editions, available to the affluent, and for their low-quality "best-sellers." Yet there was also I.D. Sytin, who catered to a less exclusive market with his "Children's Library" series, containing folktales, Russian classics, and stories by contemporary writers.[17] However, although some found Sytin's illustrated volumes a reasonable mean between the extremes of extravagant editions and cheap pulp, Marshak and Shklovskii disagreed. Marshak thought those books were "mere marketable commodities."[18]

Some of these "mere marketable commodities" do deserve another look, especially several works in verse translated from German and English. The best remembered, whether negatively or positively, is Heinrich Hoffmann's *Struwwelpeter*, an illustrated collection of didactic poetry harshly warning children against both typical and extreme misbehavior. The obstreperous German Peter was reincarnated in Russia as *Stëpka-Rastrëpka*. People like Shklovskii, remote from a child's point of view, responded vehemently to both the text of *Stëpka* and to the accompanying illustrations. "The little boy Stëpka did not comb his hair or trim his nails; his nails grew long. Besides that he picked his nose and his nose grew so large that he carried it around in front of him in a wheelbarrow. All this was expressed in impossible verse."[19] Shklovskii's "adult" reaction is certainly comprehensible. Even today not all enlightened and understanding parents find Hoffman's work suitable for children. Yet, especially with adult commentary to soften the harsh images, the book can be enjoyed by children. Referring to its graphic qualities, Maurice Sendak has called it "one of the most beautiful books in the world."[20]

Early praise came from none other than the symbolist poet Blok, when he was invited to review the book.

> on one hand, it is a very daring and vital book; on the other, it is
> completely free of banality. We must value that kind of combination,
> because daring on the whole easily crosses into effrontery and vital
> ity is often united with banality.
>     I loved this book as a child and even now find it captivating. The
> captivatingly rapid movement from cause to effect is reminiscent of
> the theater's Petrushka [Punch]. And I have been convinced over and

over again that children love Petrushka, who is constantly busy kill-
ing, deceiving, and playing dirty tricks.[21]

Much later, reminiscing toward the end of his life, Marshak recalled only one book from his earliest childhood: that disreputable
*Struwwelpeter!* Although on several occasions he criticized the
weak Russian translation, apparently done by a German who spoke
Russian poorly, he praised the spirit conveyed by the poetry: "one
remembers the brisk verse for a lifetime." It is unlikely that Marshak was exaggerating or simply conjuring up sweet memories in
his waning years, for as early as 1933 he had already expressed essentially the same opinion. "The author of *Struwwelpeter* and his
translator knew children better than did Pleshcheev of the anthologies. I am completely convinced that [they] achieved their
goal—they totally beguiled the customer. They achieved this by
means of appropriate subject matter, brisk rhythm, lively intonation. . . . they created poetry that could enter children's folklore."[22]

Another target of criticism at the beginning of this century was
children's periodicals. Condescending, insensitive approaches to
children were beginning to be challenged. Recall that one of the first
to address himself publicly to the shortcomings of children's
magazines was Chukovskii. Not only did he decry the "commercial
spirit" of the long-established, conservative *Heart-to-Heart* (*Zadushevnoe slovo,* 1877–1918), published by the prosperous Vol'f, he
was also dismayed by the low literary level of better intentioned
periodicals such as *The Glowworm* (*Svetliachok,* 1902–1918). Importantly, Chukovskii's criticism was much more than merely a
derogatory commentary on the existing situation. His evaluation,
including a perceptive description of the nature of children, pointed
the way to new attitudes toward children and their literature.
"Children live in the fourth dimension; they are in their own way
crazy, because for them solid and permanent phenomena are shaky,
unstable, and fluid. For them the world is truly a 'created legend'.
Everything is unusual, just beginning."[23] Here Chukovskii dis-
closed a view of children far from widespread in the early 1900s. He
understood that children must be dealt with in terms of their own
capabilities.

Even those who earnestly sought to offer children works of higher
aesthetic quality had difficulty approaching children on their own
terms. Such was the case with *The Path* (*Tropinka,* 1906–1912), a
children's magazine published by Poliksena Solov'ëva—the youngest sister of the famous philosopher and poet Vladimir Solov'ëv
—and Natal'ia Manaseina. Appearing at the end of the symbolist

period, *The Path* attracted well-known writers of that movement. Konstantin Bal'mont, Blok, and Viacheslav Ivanov were among the poets whose work appeared with some frequency on its pages. Among the prose writers represented were Aleksei Remizov, Fëdor Sologub, and Zinaida Gippius. Solov'ëva, who used the pen name "Allegro," was herself a minor writer and contributed sentimental and religious poetry, tales, and plays. It was in *The Path* that Chukovskii published his first poem for children.

In 1905, before the founding of *The Path*, to which he became a regular contributor, Konstantin Bal'mont (1867–1943) published *Fairy's Tales* (*Feinye skazki*), a substantial collection of sixty-six poems subtitled *Children's Little Songs* (*Detskie pesenki*) and dedicated to his daughter Nina, born in 1901. The younger symbolist Aleksandr Blok (1880–1921), a friend of coeditor Solov'ëva, first published his poems for children in *The Path*. Following the demise of that magazine, he went on to publish two slim volumes at the Sytin Publishing House—one for preschool children: *All Year Round* (*Kruglyi god*), the other for slightly older ones: *Tales* (*Skazki*). Most of the poems reprinted today in Soviet editions for children come from *All Year Round*.[24]

While complaining of its excessively religious orientation, Chukovskii warmly praised *The Path* and the writers associated with it. He was especially pleased by a few poems by Blok and the future acmeist Sergei Gorodetskii.[25] Yet Chukovskii's high opinion must be seen in a larger context. *The Path* was in many ways an improvement upon other children's magazines, but it cannot be said that what appeared there had lasting appeal for children. And if the children's poems of Blok and Bal'mont have virtually disappeared into oblivion, one can well imagine what their less talented contemporaries were producing. The essence of that poetry was scathingly but nevertheless accurately described by Tynianov and Marshak. "There were no children; there were only lilliputians. From the whole world prerevolutionary children's poetry selected the little objects then found in toy shops, the very smallest minutiae of nature: snowflakes, dew drops. From all the riches of folktales they captured only a commercial assortment of angels, fairies, mermaids, elves, gnomes, trolls, woodsprites, princesses, and talking frogs."[26]

The severity of these judgments was well deserved, but the Russians were not alone in their guilt. While the later Victorian era in England produced some excellent poetry, sensitive to a child's point of view (Robert Louis Stevenson's *A Child's Garden of Verses*, for example), there are also works that come close to reproducing Marshak's catalogue of angels, fairies, mermaids, and elves. In 1902, the same year that Rudyard Kipling published his wonderfully imaginative *Just So Stories,* Walter de la Mare came out with his first volume of children's poetry, *Songs of Childhood.* In their attitude toward children, the two works were far apart indeed. Kipling's fanciful blend of rhythmic prose, poetry, and amusingly annotated illustrations signaled an acute understanding of how children's minds operate. De la Mare's lyrics, in contrast, were often "drenched in an otherworldly mood"[27]—as an anonymous dust jacket reviewer so aptly put it—similar to the atmosphere of Bal'mont's *Fairy's Tales.* Fortunately, in the later collection *Peacock Pie* (1913), subtitled *A Book of Rhymes* and certainly reminiscent of nursery rhymes, de la Mare displayed a better understanding of children.

However minor their contributions, it is nevertheless significant that several symbolists tried writing poetry for children. Although the symbolists' efforts on the whole were less than successful, they were an improvement upon what had preceded them. They also indicate that by the beginning of the twentieth century the child was fast gaining recognition in Russia, as in the West. If the symbolists did not consistently apply the lessons inherent in folklore and the *skazki* of Pushkin and Ershov, some of their contemporaries would soon do so, proving that poetry could in fact be written in a manner appealing to children. Not long after Chukovskii in 1907 first criticized the prevailing low level of children's poetry, his admonitions were heeded by his colleague and sometime friend Sasha Chërnyi.

The place of Sasha Chërnyi (1880–1932) in the tradition of Russian children's poetry is not easy to assess. He was very much a transitional figure whose original and best writing for children predated the revolution and anticipated the work of Chukovskii and Marshak in the 1920s. Yet he is more often remembered as an émigré writer than as a Russian one. Born Aleksandr Glikberg, he came to St. Petersburg from Odessa in 1905 at the height of early revolutionary activity to become an important contributor to several of the most popular satirical periodicals of the day.[28] In connection with this work he met Kornei Chukovskii, who was also very involved in the satirical press. Unfortunately, the details of their acquaintance are vague. Apparently in 1909 Chërnyi took serious exception to something Chukovskii had written about him, which led to their estrangement for several years. As Chukovskii later described, there eventually came a rapprochement: "We nevertheless met again. We were reconciled by little children, since almost simultaneously [Chërnyi] had become a children's writer and I an editor of almanacs and collections for children."[29]

While continuing to write for adults, Chërnyi turned more and more to the world of children. In 1912 he contributed poetry and prose to two collections. The following year he published his first volume of children's poems.[30] In 1917 he collaborated with Chukovskii on the twelve issues of For Children, supplement to Plowland. Soon after that one of his poems was included in The Fir Tree. With their interest in children's literature, it would appear that Chërnyi and Chukovskii might have become a successful creative team. Unfortunately, such a possibility was cut off in 1920 by Sasha Chërnyi's emigration from Russia, first to Berlin and ultimately to Paris.

In his first years as an émigré, Chërnyi devoted himself primarily to children's literature. Children's Island (Detskii ostrov), his most complete collection of poems for children, was published in 1921. He also edited several volumes of a children's series of Russian classics.[31] Although he continued to write for children until the end of his life, he never surpassed the creative peak attained in Children's Island. Chukovskii speculated that in the alien environment of western Europe, Chërnyi gradually lost his sensitive understanding of the poetic expectations of Russian children. "His tragic alienation from the reading masses began to be felt even [in children's literature]. By the middle of the 1920s Russian émigré children no longer composed a monolithic whole. They were scattered over the entire world and were quickly assimilated into their foreign surroundings. The poet found himself in a vacuum—without any readers, without a future, with only a past."[32] Although Chukovskii probably overdramatized the situation, he was essentially correct. The inherent problems of any writer in emigration are greater yet for a children's writer.

Although Sasha Chërnyi's poetry is not readily available to the average Soviet child, it is far from insignificant in the broader spectrum of Russian children's poetry. Of the poets preceding Chukovskii, Chërnyi was the only one who clearly perceived the aesthetic and emotional needs of children. From his poetry alone, one easily senses that Chërnyi really understood the way a child's psyche operates. Documenting his sensitivity, Chërnyi's contemporaries, including Chukovskii, have described how he loved to play with children.

> In general his behavior was proud and introverted. He allowed himself to be familiar with no one. Therefore I was greatly surprised when one hot summer Sunday . . . I heard some voices resoundingly

shouting to him: "Sasha, Sasha, quick, come here!", and I saw that
not only did he not feel offended, but that he willingly reacted to
those entreaties. He was sitting half-naked in an obviously rented
boat, his black eyes sparkling like olives. The boat was full of little
kids about seven years old or a bit older whom he had just rowed to
the bridge and back; now others, crowding close by on the pier, were
waiting for him: "Sasha, come here, come here!" He cautiously un-
loaded one group of passengers and filled his boat with the others.
Then he immediately set off on another trip.[33]

Most of the poems in *Children's Island* confirm the side of Chërnyi's nature Chukovskii witnessed.

Chërnyi's poetry for children does in fact reflect the emotional
rapport he must have felt with his young friends. Understandably,
the sentimental, condescending, unchildlike poetry others were
writing disturbed his sensibility, as it did Chukovskii's. Chërnyi's
first response was the epigram "Syruplet" ("Siropchik"), addressed
to "children's poetesses" under the pseudonym "Ivan Chizhik."

> Dáma, kacháias' na vétke,
> Píkala: Mílye détki!
> Sólnyshko chmóknulo kústik
> Ptíchka oprávila biústik
> I, obnimáia romáshku,
> Kúshaet mánnuiu káshku . . . .
>
> Déti, v okónnye rámy
> Khmúro ustávias' glazámi,
> Pólny nedétskoi pecháli,
> Dáme v molchán'i vnimáli.
> Vdrúg zazvenél golosóchek:
> "Skól'ko napíkala stróchek?"[34]

(A lady swaying on a branch / chirped: Dear little children! / The little sun kissed the little bush with a smack, / the little bird
straightened out its bodice / and embracing a daisy, / is eating cream
of wheat . . . // The children, gloomily staring / at window frames, /
full of unchildlike sadness, / listened to the lady in silence. /
Suddenly a little voice rang out: / "How many little lines had she
chirped?")

Throughly annoyed by the work of those spiritual enemies impli-
cated in his epigram, Chërnyi became the first Russian poet to
dedicate himself consciously to the creation of poetry truly accessible to children. He was a successful pioneer in the territory that
came to be more widely explored after the revolution.[35]

As Chukovskii and Marshak would do a few years later, Chërnyi embodied in his children's poetry a playful, humorous spirit. He worked with relatively small forms, typically twenty to forty lines long, where the controlling point of view is most often that of a child. In each of the three sections of *Children's Island*—"Merry Little Eyes" ("Vesëlye glazki"), "Little Animals" ("Zveriushki"), and "Little Songs" ("Pesenki")—there are several poems that have play as their central focus. This element is decidedly stronger in the poems written between 1911 and 1917, but it is still discernible in those written in 1920–1921. Some of the poems directly convey the feeling of a children's game; that is, the poem itself could be a transcription of the verbal accompaniment to a game. A good example of this is the early poem "Train" ("Poezd," 1912), which begins:

> Trétii zvonók, Fón-fón-fón!
> Passazhíry, kóshki i kúkly, v vagón!
> Do svidán'ia, pishíte!
> Mashíte platkámi, mashíte!
> Mashiníst, svistí!
> Paravóz, pykhtí:
> Tsákh-tákh!
> Poékhali-poékhali,
> Taákh-tákh-tákh!
> Kochegár, ne zevái!
> Tsákh-tákh-tákh-tákh![36]

(The third bell, ding-a-ling! / Passengers, cats, and dolls, get in the car! / Good-bye, do write! / Wave your hankies, wave! / Engineer, give a whistle! / Steam Engine, puff: / Choo, choo! / Let's go, let's go, / Choo, choo, choo! / Stoker, pay attention! / Choo, choo, choo, choo!)

Play of a less dynamic sort is treated through simple description or reference, usually from a child's but sometimes from an adult's point of view. The latter is exemplified by "About Kathy" ("Pro Katiushu"), where the lyric voice conveys an image of a little girl playing at "laundry."

> Ai, skól'ko pény!
> Zabrýzgany stény,
> Tázik pishchít,
> Vodá boltáetsia,
> Katiúsha pykhtít,
> Taburét kacháetsia . . .
> Krásnye lápki
> Polóshchut triápki,
> Nad vodóiu mýl'noi
> Vyzhimáiut síl'no-presíl'no—

> I v vódu snóva!
> Gotóvo!
>
> (501)

(Oh, how many suds! / The walls are splashed up, / the basin is squeaking, / the water is sloshing, / Kathy is puffing, / The stool is swaying . . . / Little red hands / are rinsing clothes, / above the soapy water / they are wringing strongly, so strongly— / and back in the water! / Done!)

The tone is continually a happy one, capturing well the spirit of water play, one of children's favorite pastimes.

Children's fascination with the animal kingdom is acknowledged by Chërnyi in his cycle of animal poems. His menagerie is a large one, ranging from domestic kittens to barnyard animals, from common birds to the monkey and elephant of Africa. All that is missing is a crocodile! While his impulse to treat a favorite child theme is a good one, most of the animal poems do not really succeed in capturing the same lively spirit as do those that treat play directly. As soon as Chërnyi sets about describing animals, he is tempted to use them to convey rather more didactic themes, sometimes in a way vaguely reminiscent of the fable tradition.

In some poems a question-answer structure is used, reminding one of folk riddles and legitimately deriving from children's well-known, insatiable curiosity about their environment. "The Chimney Sweep" ("Trubochist," 1918) begins in a manner later immortalized by Chukovskii in "The Telephone."

> Któ prishél?—Trubochíst.
> Dlia chegó?—Chístit' trúby.
>
> (498)

(Who came?—The chimney sweep. / What for?—To sweep the chimneys.)

While an educational message lies at its base, that message—the destruction of the myth of the chimney sweep as bogey—is subordinate to the lively verbal play that predominates throughout. "Oinker" ("Khriushka"), a similar poem, maintaining a stronger sense of dialogue beyond the initial question and answer, betrays little more than pure fun in a style which Chukovskii was to exploit in "The Telephone."

> "Khavrón'ia Petróvna, kák váshe zdoróv'e?"
> —"Odýshka i malokróv'e . . . ."
> "V samom déle?
> A vý by poból'she éli! . . .

—"Khriu-khriú! Nét appetíta . . .
Éle doéla shestóe korýto:
Vedró pomóev,
Reshetó s shelukhóiu,
Púd varḗnoi kartóshki,
Mísku okróshki . . . "

(510)

("Khavronia Petrovna, how is your health?" / "I'm short of breath and
have anaemia . . . " "Really? / You should eat more!. . ." / "Oink,
oink! I have no appetite . . . / I barely ate six troughfuls: / A bucket of
slops, / A sieveful of husks, / A pood of boiled potatoes, / A bowl of
kvass soup . . . .")

Before Chërnyi, of course, humorous dialogue was frequent in children's folk rhymes and tales.

Chërnyi's poetry was the first within the written tradition to
respond consistently well to children's verbal abilities and emotional needs. To a great extent this is true because he did incorporate
many devices similar to those found in children's folklore. In this
respect two important factors distinguish the structure of his poetry
from that of his justifiably maligned contemporaries. Most of his
poems are permeated by lively rhythms and unusually rich sound
textures, both areas highly developed in folk poetry. Although in his
later poems there is a strong tendency toward regular trochaic meter, some of the earliest poems display a remarkable metrical variety. Even in shorter poems metrical shifts contribute to a varied
rhythm, which helps keep a child's attention by occasionally catch-
ing him off guard.

If Sasha Chërnyi had not emigrated but had remained in the
Soviet Union and continued his friendship with Chukovskii,
perhaps the popular "duumvirate" of children's poets—Chukovskii
and Marshak—would have been a triumvirate instead. But the
exigencies of historical reality produced a different situation.
Nevertheless, while Chërnyi's poetry has not entered the living
literary tradition of Russian children, its spirit has been continued
in the best postrevolutionary poetry written for them. With his
genuine understanding of the child psyche, Chërnyi created poetry
in a manner unprecedented before Chukovskii's "The Crocodile."
Moving away from the misguided direction of Bal'mont, Blok, and
their still less talented colleagues, he intuitively turned to the oral
tradition, thereby linking his poetry with a source of verbal creativity proven accessible to children. Beside the continuing strong tradition of children's folklore in Russia, the fate of Pushkin's and Er-

shov's *skazki* had shown that children love the oral mode, original or stylized. But before Chërnyi, only Nekrasov had attempted to incorporate folk elements in poetry written specifically for children. No one before Chërnyi drew upon the oral tradition with his understanding. His use of children's folklore, together with his appreciation of child psychology, created a model for the further development of children's poetry in Russia. Outstanding among those to profit from Chërnyi's example was Kornei Chukovskii.

**4**

## CHUKOVSKII'S *SKAZKI*

To his poetry for children Chukovskii brought three crucial ingredients: a solid background in both classical and modern Russian poetry, an extensive knowledge of Russian folklore, and boundless, loving curiosity about the children—his own and others—who were constantly near him. From his youth he was immersed in poetry. Not only was he a voracious reader, but he was also fortunate enough to be living in that magic age when it was possible to hear poetry read by such masters as Blok, Akhmatova, Ivan Bunin, Maiakovskii, Mikhail Kuzmin, and Innokentii Annenskii.[1] But Chukovskii was not merely a passive reader or listener. Already in his youth he responded as an active critic, writing numerous articles about contemporary poetry. These experiences assured his thorough familiarity with Russian poetry, and were—as he noted himself—of great importance for his own development. "It is unthinkable that without having assimilated this 'adult' poetry I could have written a single line of my 'Wash'em Clean' or 'Chatterbox Fly.' "[2]

His knowledge of contemporary poetry was matched by an avid interest in the oral tradition. The most immediate source of aesthetic inspiration, and of formal influence, for his poetry for children was folklore, and especially children's folklore. "I had . . . discovered that great life-giving miracle of art: the magnificent Russian folklore. The books of Snegirëv, Kireevskii, Rybnikov, Gil'ferding, Afanas'ev, Barsov, Shein had long since been my reference books. They accustomed me to folk aesthetics and gave me the promising foundation of common-sense, normative taste."[3] Nor was his discovery limited to the Russian tradition. Recall that more than a decade before he began to write for children, his far-ranging curiosity had led him to English nursery rhymes.

Among the dominant features of the cultural renaissance that burst forth in Russia at the turn of the century was a turning to the past, to Russian history and folklore, for artistic inspiration. One of the natural corollaries of this interest was a fascination with the primitive in general, hence with the childlike. Chukovskii's interest in children, their language, and their folklore therefore had certain elements in common with the interests of his fellow writers and artists, especially the futurists. In an article about the latter in 1914, Chukovskii wrote: "The present thirst for the primitive has led people to children, to the child's soul. Artists, especially the cubists, study children's drawings, attempt to imitate them; poets devotedly print little samples of children's verses."[4] The last statement was prompted by the inclusion of a child's poem in *A Trap for Judges* (*Sadok sudei*, 1910), the first miscellany of the Hylaea group. This precedent was followed by Aleksei Kruchënykh's anthology *Children's Own Stories and Drawings* (*Sobstvennye rasskazy i risunki detei*, 1914), expanded and republished in 1923.[5] At times the child-spirit penetrated a poet's own work, as was the case with Elena Guro. As Vladimir Markov has pointed out, in her strong attraction to the theme of childhood, Guro often presented things "as perceived or imagined by a child." In her last collection, *Baby Camels of the Sky* (*Nebesnye verbliuzhata*, 1914), she used a number of neologisms, of which "the most successful ones," according to Markov, "are created in the manner of the language of children."[6]

In recent scholarship the infantilism and childlike perception of her works has been found to be close to that of Velimir Khlebnikov (1885–1922),[7] whose central role in the creation of modern Russian poetry has been recognized all too slowly both in his own country and abroad.

In his critical articles Chukovskii judged the futurists severely, although his later reminiscences affirm his underlying respect for those poets. "Futurism was alien to me; but I repeat, this did not prevent me from being friends with the futurists, valuing many of their poems, and giving deserved credit to their individual talents."[8] He scorned above all the futurists' destructive tendencies. The harsh nonsense syllables of Kruchënykh were repulsive to him. But such an imaginatively challenging experiment as Khlebnikov's "Incantation by Laughter" ("Zakliatie smekhom")—eleven lines created entirely of neologisms derived from the word *smekh* (laughter)—received his highest praise. "Khlebnikov's *smekhun-chiki* is only rebellion against reason, but Kruchënykh's *dver bul shchyl ziu tsiu è tsprut* is rebellion against both reason and beauty."[9] Khlebnikov's experiment was highly reminiscent of children's linguistic neologisms and nonsensical word play, phenomena in which Chukovskii had developed an interest by the time this poem appeared in 1910. Chukovskii himself could not have denied that the futurists' preoccupation with "the word as such" in part encouraged this interest and further contributed to his own childlike sensitivity to the sound value of individual words.

Most interpretive studies of Khlebnikov's work rely heavily on adjectives such as "infantile" and "childlike." Tynianov described Khlebnikov in these terms: "A child's prism, infantileness of the poetic word, was found in his poetry not as 'psychology'—it was in the elements themselves, in the small phrases and verbal segments. The child and the savage were a new poetic face, suddenly mixing the solid norms of meter and word."[10] Nikolai Stepanov has compared Khlebnikov's poems to the paintings of the "primitive" school and to the drawings of children. "They have the same naive composition, devoid of perspective; a conditional, linear scheme in the portrayal of figures goes along with the scrupulous copying of individual details. And along with this in all the landscapes there is a marvelous sense of nature."[11] In a formal sense much of the childlike quality, or "infantilist technique" as Markov calls it, comes from simple repetitive sound patterns, and the use of wrong words and grammatical forms.[12]

Connecting Nekrasov's poetry with the folk tradition has long been a commonplace. Khlebnikov's work could be treated similarly, although of course from a different point of view. Yet it has not been investigated adequately, which in part explains why the relationship of Khlebnikov's work to Chukovskii's *skazki* remains to be explored. Almost as frequently as he describes Khlebnikov's poetry as "childlike", Stepanov reminds one of his interest in folklore: "Khlebnikov began with folklore. That connection was never to be broken. Folk images, rhythms and melodies, epithets and parallelisms, are part of [his] poetic system."[13]

Tangible evidence of Khlebnikov's interest in folklore can be traced directly to his acquaintance with Chukovskii. When visiting, Khlebnikov would retreat to his hosts's study to immerse himself in collections of folklore. He was especially fascinated by children's oral rhymes.[14] Chukovskii recalled transcribing for his futurist friend many of the trans-sense lines he overheard in children's speech.[15]

In contrast to the symbolists and others for whom folk poetry was largely a model for stylization, for Khlebnikov folklore served as an organizing structural principle.[16] The same contrast can be perceived in the history of children's poetry. Before Chukovskii, some children's poems were stylized in the folk manner, or in what their authors felt was the folk manner. But an appreciation of folklore as a source of intelligent inspiration to be applied to the writing of children's poetry came later.

More than the folk element in Khlebnikov's poetry finds reflection in Chukovskii's *skazki*. Chukovskii's familiarity with the work of Khlebnikov affected his own poetry in other ways. Khlebnikov's long poems, which some consider his most important and successful genre,[17] are generally constructed in a montage-like manner. According to Stepanov, he "opened new possibilities, new compositional principles, based on unexpected combinations and 'linkage' of fragments, that varied in theme and stylistic tonality. Within the bounds of a single . . . section there are shifts in stylistic levels, metrical patterns, and imagery."[18] One of the innovative characteristics frequently noted in Chukovskii's poems is precisely their montage-like composition. Furthermore, Chukovskii easily borrowed specific metrical patterns, not only from folklore, but from the written tradition as well. His knowledge of Khlebnikov's work was important in this respect too.

As later examples will make clear, Chukovskii's work for children was obviously touched by the poetry of his futurist friends. Yet it is important not to confuse structural and stylistic echoes with a poet's essential frame of reference. Chukovskii's interest in children was on a very different plane from that of the futurists who, with the exception of Maiakovskii, did not regard children as a potential poetic audience. As Chukovskii pointed out, their preoccupation with children's creativity arose primarily from their own pursuit of novelty—a search that led both forward into the future and backward into the primitive past. The latter, embracing both the history of mankind as a whole and the history of individual human lives, necessarily includes childhood. They were fascinated with children's artistic endeavors in relation to their adult point of view. Chukovskii, on the other hand, successfully interacted with children on their own level and was interested in them for their own sake. For him they were a significant, too often misunderstood, and even neglected audience, in need of good aesthetic nourishment. It might be said that Chukovskii dealt with "the child as such."

Chukovskii's outstanding contribution to children's poetry is the twelve *skazki* he wrote between 1916 and 1934. All are relatively long poems, with the extremes ranging from "The Crocodile" (539 lines) to "Wonder Tree" (39 lines). The average length of the others is 150 lines. The unique quality of these poems and the variation among them makes it difficult to assign them to a single category. Tynianov once described them in sum as "a child's comic epic,"[19] certainly a viable definition. Seven of them ("The Crocodile," "The Cockroach," "Chatterbox Fly," "Barmalei," "Fedora's Misfortune," "The Stolen Sun," and "Ouch-it-hurts") are indeed tales of epic adventure, echoing at times such a venerable folk genre as the *bylina* (the Russian oral epic). Three are engaging verbal games ("Wonder Tree," "The Muddle," and "The Telephone"), "Wash'em Clean" is an unconventional didactic tale, and the last and least successful ("Toptygin and the Fox") is a fable.

The narrative point of view is largely in keeping with the expectations of the epic genre, qualified, of course, by consideration for a special audience. Only "Wash'em Clean" is narrated entirely in the first person, ostensibly from the point of view of a capricious child who has neglected his cleanliness. The other tales flow from an omniscient adult narrator whose sympathies obviously lie with children. Although the poetic structure is far too complex for it ever to have been created by children, it is replete with sounds and concepts pleasing to them. A clever adult presence lurks constantly behind the scenes, only rarely introducing himself directly, as in "The Telephone."

> U meniá zazvoníl telefón. . . .[20]
> Ia tri nóchi ne spál,
> Ia ustál.
> Mné by zasnút',
> Otdokhnút' . . .
> No tól'ko ia lëg—
> Zvonók!
>
> (205)

(My telephone rang. // I haven't slept for three nights. / I'm tired. / I'd like to fall asleep, / to rest . . . / But as soon as I lie down— / the bell!)

The narrator's "I" already creeps in at the end of "The Crocodile." (In the original version, Re-Mi's drawing unmistakably depicts Chukovskii in caricature.)[21]

> Nýnche s vizítom ko mné prikhodíl—
> Któ vy dúmali?—sám Krokodíl.
>
> Iá usadíl stariká na divánchik,
> Dál emu sládkogo cháiu stakánchik.
>
> (295)

(To visit me today came— / Who do you think? Crocodile himself. // I seated the old man on the little sofa; / I gave him a little glass of sweet tea.)

Usually, however, his presence is indicated not by direct or indirect intrusion, but by the myriad concessions he makes to the spirit of childhood, which all contribute to the lively and imaginative unfolding of the tales. Since the whole of the poetry is permeated by this attitude, we will treat specific examples as they arise in the course of this analysis.

Neither the structure nor the thematics of Chukovskii's tales comes straight from any earlier established tradition. Their innovative quality is precisely one of their outstanding features. Nevertheless, echoes from folklore reverberate throughout, and to some extent there are recognizable traces from the written tradition.

Soviet critics and scholars have identified the similarity of some lines in "The Crocodile" with those of earlier poets. The unforgettable anapestic beginning has been traced to Nikolai Agnivtsev (1888–1932), little known today but popular in his time, who once wrote a poem which begins:

> Udivítel'no míl
> Zhil da býl Krokodíl—
> Ètak fúta chetýre, ne ból'she . . .[22]

(Once upon a time there lived / an amazingly nice crocodile— / about four feet long, not more . . .)

A stanza in very regular trochaic tetrameter:

> Vsé likúiut i tantsúiut,
> Vániu mílogo tselúiut.
> I iz kázhdogo dvorá
> Slýshno grómkoe "urá."
> (278–79)

(All are rejoicing and dancing, / and kissing dear Vania. / And from every courtyard / is heard a loud "hurrah".)

is reminiscent of those monotonously uniform trochaic lines of Ershov's "The Little Humpbacked Horse." Chukovskii's famous laconic portrayal of war—""I grianul boi! Voina! Voina!" (292) (And the battle broke out! War! War!)—unmistakably echoes Pushkin's "Poltava": "I grianul boi. Poltavskii boi!"[23] (And the battle broke out! Poltava's war!"). Some lines of dactylic tetrameter—

> Kínulsia Vánia za zlými zveriámi:
> "Zvéri otdáite mne Liáliu nazád!"
> (201)

(Vania rushed at the wicked beasts: / "Beasts, give me back Lolly!"

are rhythmically reminiscent of Nekrasov: "Trud ètot, Vania, byl strashno gromaden"[24] (That labor, Vania, was terribly enormous). Other lines are so typical of the Ego-futurist Igor' Severianin they need no exact rhythmic analogy to bring his work to mind. Consider, for example, Severianin's treatment of the child theme.

> V párke plákala dévochka: "Posmotrí-ka ty, pápochka,
> U khoróshenkoi lástochki perelómena lápochka,
> Iá voz'mú ptítsu bédnuiu i v platóchek ukútaiu . . . ."
> I otéts prizadúmalsia, potriasénnyi minútoiu,
> I prostíl vse griadúshchie i kaprízy i shálosti
> Míloi málen'koi dócheri, zarydávshei ot zhálosti.[25]

(In the park a little girl was crying: "Look, Papa, / that nice little swallow has broken its little leg, / I'll take the poor bird and wrap it in my hanky . . . ." / And the father became thoughtful, touched by the moment, / and forgave all the future whims and pranks / of his dear little daughter who wept from pity.)

A similar intonation is discernible in the first two lines of these stanzas from "The Crocodile":

Mílaia dévochka Liálechka!
S kúkloi guliála oná
I na Tavrícheskoi úlitse
Vdrúg uvidála Sloná.

Bózhe, kakóe strashílishche!
Liália bezhít i krichít.
Gliád', pered néi iz-pod móstika
Výsunul gólovu Kít.

(288)

(The sweet little girl Lolly / With her doll she was strolling, / and on
Tauride Street / she suddenly saw an elephant. // Gosh, what a fright-
ful thing! / Lolly ran and screamed. / Suddenly in front of her from
under a bridge / a whale stuck out its head.)

The image of the little girl strolling, the adjective *milaia,* and the
diminutives all recall Severianin.[26] With the word *vdrug,* however,
the similarity abruptly ends. Chukovskii's Lialechka is in quite
another world!

How do such literary echoes or borrowings fit into the structural
conception of "The Crocodile"? Petrovskii, who felt none of the
other tales to be so directly indebted to earlier poetry, chose to
interpret the familiar echoes in "The Crocodile" as a young writer's
parodistic method of mastering the art of poetry.[27] Rassadin took
issue with this theory, claiming that Chukovskii's borrowings,
though conscious, fit organically into their new and unique poetic
environment. Associated with a definite mood and clothed in a
definite lexicon, the rhythmic-syntactic figures of Nekrasov or
Lermontov were necessary to Chukovskii in those moments when
similar moods arose in his *skazka.*[28] Both critics made valid, compatible points. Creating children's poetry for the first time,
Chukovskii called upon the earlier tradition whenever it was suitable. This is especially understandable if one bears in mind the original circumstances of composition. But these borrowings do not
strike one as typical parody, where an earlier literary work is consciously ridiculed. Here the emphasis is rather on their integration
into a new poetic structure.

A better example of real parody can be found in "Barmalei."

Mílyi, mílyi liudoéd,
Smíluisia nad námi,
Mý dadím tebé konfét,
Cháiu s sukhariámi!

(217)

(Dear, dear cannibal, / have mercy on us; / we will give you candy, / and tea with rusks!)

Here Chukovskii directly mocks that older, turn-of-the-century tradition of sugary-sweet poetry for children, exemplified by the poem "Birdie" ("Ptichka"), found in many earlier anthologies. The last two lines of the stanza come straight from the following one:

> Akh, ne pústim, ptíchka, nét!
> Ostaváisia s námi.
> Mý dadím tebé konfét,
> Cháiu s sukhariámi . . . .[29]

(Oh, we won't let you go, birdie, no! / Stay with us. / We will give you candy / and tea with rusks!)

The case of parody is one where obvious divergence between child and adult perception arises. Literary parody is inaccessible to small children, for they are not likely to be familiar with adult poetry. Those lines which for an adult evoke Lermontov or Nekrasov, for a child simply convey a direct emotion, to be taken at face value. It is possible, however, that some children of the 1920s caught the humorous intonation of the line "tea with rusks," since "Birdie" was still a popular poem then.

While Soviet critics have pointed out myriad echoes of nineteenth-century Russian poetry in "The Crocodile," no one has so much as suggested some obvious and striking correspondences between "Wash'em Clean" and one of Khlebnikov's long poems. It is true that Chukovskii was working on Nekrasov's long satirical poem "The Contemporaries" at the time he wrote "Wash'em Clean" and "The Cockroach" in 1921. But equally importantly, he must also have read Khlebnikov's "Harmony World" ("Ladomir," 1920).[30] Not only does the title of Chukovskii's work echo Khlebnikov's, but major parts of the text, from beginning to end, do as well. In fact, "Wash'em Clean" in so many instances evokes "Harmony World," one senses that Khlebnikov's work must have been a primary source of inspiration for Chukovskii. This is not to suggest there are any thematic similarities between the works. Khlebnikov's complex utopian vision is very remote from Chukovskii's lighthearted didactic tale for children. But some of Khlebnikov's sounds, words, and rhythms seem to have sparked Chukovskii's creative imagination.

The most explicit connection between the two works is a short line in the closing triplet of "Wash'em Clean," which, it appears, Chukovskii took directly from Khlebnikov.

I v vánne i v báne,
Vsegdá i vezdé—
Véchnaia sláva vodé!

(189)

(And in the bathtub and at the public baths, / always and everywhere— / eternal glory to water!)

Compare this with three lines from "Harmony World" following a section devoted to rivers.

Vsegdá, navsegdá, tam i zdés'!
Vsem vsě, vsegdá i vezdé,—
Nash klích proletít po zvezdé![31]

(Always, forever, here and there! / Everything to all, always and everywhere— / our cry will reach into the cosmos!)

They also share an underlying amphibrachic rhythm. Even the famous beginning of "Wash'em Clean" bears a certain acoustic and syntactic resemblance to lines in "Harmony World." The first example is from Chukovskii, the second from Khlebnikov.

Odeiálo
  Ubezhálo,
Uletéla prostyniá,
  I podúshka,
  Kak liagúshka,
Uskakála ot meniá.

(181)

(The blanket / ran away, / away flew the sheet, / and the pillow / like a frog / leaped away from me.)

Upálo Gé Germánii
I rússkikh Eŕ upálo.
I vizhu El' v tumáne iá
Pozhára v nóch' Kupála.[32]

(The G of Germany fell / and the R of the Russians fell. / And I see L in the fog / of a fire on St. John's eve.)

The meter of the washstand's monologue largely duplicates that in a passage from "Harmony World." Both are trochaic tetrameter.

Ia—Velíkii Umyvál'nik,      ‒ ‒ ´ ‒ ‒ ‒ ‒ ´ ‒
Znamenítyi Moidodýr,        ‒ ‒ ´ ‒ ‒ ‒ ‒ ´
Umyvál'nikov Nachál'nik     ‒ ‒ ´ ‒ ‒ ‒ ‒ ´ ‒
I mochálok Komandír!        ‒ ‒ ´ ‒ ‒ ‒ ‒ ´
Esli tópnu ia nogóiu,       ‒ ‒ ´ ‒ ‒ ‒ ‒ ´ ‒

Pozovú moikh soldát,

V ètu kómnatu tolpóiu

Umyvál'niki vletiát,

I zaláiut, i zavóiut,

I nogámi zastuchát,

I tebé golovomóiku,

Neumýtomu, dadút—

(184)

(I am the Great Washstand, / the famous Wash'em Clean, / chief of washstands / and commander of sponges! / If I stamp my foot / and call my soldiers, / into this room will fly / a crowd of washstands. / And they'll begin to bark and they'll begin to howl, / and they'll begin to stamp their feet, / and they'll give you a dressing down [literally, head washing], / you dirty one.)

Èto shéstvuiut tvoriáne,

Znamenívshi D na T́,

Ladomíra soboriáne

S Trudomírom na shesté.

Èto Rázina miatézh,

Doletév do néba Névskogo,

Uvlekáet i chertézh

I prostránstvo Lobachévskogo.

Pust' Lobachévskogo krivýe

Ukrásiat gorodá

Dugóiu nad rabóchei výei

Vsemírnogo trudá.[33]

(I have not provided a translation since the similarity exists only in Russian.)

Besides the metrical coincidence of these two passages, there are several strong phonetic and morphological echoes. In the second line Chukovskii uses *znamenityi* in the position of Khlebnikov's *zamenivshi*. In the third line both poets syntactically invert a possessive construction (genitive–nominative). *Komandir* in the fourth line of "Wash'em Clean" echoes *trudomirom* in the same line of "Harmony World." After this, one becomes acutely sensitive to the simplest words or short phrases in Khlebnikov's poem that find some reverberation in Chukovskii.

Unfortunately, Chukovskii left no direct clues to how Khlebnikov's poem may have served as a catalyst for "Wash'em Clean," which it seems to have done. One is left to speculate about the mysterious ways of artistic inspiration. No one would dream of calling "Wash'em Clean" derivative, even knowing of its connections with Khlebnikov. It is clearly a masterpiece, perhaps

Chukovskii's best work for young children. They love it and easily commit it to memory. A topic that might otherwise lead to dull sermonizing—"Children, be clean!"—is presented in a highly pleasurable manner. Nevertheless, on some level children have esoteric adult poetry to thank for this.

With the possible exception of "The Telephone," which has some echoes of Khlebnikov and Sasha Chërnyi, only "The Crocodile" and "Wash'em Clean" are so obviously indebted to the written literary tradition.[34] Ultimately the oral tradition, especially children's folklore, prevails. While Chukovskii's *skazki* do not conform to the consistently regular pattern one finds in the oral epic or folktale, in the seven "adventure" tales, a general structural principle reminiscent of the oral epic and folktale can be discerned. In all of them there is the unexpected appearance of danger, the search for a defender, a short battle, victory of the small hero, and collective merrymaking and pardon of the guilty. Even "Ouch-it-hurts" fits into that schema in a most general way, although there the battle is that of a doctor against illness. The qualities of suspense, the hero's apparent inadequacy at the beginning, and the invariable happy ending are all shared with the oral epic and the folktale.

With the exception of "The Crocodile," all of Chukovskii's *skazki* were written in the Soviet era, when collective readings became a part of the poetic experience for children, as well as adults. "When we write, we imagine ourselves on stage . . . I would have written the *skazki* entirely differently, if while writing I did not feel that I would have to read them in huge halls before a multitude of young listeners. From there comes the poetry's quality which I would call theatrical . . . the plots unfold according to the laws of dramatic action."[35] Chukovskii himself reveals that both "Ouch-it-hurts" and "The Stolen Sun" originally were much longer than the final versions. Although he certainly did not discourage solitary reading, his first consideration was for a listening audience. After all, the typical audience for such works does not yet know how to read. Long, slowly paced poems would be especially ineffective. In retrospect, therefore, Chukovskii was dissatisfied with that part of "The Crocodile" where "inexperience" allowed him to introduce the crocodile's long monologue about the animals suffering in the zoo. "In the tale's new edition I wanted to replace that monologue with a brief eight-line stanza conveying the same subject, but the editors opposed this change. In their words, a tradition had already been established which was impossible to destroy. . . . Nevertheless, I consider the monologue a mistake on my part."[36]

One of the most striking features of Chukovskii's poetry is the

variety of rhythmic patterns within a single work. His use of shifting stanzaic structure and metrical patterns was a startling new
approach to children's poetry. It is true that by 1916, when
Chukovskii wrote "The Crocodile," metrical experimentation was
an accepted element of Russian poetry. Beginning with the symbolists, deviations from the canonized syllabo-tonic system of the
eighteenth and nineteenth centuries became the norm. In a relatively short time the disintegration of tradition led from the mod-
ified syllabo-tonic lines of Gippius and Blok, through the experiments of Khlebnikov, to the purely accentual lines of Maiakovskii.
But it is not those developments that Chukovskii pursued. Taking
individual lines and even complete stanzas, one finds his meter is
quite regular. What may be considered innovative, however, are the
metrical shifts between stanzas. In a way, Chukovskii's stanzaic
structure may be compared with that of Blok's "The Twelve"
("Dvenadtsat' "), which in turn harks back to Nekrasov's "Contemporaries" and "Who Lives Well in Russia?"[37] Chukovskii's
montage-like structure must also be considered in light of Khlebnikov's long poems. They are typically written in quite regular metrical patterns, but with shifts from one to another within a single
poem. "Harmony World," for example, is predominantly iambic
tetrameter. Yet the stanza echoed in "Wash'em Clean" is trochaic.

In his study "Rhythmic Shifts," Vladislav Kholshevnikov isolated
several factors in poetry that contribute to what he called the "effect
of expectation deceived" (èffekt obmanutogo ozhidaniia)—
the jolting of the audience's attention. From weaker to stronger,
these rhythmic breaks are: changes in rhyme order, in line length, in
the number of lines in a stanza, enjambment, caesura, and sudden
changes in meter. The last may be either a line of different meter
included in a text of more or less regular meter, or the juxtaposition
in a long poem of small fragments in contrasting meter, usually
emphasizing a thematic or expressive break.[38] Of these shifts, the
one Chukovskii uses least of all is change in the order of rhyme. In
accordance with children's proclivity for rhyme, his tales are written largely in paired rhyme. There are, of course, some deviations,
but those can usually be best explained on the level of verbal play.
Enjambment is rare, as is caesura, which hardly occurs, since most
lines are relatively short. Line length and stanza shape, however, are
very significant.

One need only quickly leaf through a book of Chukovskii's *skazki*
to discover that his lines and stanzas are graphically arranged; many

of the rhythmic shifts are visually discernible. Some lines are very short—sometimes only one syllable long. Others stretch out to as many as fifteen syllables. Those are the extremes; average lines run from two to four feet, as they do in children's folklore. Some stanzas are brief, others are much longer. Lines and stanzas are often placed distinctively on the page. A stanza from "Toptygin and the Fox," which includes a rare one-syllable line, also provides an instance where a case may be made for linking a change in line length to the subject matter.

| | | |
|---|---|---|
| I vót po gorám, po dolínam | – – ´ – – – ´ – – – ´ – | A |
| Míshka shagáet pavlínom, | – ´ – – – ´ – – – ´ – | A |
| I blestít u negó za spinói | – – – ´ – – – ´ – – – ´ | b |
| Zolotói-zolotói, | – – – ´ – – – ´ | c |
| Raspisnói, | – – – ´ | b |
| Sínii-sínii | ´ – – ´ – | D |
| Pavlínii | – – ´ – | D |
| Khvóst. | – ´ | e |

(209)

(And there along mountains and valleys / bruin struts like a peacock, / and shining behind his back is / a very golden, / decorated, / very blue, / peacock / tail.)

An air of suspense is maintained until the very end of the stanza, where the noun finally appears. The emphasis achieved by the one-syllable line is further underscored by the use of a nonrhyme, (*khvost*), after a series of insistent rhymes. By its unconventional arrangement, the underlying anapestic meter enhances the meaning of the stanza.

"Wash'em Clean" also illustrates well Chukovskii's use of the juxtaposition of stanzas to create varying effects. Until the last three stanzas, metrical rhythmic variation is conveyed through changes in line length, most obviously between stanzas, but sometimes within them as well. Two-foot trochaic lines alternate irregularly with four-foot trochees. The length of the stanzas varies, as does the rhyme scheme.

| | | |
|---|---|---|
| Iá za svéchku, | ´ – – ´ – | A |
| Svéchka—v péchku! | ´ – – ´ – | A |
| Iá za knízhku, | ´ – – ´ – | B |
| Tá—bezhát' | ´ – – ´ | c |
| Í vpriprýzhku | ´ – – ´ – | B |
| Pod krovát'! | – – – ´ | c |

Iá khochú napít'sia cháiu,    $\smile - \smile - \smile - \smile -$    D
K samováru podbegáiu,     $- - \smile - - - \smile -$    D
No puzíatyi ot meniá       $- - \smile - - - - \smile$    e
Ubezhál, kak ot ogniá.      $- - \smile - - - - \smile$    e
(181–82)

(I go to get a candle; / it goes into the oven! / I go to get a book; / it goes / leaping / under the bed! // I want to drink some tea. / I run up to the samovar, / but the paunchy thing / runs away from me, as from fire.)

Some might argue that the shorter lines can actually be read together as longer ones. This is in fact sometimes possible when the metrical pattern does not coincide with the end of the line but carries over to the next line. However, when the meter fits the line, as in the above stanzas, the line must be accepted as Chukovskii presented it on the page, since the division into lines does (or should) affect the way poetry is read.

The stanza in "Wash'em Clean" that directly follows the two quoted above further demonstrates the way Chukovskii's stanzas work in contrast to one another.

Bózhe, bózhe!         $\smile - - \smile -$    A
Chtó sluchílos'?      $\smile - - \smile -$    B
Otchegó zhe        $- - - \smile -$    A
Vsë Krugóm         $\smile - - \smile$    c
Zavertélos'        $- - - \smile -$    D
Zakruzhílos'       $\smile - - \smile \smile$    B
I pomchálos' kolesóm?  $- - \smile - - - \smile$    c
(182)

(My, my! / What has happened? / Why has / everything around / started whirling / started twirling / and rushed off in a cartwheel?)

The two-foot lines work naturally to underscore the excited intonation, possibly even conveying a feeling of breathlessness. Therefore, it does not seem artificial that the last four lines are actually one sentence. Further, such line division offers an opportunity to emphasize as end rhyme what otherwise would be internal rhyme. And, of course, short lines are more appropriate for small children than long ones.

Chukovskii's longest lines appear in "The Crocodile." As he grew experienced in writing for children, he was less likely to use twelve- to fourteen-syllable lines. During the narrator's encounter with the crocodile in "Wash'em Clean," the previous stanzas of predominantly four-foot trochees are interrupted by the crocodile's admonition:

> A potóm kak zarychít      — — –́ — — — –́
> Na meniá,      — — –́
>
> Kak nogámi zastuchít
> Na meniá:
>
> "Ukhodí-ka ty domói,
> Govorít,
>
> Da litsó svoë umoí,
> Govorít,
>
> A ne tó kak nalechú,
> Govorít,
>
> Rastopchú i proglochú!—
> Govorít."
>
> (185–86)

(And then he really began to roar / at me; // he really began to stamp his feet / at me! // "You go home," / he said, // "and wash your face," / he said. // "Otherwise I'll rush at you," / he said. // "I'll trample and swallow you!" / he said.)

The significance of each long line is emphasized by the short, repetitious one following it.

Perhaps the easiest and most obvious means of introducing rhythmic variety is through definite metrical shifts. In Chukovskii's *skazki* this occurs in both of the ways described by Kholshevnikov. Most marked is the juxtaposition of whole stanzas in different meters. In the final three stanzas of "Wash'em Clean," for example, from the binary meter used exclusively up to that point, there is a shift to ternary meter.

> Da zdrávstvuet mýlo dushístoe,    — –́ — — –́ — — –́ — —
> I poloténtse pushístoe,    — — — –́ — — –́ — —
> I zubnói poroshók,    — — –́ — — –́
> I gustói grebeshók!    — — –́ — — –́
> Daváite zhe mýt'sia, pleskát'sia,    — –́ — — — –́ — — –́ —
> Kupát'sia, nyriát', kuvyrkát'sia,    — –́ — — –́ — — –́ —
> V usháte, v korýte, v lokháni,    — –́ — — –́ — — –́ —
> V reké, v rechéike, v okeáne,    — –́ — –́ — — — –́ —
>
> I v vánne i v báne    — –́ — — –́ —
> Vsegdá i vezdé    — –́ — — –́
> Véchnaia sláva vodé!    –́ — — –́ — — –́
>
> (188–89)

(Long live fragrant soap, / and fluffy towels, / and tooth paste, / and thick combs! // Let's wash and splash, / bathe, dive, / and turn somersaults / in wooden tubs, in troughs, in wash buckets, / in rivers, / in streams, / in the ocean, // in the bathtub and at the public baths, / always and everywhere— / eternal glory to water!)

The negative aspect of the morality tale is over. Now it is time for solemn instruction. That tone is enhanced by such expressions as "long live" and "eternal glory to water." Although an element of play persists to the end in the catalogue of verbs and washing places, the point of view becomes that of an adult after Wash'em Clean's last speech. Until then the point of view was that of a child.

Similar links between metrical shifts and thematic content exist throughout the *skazki*. Chukovskii clearly used the technique to achieve more than mechanical variety. This is not to suggest that each shift is necessarily accompanied by an obvious tonal transition. Such consistently developed transitions are more likely in adult poetry, where variety as such is not a major issue. Nonetheless, there is in Chukovskii's poetry more than a random connection between content and changes in meter, especially when the changes occur between stanzas. It is not that any given meter can be directly linked with any one mood or tone.[39] Rather, it is the presence of the shift, the very juxtaposition of different metrical patterns, whatever they may be, that is important. Their significance derives from the individual context.

Besides the "shifts" described by Kholshevnikov, other factors contribute to rhythmic variation in poetry. Among them is syntax, which plays an important role. Chukovskii adhered to the lessons he learned from his observations of children at play and from his knowledge of their folklore. Most frequently he divided a sentence into two lines of verse. Long sentences tend to be series of independent clauses, resulting in compound, never complex, syntactical structure. Almost never is there enjambment, which destroys the coincidence of verse line and syntactic unit. Complex verb formations occur only in "The Crocodile." After his first work Chukovskii recognized the error and in the future not only avoided cumbersome participles, but rarely used simpler verbal adverbs.

Among Chukovskii's most common rhythmic devices are repetition and parallel construction. Simple single-word repetition evokes children's folklore above all.

> Múkha, Múkha-Tsokotúkha,
> Pozolóchennoe briúkho!
> (190)

(Little fly, little chatterbox fly, / with the shiny golden belly!)

Such lines are stylistically close to children's jeers. Chukovskii's virtuoso "take-off" on this genre occurs in three stanzas of "The Telephone," where he plays with a basic taunting pattern.

> A nedávno dve gazéli
> Pozvoníli i zapéli:
> —Neuzhéli
> V samom déle
> Vse sgoréli
> Karuséli?
>
> —Akh, v umé li vy, gazéli?
> Ne sgoréli karuséli,
> I kachéli utseléli!
> Vy b, gazéli, ne galdéli,
> A na budúshchei nedéle
> Priskakáli by i séli
> Na kachéli-karuséli!
>
> No ne slúshali gazéli
> I po-prézhnemu galdéli:
> —Neuzhéli
> V samom déle
> Vse kachéli
> Pogoréli!
> Chto za glúpye gazéli!
> (203)[40]

(And not long ago two gazelles / ran up and sang out: / "Really / is it true / all the carousels / burned down?" // "Oh, are you out of your minds, gazelles? The carousels didn't burn down, / and the swings were spared! / Gazelles, you shouldn't make a din, / and next week you could hop over / and sit down on the carousel-swings!" // But the gazelles didn't listen / and kept right on making a din: / "Really / is it true / all the swings burned down?" / What silly gazelles they are!)

In Chukovskii's *skazki* there are numerous instances of syntactic devices familiar from folk poetry in general. The end of one line may be repeated at the beginning of the next (a type of anadiplosis).

> Usmekhnúlsia Krokodíl
> I bedniágu proglotíl,
> Proglotíl s sapogámi i sháshkoiu.
> (275)

(The crocodile grinned / and swallowed the poor policeman; / he swallowed him with his boots and his sword.)

Or the beginning may be repeated (anaphora).

> Vse ot strákha drozhát,
> Vse ot strákha vizzhát.
> (275)

(From fear all tremble; / from fear all shriek.)

Other occasional rhythmic devices echoing folk poetry include negative definitions.

> Ne listóchki na něm,
> Ne tsvetóchki na něm,
>
> A chulkí, da bashmakí
> (195)

(There are no little leaves on it, / there are no little flowers on it: / Instead there are stockings and shoes)

and repeated prepositions:

> Vdrug iz máminoi iz spál'ni
> (183)

(Suddenly from mama's, from her bedroom).

The various metric and syntactic devices by which Chukovskii achieves rhythmic diversity operate in conjunction with intricately arranged sound patterns. As it has been said, "every work of literary art is, first of all, a series of sounds out of which arises the meaning."[41] In poetry, unless one is dealing with extreme trans-sense language, such as that of Kruchënykh, the emergence of semantic content from that series of sounds is an all-important issue. In contrast to most adult poetry, however, children's poetry often approaches pure sound. Furthermore, the subject matter may be very elementary. Thus, while conceptual relationships in Chukovskii's poetry are dramatically but simply drawn, the structural relationships are amazingly complex.

In the early twentieth century, poets were actively exploring the connection between the phonetic and semantic sides of language. Marina Tsvetaeva, for example, once reacted to the word èstrada (stage) in a very childlike way: "Èstrada. Èstrada mesto iavnoe. Iavlennost' zhe i v samom zvuke. 'Zdrastvui! Raduites'!' "[42] (The stage is a place for display. Its "displayfulness" is in the sound itself. "Hooray! Let's be gay!") It is in the same spirit that Chukovskii created the crocodile, whose defining trait and chief preoccupation

is to swallow (*proglotit'*). In whatever situation he appears, he is
gulping down someone or something.

> Oglianúlsia Krokodíl
> I barbósa proglotíl,
> Proglotíl ego vméste s oshéinikom.
>
> (274)[43]

(The crocodile looked round / and swallowed the hound; / he swallowed him along with his collar.)

So it is with all of Chukovskii's animals—their primary characteristics are determined by considerations of sound. Underlying sound
patterns also clarify the following note Chukovskii included in
"The Crocodile": "Some people think that *Gippopotam* (hippopotamus) and *Begemot* (behemoth) are one and the same. In tales
this is not so: *Begemot* is the pharmacist and *Gippopotam* is the
tsar" (284).

Together with features of rhythmic variation, carefully organized
sound patterns play as important a role in Chukovskii's poetry as
they do in children's folklore. Sensitive to children's need for close
rhymes, Chukovskii incorporated regular rhyme as a fundamental
part of his poetry. And in view of children's own proclivities, he
frequently used paired rhyme schemes, a tendency he shares with
folk poetry and literary imitations of folk poetry. Paired rhymes
never dominate to the point of monotony, however. In "The
Crocodile," for example, there are traditional stanzaic patterns,
suggesting a more literary origin.

| | |
|---|---|
| Díkaia Gorílla | A |
| Liáliu utashchíla | A |
| I po trotuáru | B |
| Pobezhála vskách'. | c |
| | |
| Výshe, výshe, výshe, | D |
| Vot oná na krýshe, | D |
| Na sed'móm ètazhé | e |
| Prýgaet, kak miách. | c |

(289)

(The wild gorilla / made off with Lolly / and set off at a gallop / down
the sidewalk. // Higher, higher, higher, / now he's on the roof; / above
the seventh floor, / he's bounding like a ball.)

In later poems an underlying paired rhyme scheme may be broken
by brilliant bursts of sound.

| Vot i výlechil on íkh, | a |
| Limpopó! | b |
| Vot i výlechil bol'nýkh | a |
| Limpopó! | b |
| I poshlí oni smeiát'sia, | C |
| Limpopó! | b |
| I pliasát' i balovát'sia, | C |
| Limpopó! | b |

(247)

(Now he healed them, / Limpopo! / Now he healed the sick ones, / Limpopo! / And they went to laugh, / Limpopo! / and to dance and frolic, / Limpopo!)

Already in "The Crocodile," just a few stanzas before the crocodile's bookish monologue, there appears the following stanza, which is hypnotic as a result of its repeated rhymes:

| "K nám— | a |
| Gippopotám?!" | a |
| "Sám— | a |
| Gippopotám?!" | a |
| "Tám— | a |
| Gippopotám?!" | a |

("To us— / the hippopotamus?!" / "Himself [boss]— / the hippopotamus?!" / "There— / the hippopotamus?!")

(It is often in this type of sound pattern that Chukovskii's influence can be felt in the work of subsequent children's poets.) And of course, the famous first stanza uses only one rhyme, broken in the end by a nonrhyming line.

| Zhil da býl | a |
| Krokodíl. | a |
| On po úlitsam khodíl, | a |
| Papirósy kuríl, | a |
| Po-turétski govoríl,— | a |
| Krokodíl, Krokodíl Krokodílovich! | B (dactylic) |

(273)

(Once upon a time / there lived a crocodile. / He strolled the streets, / he smoked cigarettes, / and spoke Turkish— / Crocodile, Crocodile Son of Crocodile!)

Stanzas with a last unrhymed line occur frequently. In an environment of consistent rhyme, the nonrhyming line attracts special attention.

Again as in children's folklore, internal rhyme is almost as prevalent as end rhyme. Chukovskii took advantage of every opportunity to satisfy children's expectations. In the rare instances where a rhyme may not be regular or rich, there is internal rhyme, which shifts some of the burden from the end of the lines.

| | A | A |
|---|---|---|
| To-to ráda, to-to ráda | | |
| vsia zverínaia sem'iá, | b | b |
| Proslavliáiut, pozdravliáiut | C | C |
| udalógo Vorob'iá! | | b |
| (179) | | |

(Now the whole family of beasts / is happy; / they glorify and congratulate / the daring sparrow!)

Internal rhyme is a constantly recurring phenomenon in this poetry that enraptures the listener with its repeated sounds. One of the most memorable stanzas from "Wash'em Clean" illustrates Chukovskii's rhyming principle with full grammatical rhymes and also serves as an example of how the feeling of motion can be conveyed without any verbs. It is true that verbs precede and follow this passage, but they merely serve to supplement a rhythm easily established without them.

> Utiugí
>> za
>>> sapogámi,
>
> Sapogí
>> za
>>> pirogámi,
>
> Pirogí
>> za
>>> utiugámi . . .
>>>> (182)

(The irons / chase after / the boots.//.the boots / chase after / the pies, // the pies / chase after / the irons. . . .)

The above stanza is also a good example of the role played by special typographic arrangement on the page, a favorite device of Maiakovskii's.

Rhyme is merely the most obvious acoustic feature in this poetry. The sensitive ears of children are delighted by all imaginative sound combinations. Deeply immersed in the process of learning to manipulate the language of their environment, they often are even more aware than adults of the language's peculiar features. They are alert

to alliteration and sound orchestration in general, which may serve
to emphasize a mood. They are especially enchanted by sound-
imitation, which occurs frequently in Chukovskii's poetry, after the
pattern of children's folklore.

> A za nı́mi bliǔdtsa, bliǔdtsa—
> Dzyn'-lia-liá! Dzyn'-lia-liá!
> Vdol' po ǔlitse nesǔtsia—
> Dzyn'-lia-liá! Dzyn'-lia-liá!
>                                   ("Fedora's Misfortune," 232)

(And after them chase saucers, saucers— / Ding-a-ling! Ding-a-
ling! / They're rushing down the street— / Ding-a-ling! Ding-a-ling!)

When Chukovskii spoke of the musical quality of poetry for children, he was referring to a special fluidity of sound attained chiefly
by an avoidance of excessive consonant clusters. "In their own
poetry children never tolerate the accumulation of consonants that
so often disfigures our 'adult' poetry for children."[44] In Chukovskii's
verse there are usually at least as many vowels as consonants, and
sometimes there is even a higher proportion of vowels.[45]

As Osip Brik, formalist critic and close friend of Maiakovskii,
emphasized in his pioneering essay "Acoustic Repetition," poetic
sound texture depends on more than the traditionally recognized
features of rhyme, alliteration, and sound imitation.[46] All poetry is
structured upon the alternation of consonants and vowels. In adult
poetry there is often an integral relationship between the acoustic
and semantic levels. In most children's poetry, especially in Chukovskii's, the connection between these two levels is less significant. Instead, exploiting children's sensitivity to acoustic effects,
Chukovskii emphasized cleverly arranged sound patterns.
Throughout his poetry there is identifiable, often intricate, repetition in individual lines, in single stanzas, and even beyond stanzaic
boundaries. To a large extent the meaning of this poetry, as of children's folklore, derives from its purely musical flow.

In these skazki certain types of words abound, words calculated to
appeal especially to small children. One prevailing criterion is children's addiction to movement, which Chukovskii frequently acknowledged in From Two to Five. Many critics have insisted that
this means verbs above all. But verbal energy exists in nouns too;
moreover, it often depends on syntax. Admittedly, some passages
in Chukovskii's poetry overflow with verbs. The beginning of
"Wash'em Clean" is unusually full of them. Chukovskii himself
acknowledged consciously structuring that work with many

verbs.[47] Yet sometimes a single verb establishes sufficient momentum to carry through several verbless couplets.

One of Chukovskii's "commandments" urges children's poets to avoid using too many adjectives, a part of speech that he felt plays only a small role in children's early vocabulary.[48] He himself followed this "commandment" up to a point. "The Muddle" comes closest to perfection with only one adjective (repeated several times), well-known as a fixed epithet from folklore.

> K móriu sínemu poshlí,
> Móre sínee zazhglí.
> (223)

(To the blue sea they went, / the blue sea they set on fire.)

"Toptygin and the Fox," on the other hand, tends toward the opposite extreme and in this respect is atypical among Chukovskii's *skazki*. The central figure of this fable is a vain bear in search of a tail who succumbs to a fox's flattery. Their discussion of tails provides a good opportunity for abundant adjectives, all of which are concrete and understandable to children.

> Est' kozlínye, est' loshadínye,
> Est' oslínye, dlínnye-dlínnye.
>
> Ty voz'mí sebe lúchshe pavlínii:
> Zolotói on, zelënyi i sínii.
> (208)

(There are goat tails, horse tails, / there are donkey tails, long, long ones. // Why don't you take a peacock tail? / It's golden, green, and blue.)

In his other *skazki* Chukovskii used adjectives with moderation. While those he repeated most regularly are often banal, they happen to be words children readily use themselves. The adjective *bednyi* (poor) occurs twenty-five times. Less frequent but still quite noticeable are words such as *milyi* (nice), *neschastnyi* (unhappy), *glupyi* (stupid), *gadkii* (nasty), and *malen'kii* (little). These adjectives are undoubtedly one of Chukovskii's strongest links with previous poetry for children. Yet there are also less common and more complex adjectives, typically occuring in rhymed pairs.

> Vy—zubástye,
> Vy—klykástye . . .
> ("The Cockroach," 178)

(You are toothy, / you are fangy . . . )

Iá krovozhádnyi,
Iá besposhchádnyi,
Iá zloi razbóinik Barmaléi!
                    ("Barmalei," 216)

(I'm blood-thirsty / I'm merciless, / I'm the wicked bandit Barmalei!)

Folklore directly contributes to Chukovskii's lexicon its tradition of compound words. Most often they are nouns, including the titles of two of the tales—"Chudo-derevo" and "Mukha-tsokotukha." And, of course, there are diminutives uniting the folk and children's traditions. Although Chukovskii used them abundantly, they never create the saccharine atmosphere of much of the earlier turn-of-the-century poetry for children, since they rarely occur exclusively. Usually they are balanced by nondiminutive forms.

Pliáshut chízhiki i záichiki v lesákh,
Pliáshut ráki, pliáshut ókuni v moriákh,
Pliáshut v póle cherviachkí i pauchkí,
Pliáshut bózhii koróvki i zhuchkí.
                    ("The Crocodile," 283)

(Finches and bunnies are dancing in the woods, / crayfish and perch are dancing in the seas, / little worms and little spiders are dancing in the field, / ladybugs and little beetles are dancing.)

Another lexical feature of Chukovskii's *skazki* found also in the realm of children's lore is the frequent occurrence of food, especially gingerbread and other sweets.

Ia za tó podariú tebe priánichka.
                    ("The Crocodile," 277)

(In exchange I will give you gingerbread.)

Édut i smeiútsia,
Priániki zhúiut.
                    ("The Cockroach," 174)

(They're riding and laughing, / they're chewing gingerbread.)

A dlia Vánechki
I dlia Tánechki
Búdut, búdut u meniá
Miátny priánichki!
                    ("Barmalei," 220)

(For little Vania / for little Tania / I'll have, I'll have / fancy gingerbread!)

I vsém po poriádku
Daët shokoládku.
("Ouch-it-hurts," 246)

(And one after the other / he gives them chocolate candy.)

Invariably pleased by an offer of sweet treats, children have no difficulty identifying with these situations.

As a variety of examples has shown, Chukovskii used diction readily comprehensible to young children. Many of his words are colloquial. Rarely did he resort to archaisms or expressions restricted to poetic usage. And when archaisms or poeticisms do appear, as in "The Crocodile," they are near words from popular speech, producing a striking juxtaposition, at least to the more sophisticated ear.

I govorít Gippopotám:
"Ó Krokodíl, *povédai* nám,
Chto vídel ty v chuzhóm kraiú,
A iá *pokúda* podremliú."
(285)

(And the hippopotamus says: / "Oh crocodile, let us know what you saw in that foreign land, / and meanwhile I'll take a snooze.")

*Provedat'* is an archaism, *pokuda* is colloquial.

Among most children's earliest acquired recognizable "words" are imitations of animal sounds, which Chukovskii cleverly incorporated into his poetry.

Prýg da prýg,
Da chík-chirík,
Chíki-ríki-chík-chirík!
("The Cockroach," 178)

(Hoppity hop, / and chirpity chirp, / chirpy whirpy chirpity chirp!)

"Kud-kudá! kud-kudá!
Vy otkúda i kudá?"
("Fedora's Misfortune," 228)

(Cluckity cluck, cluckity cluck! / Where are you from and where are you going?)

Although children themselves may surpass Chukovskii when it comes to inventing pure nonsense sounds, he prevails as an imaginative expert in the concoction of proper names: Moidodyr (Wash'em Clean), Mukha-tsokotukha (Chatterbox Fly), Barmalei,

Akula-karakula. And of course there is the immortal Aibolit
(Ouch-it-hurts), a special delight to small children when they succeed in deciphering the code.[49]

In accordance with his audience's stage of development, Chukovskii made minimal use of figurative language. The only recurring trope in his tales is the simile, also common in folklore. And
even similes are infrequent and invariably taken from the world of
things familiar to children. They are concrete and determined
largely by sound.

> . . . shchëtki
> Zatreshcháli, kak treshchëtki . . .
> ("Wash'em Clean," 184)

( . . . the brushes / began to rattle like rattles . . . )

> A ot béshenoi mochálki
> Ia pomchálsia, kak ot pálki . . .
> (185)

(And from the mad sponge / I dashed away as from a stick . . . )

Such comparisons frequently are made by children.[50]

Hyperbole and realized metaphor—favorite devices of the
futurists, especially Maiakovskii—also play a role in Chukovskii's
*skazki.* The underlying tone of all the tales can be characterized as
hyperbolic. The world of these creatures often exhibits larger-than-
life dimensions. Thus the dance that celebrates the cockroach's
defeat leads to more than earth-shattering consequences.

> A sloníkha-shchegolíkha
> Tak otpliásyvaet líkho,
> Chto rumiánaia luná
> V nébe zadrozhála
> I na bédnogo sloná
> Kúbarem upála.
>
> Vot bylá potóm zabóta—
> Za lunói nyriát' v bolóte
> I gvozdiámi k nebesám prikoláchivat'!
> (179–80)

(And the fashionable lady elephant / danced so wildly, / that the rosy
moon / began to sway in the sky / and fell head over heels / upon the
poor elephant. // Then there was trouble— / [they had] to dive into
the swamp after the moon / and nail it back up in the heavens!)

One entire tale, "The Stolen Sun," unfolds as a realized metaphor.

The silly magpies' interpretation of the sun hidden behind a cloud quickly becomes poetic reality.

> "Góre! Góre! Krokodíl
> Sólntse v nébe proglotíl!"
>
> (233)

(Oh woe! The crocodile / swallowed the sun in the sky!)

From the third verse on, the problem becomes one of forcing the crocodile to return the sun to its proper position.

While a major part of the impact of Chukovskii's tales derives from their structural qualities, by no means can their essence be reduced to manner alone. The content of these works is also significant. Thematically, as well as structurally, Chukovskii made important breaks with tradition. Following the tentative precedent of Sasha Chërnyi, he cleverly exploited children's delight in play. In his hands, age-old didactic themes are ingeniously transformed.

In "Wash'em Clean," dealing with a recalcitrant child who refuses to wash becomes a game.

> "Akh ty gádkii, akh ty griáznyi,
>     Neumýtyi porosënok!
> Ty chernée trubochísta,
>     Poliubúisia na sebiá;
> U tebiá na shée váksa,
>     U tebiá pod nósom kliáksa,
> U tebiá takíe rúki,
>     Chto sbezháli dázhe briúki,
> Dazhe briúki, dazhe briúki
>     Ubezháli ot tebiá.
>
> (183)

("Oh you nasty, oh you dirty, / unwashed piglet! / You're blacker than a chimney sweep. / Just look at yourself: / On your neck there is shoe polish, / below your nose there's an ink spot, / your hands are so dirty / that even your trousers have run away, / even your trousers, even your trousers / have run away from you.)

The same approach is found in "Fedora's Misfortune," which subtly urges children to take proper care of their belongings.

> Dólgo, dólgo tselovála
> I laskála ikh oná,
> Polivála, umyvála,
> Poloskála ikh oná.

"Uzh ne búdu, uzh ne búdu
Ia posúdu obizhát',
Búdu, búdu ia posúdu
I liubít' i uvazhát'!"
                                    (231–32)

(For a long, long time she kissed / and caressed them; / she poured
water on them, washed them, / and rinsed them. // "Never again,
never again will I / offend the plates and dishes; / I will, I will love /
and respect the plates and dishes!")

Indeed, it is more than inanimate possessions that this poem
encourages children to love and respect. In their anthropomorphized
state the objects suggest living beings, a transference readily made
by children, who attribute life to everything.

"Barmalei" begins as a variation on the old didactic theme of
children's obedience to their parents.

I pápochka i mámochka
Détiam govoriát: . . .

Ne khodíte, v Áfriku,
Déti, nikogdá!"
                            (213)

(And daddy and mommy / say to their children: . . . / "Do not go to
Africa, / children, ever!")

But quickly the poem pursues the whims of capricious children and
unfolds as an exotic adventure story: Tania and Vania go to Africa by
stealth. Somehow the fact that they not only disobey their parents
but bring on their own potential ruin by taunting the shark is over-
shadowed by Barmalei's unmitigated ferocity. After all, he even
seizes the compassionate Doctor Ouch-it-hurts.

No zlodéi Aibolíta khvatáet
I v kostér Aibolíta brosáet.
I gorít i krichít Aibolít:
"Aí, bolít! Aí, bolít! Aí, bolít!"
                                    (218)

(But the villain grabs Ouch-it-hurts / and onto the bonfire throws
Ouch-it-hurts. / And Ouch-it-hurts burns and screams: / "Ouch, it
hurts! Ouch, it hurts! Ouch, it hurts!")

At the end of the ordeal, there is no reference to the children's
misbehavior. Barmalei's punishment and subsequent repentance
serves as a more subtle and effective lesson. "Búdu, búdu ia dobréi,
da dobréi!" (220) (I will, I will be kinder, yes kinder!) The theme of

repentance and forgiveness also plays a large role in "The Crocodile" and "Fedora's Misfortune."

The contest between Barmalei and the children, with the latter's ultimate victory, follows a pattern recurrent in most of Chukovskii's *skazki*: the traditional struggle between good and evil, with the victory of the weak and good over the powerful and evil. This theme is central in "The Crocodile," "The Cockroach," "Chatterbox Fly," "The Stolen Sun," and, in a sense, "Ouch-it-hurts," although in the latter the obstacles are the elements of nature, not living creatures.

"The Cockroach" and "Chatterbox Fly" both deal with malevolence. The cockroach and the spider mercilessly tyrannize their victims, whether it be the whole animal collective or a single helpless little fly. In other instances the relationship between good and evil is less unconditional, as in "Barmalei," where the weak themselves unnecessarily arouse the wrath of the tyrannical giant. Likewise, in "The Crocodile" the struggle between the animals and the population of Petrograd is initiated by unprovoked taunts of the crocodile. From then on the martial spirit and thirst for revenge run rampant, with terror on both sides, until the lilliputian victor, the child Vania Vasil'chikov, reinforces his triumph with the magnanimous gesture of freeing all the captive animals from the zoo. A gratuitous, irrational act is also at the center of "The Stolen Sun"— the crocodile not only swallows the sun, but gloatingly threatens to abscond with the moon as well.

Most of the settings for Chukovskii's fantasies are the abstract countryside of children's folklore, defined only by fields, meadows, or woods. There are, however, notable exceptions. In his first *skazka* "The Crocodile," Chukovskii juxtaposed an urban scene (identified as Petrograd) with a remote and exotic Africa. The urban setting reappears in "Wash'em Clean," where Petrograd is unmistakably conjured up by recognizable geographical names; and the reformed Barmalei is happy to be going to Leningrad. Modern technology in the form of airplanes, streetcars, electricity, telephones, and telegrams recurs throughout the tales. Often its presence seems determined by an undiscriminating childlike imagination, as in "The Cockroach," where a bicycle, automobile, and streetcar appear in what is otherwise a rural setting. In "Barmalei" and "Ouch-it-hurts" the African setting is similarly an imaginative place, not related in any realistic way to actual geography. Sound and rhythm are the selective factors, not any desire to portray physical reality.

The majority of characters populating Chukovskii's tales are the familiar anthropomorphized creatures of Russian folklore, especially children's folklore—bears, wolves, foxes, rabbits, chickens, cats, and a myriad of insects. To this traditional lot he added a new kingdom of exotic ones, unknown to the northern Russian landscape—crocodiles, elephants, hippopotamuses, kangaroos.[51] Besides these, in "Wash'em Clean" and "Fedora's Misfortune" inanimate objects assume the same anthropomorphized role as animals in the other tales. Finally, interacting with these objects and animals are human characters—Vania Vasil'chikov, Doctor Ouch-it-hurts, Tania and Vania, and the narrator himself. In "Wash'em Clean" all three categories appear, while in "Chatterbox Fly" there are only insects. Elsewhere, human characters mix with either animals or objects.

"The Crocodile" introduced to Russian children's literature a positive hero, Vania Vasil'chikov, a small child with whom his compatriots could easily identify.

> On boéts
> Molodéts,
> On gerói
> Udalói:
> On bez niáni guliáet po úlitsam.
>
> (276)

(He's a warrior / magnificent, / he's a hero / bold: / He can stroll the streets without his nanny.)

He is the predecessor of such heroes as the sparrow who rids the terrified animal population of their cockroach captor or the mosquito who saves the fly from further torture. In "The Muddle" there is a variation on the theme, in the figure of the delicate butterfly who succeeds in extinguishing the conflagration on the sea, a feat no other creature before her had been able to accomplish. Rather more realistically, Doctor Ouch-it-hurts also fits this category. Neither mountains, sea, nor snowstorm are insurmountable obstacles when it is a question of curing the ailing baby animals of Africa.

Although each tale is a self-contained whole, together they make up an immense fantastic cycle, unified not only by similar thematics and recurring characters, but also by an undercurrent of distinct verbal leitmotifs. Of the differentiated characters, the crocodile— with his propensity for swallowing whatever crosses his path— appears most regularly (in seven of the tales). Even his children make brief reappearances in "Wash'em Clean" and "The Telephone." Other leitmotifs expressed as characters are the shark, cockroaches, and chimney sweeps. The image of the chimney sweeps occurs first in "The Crocodile." Then in "Wash'em Clean" it is combined with the childish taunt *styd i sram* (for shame), which in turn appears also in "The Cockroach." Similarly, once Chukovskii created the shark for "Barmalei," that image easily made its way into "Ouch-it-hurts," the next tale with an African setting.

The concept of play, which runs as a unifying thread through all the *skazki*, can also be considered a leitmotif. In the three in which it is dominant—"Wonder Tree," "The Muddle," and "The Telephone"—the prevailing spirit is one of nonsense and the absurd. These stories reflect the two most important influences upon Chukovskii's poetry—futurism and folklore. "The Telephone"—a series of funny conversations with animals who make incredible demands—is best classified as purely verbal play. In it Chukovskii experimented with sound combinations in the manner of Khlebnikov. "The Muddle," on the other hand, is a fine example of a modern topsy-turvy rhyme. With it he simply introduced a well-established folk tradition into children's literature. Of course, neither of these sources was acceptable to those who criticized him in the 1920s. With their limited and highly political perspectives, they scorned the imaginative flights of both ancient and modern Russian culture.

These same critics, and others since, were and continue to be concerned with the question of satire in Chukovskii's *skazki*. Of course, satire, like parody, is accessible primarily to adults. That there are in fact satirical undercurrents in several of the tales is indisputable. This is one of the elements that broadens their appeal. Yet some critics have insisted upon overemphasizing and overinterpreting satirical allusions. One contemporary critic, for example, finds "The Crocodile" dated, full of coded satire. She identifies Vania Vasil'chikov with a certain pseudo-hero who used to perform miraculous feats on the pages of popular adult and children's magazines during World War I.[52] Others have variously accused it of satirizing Kaiser Wilhelm, Kerenskii of the Provisional Government, and General Denikin of the White Army.[53] It is not difficult to point out that the tale was written before the latter two figures had risen to prominence. Such attempts to isolate concrete satirical objectives, here or in any of the other tales, seem a fruitless pursuit.

The satirical thrust of "The Crocodile" is undated, abstracted, and exposes warlike conflict in general, not World War I in particular. Similar interpretations may be applied to Chukovskii's other tales that focus upon a bully's tyrannical use of force or pretense of force against a weak, captive population, as in "The Cockroach" and "The Stolen Sun," or against individual victims, as in "Chatterbox

Fly" or "Barmalei." Chukovskii's satire strikes out against evil and
bad will in general. It does not carry the same political implications
as do, for example, direct poetic attacks, shrouded in Aesopian language.[54] Yet, guilt-ridden beings often have a tendency to project
their own fears everywhere. One wonders, therefore, whether the
exclusion of the following passage in "The Telephone" from some
editions of Chukovskii's works was due to adverse political interpretations.

> A potóm pozvoníla svin'iá:
> —Nel'ziá li prislát' solov'iá?
> My segódnia vdvoém
> S solov'ём
> Chudésnuiu pésniu
> Spoём.
> —Net, nét! Solovéi
> Ne poёt dlia svinéi!
> Pozoví-ka ty lúchshe vorónu![55]

(and then the pig called: / "Couldn't you sent a nightingale? / Today I
will sing / a marvelous song / together with the nightingale." / "No,
No! Nightingales / don't sing for pigs! / You should call a crow instead!")

Anyone who, for whatever reason, identifies with the caller—the
pig—might feel offended at being offered the song of a crow rather
than a nightingale. Such an explanation seems farfetched indeed,
yet fearful political leaders and their underlings have been known to
find criticism of their regime in the most unlikely places.

Despite some people's interpretations, Chukovskii was not an
ideologically engaged writer. The same can be said of his closest
"follower," Daniil Kharms. Some writers, like Marshak, were capable of submitting to external dictates without completely sacrific-
ing their creativity. Others, such as Maiakovskii, submitted with
disastrous consequences. Chukovskii chose essentially to retreat in
face of the changing conditions. In retrospect, despite the vicious
campaign against him in the 1920s, he not only dominates that first
decade of Soviet children's poetry but continues to be its finest
figure to the present day. Furthermore, his pioneering work has been
the single most important creative influence on subsequent poets.
His poems have so penetrated the popular consciousness that lines
from them have become everyday sayings. As Veniamin Kaverin put
it, "Chukovskii's poetry came from folklore and returned to folklore—a fortune that falls upon few."[56]

# 5

## SAMUIL MARSHAK

$T$HERE IS HARDLY a context in Russia today in which the name of Chukovskii arises without at least an allusion to his equally famous contemporary, Samuil Marshak (1887–1964). The two became acquainted in Petrograd in 1922 and immediately became close friends. Both of them later left reminiscences of the early days of their friendship. Marshak remembered their first encounter: "I first met that veteran of our children's poetry, elder critic and literary scholar . . . at the seashore, with a whole band of kids who could hardly keep up with him. Barefoot and tan, he was on a walk with them; or perhaps it was business that he turned into play, giving every ordinary business-like word the merry rhythm of a

counting-out rhyme."[1] Chukovskii warmly recalled the many
hours the two of them spent wandering the streets of Petrograd on
misty white nights, reciting poetry to one another—their own and
that of others.[2] They shared their uncontainable poetic impulses,
impressing one another with their creativity. More than three decades later Chukovskii recorded: "Even now I remember all of Marshak's children's poems by heart, because Marshak created them
literally before my eyes. Every new piece he wrote for children I
perceived as an event."[3]

At first Chukovskii and Marshak were close friends. Marshak
alleged that they even planned a children's magazine together, to be
published by their mutual acquaintance Lev Kliachko. The
magazine *Rainbow*, however, never materialized, perhaps due to
Kliachko's organizational shortcomings. According to Marshak,
Kliachko "was a noble, talented person, but he was disorderly."[4]
Fortunately the plans were not in vain—Kliachko did establish a
small publishing house, preserving the name Rainbow and producing many of the best new books for small children. In the mid-1920s
Marshak along with Chukovskii published much of his children's
poetry there. As the decade wore on, however, Chukovskii and Marshak grew apart. The era dominated by the proletarian pedologists
was difficult for both of them, but Chukovskii encountered more
severe difficulties than Marshak. It was not until the last two decades of their lives, after World War II, that they became close friends
once again.[5]

Born in Voronezh and raised in the provincial town of Os-
trogozhsk, Marshak spent his childhood in a way untypical for the
son of a factory technician. His interest in literature, which would
ultimately lead him to a career as poet, translator, and editor, was
manifest at an early age. "As far as I can remember, my inclination
for poetry appeared when I was extremely young. In fact, I began 'to
write verse' long before I learned to write. I composed aloud to
myself two-line stanzas, sometimes even four-line stanzas, but I
quickly forgot those lines thought up out of the blue. Gradually I
progressed from this 'oral creation' to written poetry."[6] Along with
his poetic talent, Marshak displayed an early interest in editorial
work. "At the age of twelve and thirteen I composed long poems in
several parts and was a co-worker and co-editor of a literary-artistic
magazine, *First Tries (Pervye popytki).*"[7]

His family's move to St. Petersburg in 1902 brought the fifteen-
year-old Marshak to the attention of the aging art patron Vladimir
Stasov. If until then Marshak's inclinations toward a literary career

had been primarily a childhood fantasy, now they became an ir-
revocable reality. Stasov's first influential step was to arrange for
Marshak's enrollment in a classical gymnasium in St. Petersburg.[8]
Two years later, in August 1904, Stasov introduced young Marshak
to Maksim Gor'kii, who played a crucial role in innumerable writers' careers in early twentieth-century Russia. Gor'kii's most immediately helpful gesture toward Marshak, whose health was weak,
was an invitation to join his family in Yalta and finish his secondary
education there.[9] Decades later, in 1930, Gor'kii was again to inter-
vene providentially in Marshak's life, this time to defend him from
the attacks of proletarian critics.

Two years before graduation, in the winter of 1906, Marshak was
forced to leave school. With the remote hope that he might some
day nevertheless study at the university, he returned to St. Petersburg to pursue a literary career. By 1908 he began earning a
meager living as a journalist. Through his work on the magazine
*Satirikon,* he met Sasha Chërnyi, who became a good friend.[10]

Unable to gain admission to the university, Marshak was determined to continue his education, if only informally. One possibility
open to him was foreign travel. Thus, in June 1911, Marshak de-
parted for a six-month journey to the Near East. Within a year of his
return, in September 1912, he again set off, this time to Britain, for a
stay of almost two years. Like Chukovskii some nine years earlier,
Marshak arranged to work as a correspondent for several Russian
newspapers and magazines.[11] However, the results of his journalistic endeavors were subordinate to those of his philological studies at
London University. Importantly, his English language study facili-
tated his developing interest in translating English poetry. It was in
London that Marshak, again like Chukovskii, first became acquainted with English nursery rhymes, which were to be such an
influential force in his later career as a children's poet. "In the library I happened upon that marvelous English children's folklore,
full of whimsical humor. My long acquaintance with Russian children's folklore helped me recreate in Russian those classical verses
that are so difficult to translate."[12]

Marshak's professional interest in children arose in the British
countryside at the Simple Life School, an idealistic "free" school
run by Philip Oyler in Tintern, Wales. Years later, in 1927, Marshak
described the school in a letter to Gor'kii. "I came to children's
literature over a strange path. In 1913 I became acquainted with a
very curious school in southern Wales. The children lived there in
tents almost all year round; they dressed lightly, led a spartan life,

participated in the construction of the school house. I lived with them about a year—a most happy time of my life."[13] There, in a cottage named "Sunnyside," Marshak began to write poetry for children. Those first efforts—Russian renditions of English nursery rhymes—are among his best. There also was born his first child, a girl named Natanel', whose tragic accidental death came before she was two years old.[14]

In July 1914, a month before the outbreak of World War I, Marshak returned with his family to Russia and pursued a variety of occupations during the ensuing chaotic war years. After the death of Natanel', Marshak and his wife, then in Voronezh, were anxious to find work with children. Their strong desire is expressed in his letter to Gor'kii's wife in January 1916. "If I were to be involved with them, I would be very happy. It seems I even have a certain calling for that. In any case, my wife and I would fervently throw ourselves into such work. . . ."[15] That year Marshak did work with resettled orphans (bezhentsy), mostly Jews from the Ukrainian front, an experience he later cited as having contributed greatly to his growing knowledge of children.[16]

Marshak gained more experience with children in the summer of 1918, when he worked in a children's colony on the bank of Lake Onega in Petrozavodsk. In her memoirs, a fellow worker from that colony wrote with enthusiasm about Marshak's participation. "The children felt he was 'one of them'; they asked his advice about everything, shared all their secrets with him. . . ."[17]

In the spring of 1920 he was in Krasnodar, helping with the establishment of a center for homeless children (detskii gorodok).[18] With the help of his colleague Elizaveta Vasil'eva and members of the local theater, Marshak produced a play based on Oscar Wilde's tale "The Young Prince." Wanting to continue their enterprise but having no tradition of Russian children's theater to fall back upon, Marshak and Vasil'eva created an entire repertory on the spot. Together they wrote a number of plays based on Russian folklore.[19] The success of these plays confirmed for Marshak children's love of the oral tradition. He would turn to it throughout his life as a source of inspiration and material, not only for his later plays, but for much of his children's poetry as well.

By 1922 Marshak finally returned to Petrograd, where the Theater for Young Spectators (Teatr iunykh zritelei, or TIuZ) had been recently founded. With Vasil'eva as his assistant, Marshak became the head of the literary section of TIuZ, which quickly became one of the most vital theaters in the city.[20] In search of new material for

TIuZ, he turned to Ol'ga Kapitsa, the specialist on children's literature and folklore at the Institute of Preschool Education. Soon he
became one of the main participants of Kapitsa's workshop for children's writers.[21] It was while working at TIuZ that Marshak had his
first experience with intractable pedologists. A play he wrote in
collaboration with Vasil'eva—*The Golden Wheel* (*Zolotoe
koleso*)—was closed after a few performances. Its use of folk motifs
and call for some audience participation apparently displeased the
proletarians.[22] Although he continued his position at TIuZ until
1925 and served as a consultant for two more years, Marshak began
to direct more and more of his energy to the fast-growing world of
children's literature. He had met Chukovskii soon after his return to
Petrograd. Then, with the establishment of Kliachko's publishing
house, Marshak, along with Chukovskii, began regularly writing
poetry for children.

In 1923 Marshak made his debut as a children's poet with three
works: "Kids in a Cage" ("Detki v kletke"), "The Tale of the Silly
Baby Mouse" ("Skazka o glupom myshonke"), and "The Fire"
("Pozhar"). That year he also published *The House that Jack Built*
(*Dom, kotoryi postroil Dzhek*), the first edition of his translations of
English nursery rhymes, which he had begun working on in Wales
ten years earlier. That collection continued to grow as he published
more translations throughout his lifetime.[23]

Continuing the precedent set by Chukovskii and Benois with *The
Firebird*, Kliachko attracted excellent artists to illustrate the books
he published. In this way Marshak developed his successful collaboration with Vladimir Lebedev, who over the years illustrated many
first and then subsequent editions of Marshak's poetry. Their first
project was "The Circus" ("Tsirk," 1925), for which Marshak wrote
captions to accompany Lebedev's poster-like drawings. Their next
work, "Ice Cream" ("Morozhenoe," 1925), is the most integral, with
Lebedev's bright schematic pictures complementing Marshak's imaginative poem. Unfortunately, as time went on and the growing
rigidity of Stalinism demanded more realistic representation in all
the arts, the originality of both Marshak and Lebedev diminished
markedly.[24]

Not long after Marshak began publishing poetry for children he
was invited to join the editorial staff of a new children's magazine,
*Sparrow* (*Vorobei*). At first he approached the opportunity with
reluctance. "When they began calling me to join *Sparrow*, I did not
go immediately. The people who worked there were not very talented. And I did not like the title. At first I only helped from the

outside."[25] Soon Marshak used his influence to effect changes, including the name, which became New Robinson (Novyi Robinzon). With the help of his established acquaintances, he attracted to the magazine an impressive circle of children's writers. Even the names of the well-known poets Mandel'shtam and Pasternak occasionally appeared on its pages. When New Robinson ceased publication in 1925, its core of staff writers moved with Marshak to the Leningrad State Publishing House (Gosizdat), where he accepted an offer to run the children's section. For twelve years he worked as an editor and literary consultant in offices atop the old Singer Building (now the bookstore Dom knigi) on Nevskii prospekt.

Although Marshak continued writing children's poetry, at that time he was known best for his editorial work. Negative reactions on the part of the pedologists helped deemphasize the significance of his poetry. Although the campaign against Marshak was less fierce than the one Chukovskii endured, there were complaints against him as well.[26] In the post-Stalin era, when Marshak's early children's poetry was again placed in proper perspective, many warmly recalled his unusual dedication and extraordinary success as an editor.

> Marshak united us; he was the center around which everything turned. Every author passed through a stage of being in love with the main consultant. The degree of love depended on age and character, but there was no one who did not succumb to Marshak's charm. . . . Editing does not mean sitting at a desk and marking up a manuscript with a pencil. Editing means educating the author, broadening his outlook, telling in an inimitably throaty voice just *what* mankind gained in your favorite piece of work. And Marshak did that brilliantly . . . his editorial work was not a craft but an art. Why, in that process there occurred the miraculous birth not only of the book, but of the author himself."[27]

Marshak did not gather around himself only writers already involved in children's literature, such as those who had worked with him at New Robinson. More importantly, he attracted to children's literature some surprising converts. Among the most outstanding were Evgenii Shvarts and Nikolai Oleinikov and two members of the avant-garde literary group Oberiu, Daniil Kharms and Aleksandr Vvedenskii. As Marshak confessed, "They say I am striving to turn everyone into a children's writer. Well, why not try?"[28]

The years of trying, the late 1920s and early 1930s, produced two memorable children's magazines—Ëzh (Hedgehog) and Chizh

(*Finch*)—and in which Marshak's disciples, Shvarts, Oleinikov, Kharms, and Vvedenskii, figured prominently.[29] Marshak was the nominal editor-in-chief of the magazines and occasionally published in them too. In retrospect, they stand out as a last creative journalistic effort in a growing flood of forced conformity and mediocrity.[30]

With the dissolution of the Russian Association of Proletarian Writers in 1932, the adverse pressure on Marshak, and on writers in general, was somewhat alleviated. Marshak was additionally protected by Gor'kii's overt support. During his last stay in Italy, Gor'kii invited Marshak to visit him there and to write on the contemporary role of children's literature in the Soviet Union. This project included a proposal for the establishment of a specialized publishing house for children's and young people's literature. Gor'kii edited Marshak's proposal and forwarded it to the Central Committee. The result was the establishment of the Children's Publishing House (Detizdat), and the offer of its directorship to Marshak. He refused the post, however, preferring to continue his editorial work.[31]

In 1934, at the First All-Union Congress of Soviet Writers, Marshak delivered a keynote address on children's literature. (Chukovskii was also among the speakers.) Although on the whole his speech was noncontroversial, even politically acquiescent, he did contrive to slip in a defense of the *skazka* as an important genre for children; he also subtly underlined his view of the necessarily aesthetic nature of this literature. "Children's literature must be art. Many of us still do not understand that simple truth."[32]

By the mid-1930s, like many other poets at that difficult time, Marshak began turning his genuinely creative impulses toward literary translation, in his case English poetry. By 1936, the year of Gor'kii's death, even Marshak's token production of children's poetry was interrupted. The following year, marked by the second surge of Stalin's terror, loomed as an especially bleak one for many Russians. Marshak was no exception. After the forcible "demise" of his editorial staff at the Children's Publishing House, he feared for his life.[33] Then unexpectedly he was awarded the Order of Lenin. During World War II he devoted much time to journalism, but once peace came he returned to poetic translation. Although he occasionally did write children's poetry during the last two decades of his life, Marshak considered his lyric poetry the most important product of those years. He let the editorial role he had played earlier be filled by others. Nonetheless, he continued until his death to inspire and to give valuable technical assistance to the children's poets of the new generation.

Marshak tried his hand at children's poetry after having gained considerable experience as a writer for adults.

> Before I began to create tales and verse for children, for many years I wrote for adults—lyric poetry, satires, epigrams, sketches, articles. It never crossed my mind that I might someday become a children's writer. I had a condescending and condemning attitude toward the literature specifically designated for little children, toward the decorated little children's books and sweetly edifying magazines of the prerevolutionary years.[34]

Once he did become involved, his contributions both as a poet and as an editor were considerable. Despite the subversive efforts of the pedologists, he did much to help redirect Russian literature for children in the early Soviet period.

At the time of his debut as a children's writer, Marshak offered Russian children not one, but a variety of genres—plays, longer poems, some short ones, and translations of English nursery rhymes. Amidst this apparent diversity, however, there was a strong, unifying thread, identified in retrospect by Chukovskii and others. "In general, Russian folklore already at that time served [Marshak] as a base, as the compass and governor of all his works and all his translations."[35] In addition to the children's folklore that was an inevitable part of his childhood, Marshak was imbued from his early environment with what is sometimes designated as "low" folklore, genres found in urban or near-urban settings—above all, various street cries (vykriki), such as those of wandering organ grinders, craftsmen, and merchants.[36] And from his travels in Britain he was steeped in English ballads and nursery rhymes.

During his early period (1923–1928), which coincides approximately with the era of the New Economic Policy, Marshak published more than twenty original poems for children, the majority of which are longer poems, averaging just over one hundred lines. (This figure is somewhat exaggerated, since Marshak, like Maiakovskii, sometimes divided a regular line vertically down the page into short phrases or single words.) The short poems consist of as little as a single stanza and rarely exceed four or five. At first glance it seems as if Marshak's poetry might fall into two distinct categories, narrative tales and shorter lyrics. Upon closer scrutiny, however, such a distinction cannot be made, since a single structural principle pervades all of Marshak's poems. Underlying them is a concise, anecdotal form, familiar to English-speaking readers from their traditional nursery rhymes. Looking back on his early work, Marshak himself identified that structural principle. "From laconic, internally complete songs I gradually began to compose tales . . . or small narratives in verse. . . ."[37]

It is hardly fortuitous that Marshak's translations of English nursery rhymes and his first original poems for children appeared in the same year. The process involved in transforming the English poems into successful Russian ones helped refine Marshak's sensibility for children's poetry, prejudicing him in a certain direction—or, possibly, reaffirming an earlier established bias, determined by his acquaintance with Russian children's folklore. As Chukovskii pointed out, "Leaving the English colors intact, Marshak projected into his translations our Russian counting-out rhymes, riddles, nonsense rhymes, entertaining songs, and taunts."[38] It was natural that Marshak should turn to the established sounds and rhythms of his native folk culture to find equivalents for the related rhymes of the English tradition.

Marshak's discovery of nursery rhymes in England was a major contributing factor in his later becoming a children's poet. His interest in Russian folklore was activated to a great extent by his experience in England. Certainly, he came to know and to love more than the nursery rhymes. Folk ballads and the poetry of Burns, Blake, Keats, and Shakespeare all played an important part in the course of his literary career. But in the history of Marshak as a children's poet, the nursery rhymes are, naturally enough, most crucial. He began to translate them well before he ever considered writing his own poems for children. Inevitably, his familiarity with them transcended the boundaries of his translations and came to be felt in his own poetry as well, much of which displays the primary structural characteristics of the nursery rhymes.

The English rhymes Marshak translated are typically short, carefully constructed humorous anecdotes. Sometimes the anecdote is conveyed in a single stanza, reminiscent of a pointed epigram.

> Shkól'nik, shkól'nik,
> Chto tak ráno
> Ty speshísh'
> Segódnia v kláss?
> Ty vsegdá
> Prikhódish' v vósem',
> A tepér'
> Desiátyi chás.[39]

(A diller, a dollar, / A ten o'clock scholar, / What makes you come so soon? / You used to come at ten o'clock / And now you come at noon.)

Frequently they employ repetition and syntactic parallelism, common to Russian children's folklore as well.

> Shaltái-Boltái
> Sidél na stené.
> Shaltái-Boltái
> Svalílsia vo sné.
>
> Vsiá korolévskaia kónnitsa,
> Vsiá korolévskaia rát'
> Ne mózhet
> Shaltáia,
> Ne mózhet
> Boltáia,
> Shaltáia-Boltáia,
> Boltáia-Shaltáia,
> Shaltáia-Boltáia sobrát'.
>
> (84)

(Humpty Dumpty sat on a wall, / Humpty Dumpty had a great fall. / All the king's horses, / And all the king's men / Couldn't put Humpty Dumpty together again.)

Here, as in several of his reworkings, Marshak's version improves upon the original. He added a new dimension through repetition and inversion. Another good example of his creative reworking is "Mary Had a Little Lamb" ("Mèri i baran"). Marshak expanded the original four stanzas to nine into which he cleverly worked variations of the fourth line of the first stanza.

> U náshei Mèri ést' barán.
> Sobáki on vernéi.
> V grozú, i v búriu, i v tumán
> Barán bredét za néi.
>
> (97)

(Mary had a little lamb, / Its fleece was white as snow; / And everywhere that Mary went / The lamb was sure to go.)

Exploiting some of the rich possibilities of Russian motion verbs, he created a poem more thematically developed than the original and more tightly structured despite its length.

One of Marshak's best-known translations is of "This is the House that Jack Built," based on accumulative structure akin to that found in the Russian folktales "The Turnip" and "The Little

House-tower." The ninth and last stanza is a virtuoso achievement
in syntactic repetition. Each line in the stanza can easily be accompanied by an illustration.

> Vot dvá petukhá,
> Kotórye búdiat togó pastukhá,
> Kotóryi branítsia s koróvnitsei strógoiu,
> Kotóraia dóit koróvu bezróguiu,
> Liagnúvshuiu stárogo psá bez khvostá,
> Kotóryi za shívorot tréplet kotá,
> Kotóryi pugáet i lóvit sinítsu,
> Kotóraia chásto vorúet pshenítsu,
> Kotóraia v témnom chuláne khranítsia
> V dóme
> Kotóryi postróil Dzhék.
>                                    (80)

(This is the farmer sowing his corn, / That kept the cock that crowed
in the morn, / That waked the priest all shaven and shorn, / That
married the man all tattered and torn, / That kissed the maiden all
forlorn, / That milked the cow with the crumpled horn, / That tossed
the dog, / That worried the cat, / That killed the rat, / That ate the malt
/ That lay in the house that Jack built.)

Such repetition, although usually of shorter phrases or simply
words, is an important feature of Marshak's own poetry.

Monologue or dialogue is another important structural element
frequently found in children's folklore and widely used by Marshak.

> Poteriáli kotiátki
> Na doróge perchátki
> I v slezákh pribezháli domói.
> —Mama, máma, prostí,
> My ne mózhem naití,
> My ne mózhem naití
> Perchátki!
>
> —Poteriáli perchátki?
> Vot durnýe kotiátki!
> Ia vam nýnche ne dám pirogá.
> Miau-miáu, ne dám,
> Miau-miáu, ne dám,
> Ia vam nýnche ne dám pirogá!
>                                    (91)

(Three little kittens they lost their mittens, / And they began to
cry, / Oh, mother dear, we sadly fear / Our mittens we have lost. /
What! lost your mittens, you naughty kittens! / Then you shall have
no pie. / Mee-ow, mee-ow, mee-ow. / No, you shall have no pie.)

These folk rhymes served Marshak well as a foundation upon which to construct his literary superstructure. Their larger structural elements are prominent in his verse. On another level, but equally important, is his sense of humor, his love of laughter and jokes, which links his poetry with the English nursery rhymes. With rare exception, humor is a sustaining quality of his poetry.

Marshak's best poems—those written between 1923 and 1928—fall more or less equally into three structural categories. They are either single anecdotes, a collection of anecdotes, or a more developed continuous narrative. Two of these works were conceived as verse accompaniment for already existing drawings. Marshak's very first work for children, "Kids in a Cage," was his response to a series of animal drawings by an English artist.[40] Each of the twenty-two short poems is complete in itself, requiring only the single picture to which it refers. An example is "Ibis," later retitled "Little Swan" ("Lebedënok").

> Otchégo techët vodá
> S ètogo mladéntsa?
> On nedávno iz prudá,
> Dáite poloténtse![41]

(Why is water running / off this baby? / He just came from the pond. / Give him a towel!)

Some of the poems are comprehensible without any illustration. One of these is "The Elephant" ("Slon"). It is also by far the most reminiscent of a nursery rhyme, with its epigrammatic style, laconic structure, and pointed wit.

> Dali túfel'ki slonú.
> Vzial on túfel'ku odnú
> I skazál:—Nuzhný poshíre,
> I ne dvé, a vsé chetýre!
> (30)

(They gave the elephant little shoes. / He took one of the shoes / and said: "I need wider ones, / and not two, but four!")

Several of the slightly longer poems in this cycle are less successful, especially those which stray from the anecdotal toward the elegiac. Fortunately, Marshak himself recognized the problem and revised some of the poems for later editions.

Another work inspired by an artist's illustrations is "The Circus" ("Tsirk," 1925). This was the first collaborative project of Marshak and the artist Lebedev. Before meeting Marshak, Lebedev was already celebrated for the propaganda posters he had made for the

Russian Telegraph Agency (abbreviated ROSTA) in 1920–1921. His ROSTA windows in Petrograd were paralleled in Moscow by those of Maiakovskii. For Lebedev's bright and simple poster-like pictures Marshak created succinct, humorous couplets and quatrains, introduced by several longer stanzas.

> Vpervýe
> V Rossíi
> Proézdom v N'iu-Iórk
> Tsírk Tsanibóni:
> Uchěnye kóni,
> Ósliki, póni
> Vseóbshchii vostórg!
>                          (354)

(For the first time / in Russia / en route to New York / we have Caniboni's Circus: / Trained horses, / donkeys, ponies. / All will be delighted!)

One of the verses from "The Circus" became a favorite of Maiakovskii, who is reputed to have recited it frequently.[42]

> Po próvoloke dáma
> Idět kak telegrámma.
>                          (355)

(Along the wire the lady / goes like a telegram.)

Unfortunately, an English translation cannot successfully convey the Russian idiom—"a telegram goes."

"The Tale of the Silly Baby Mouse" is a single anecdote that undergoes seven variations through substitution. Dissatisfied with its mother's voice the little mouse insists on having some other nanny sing it to sleep.

> Pobezhála mýshka-mát'
> Stala útku v nián'ki zvát':
> —Prikhodí k nam, tětia útka,
> Nashu détku pokachát'.
>
> Stala pét' myshónku útka:
> —Ga-ga-gá, usní maliútka!
> Posle dózhdika v sadú
> Cherviaká tebé naidú.
>
> Glúpyi málen'kii myshónok
> Otvecháet ei sprosónok:
> —Nét, tvoi gólos nekhorósh.
> Slishkom grómko ty poésh'.
>                          (68)

(Mother mouse ran off, / she started calling the duck to come as nanny: / "Come to us, auntie duck, / to rock our baby." // The duck began to sing to the baby mouse: / "Quack, quack, quack, fall asleep, little one! / After the rain in the garden / I'll find you a worm." // The silly little baby mouse / answered her half-asleep: / "No, your voice is no good. / You sing too loudly.")

The baby mouse expresses similar dissatisfaction with several other animals. Finally the cat arrives and, naturally, devours the mouse. The syntactic parallelism of this poem is evocative of the folk tradition. Marshak revealed that he originally composed it orally. "The form of this tale with all its repetition, with its rhythm, came to me during an evening walk through the streets of Leningrad, and I composed [it] orally in its entirety. When I returned home, I made a fair copy almost at once."[43] Although Marshak may very well have conceived the form of this work orally, its carefully executed symmetry is rather a product of the written literary tradition. The more traditional syntactic devices of oral poetry, such as anaphora, occur infrequently in this poetry.

In a similar way, although less tightly ordered, "That's How Absent-minded" ("Vot kakoi rasseiannyi," 1928) is built on a series of anecdotal incidents of varying length, united by a refrain.

> Zhíl chelovék rasséiannyi
> Na úlitse Basséinoi.
>
> Sel on útrom na krovát'.
> Stal rubáshku nadevát',
> V rukavá prosúnul rúki—
> Okazálos', èto briúki.
>
> Vót kakói rasséiannyi
> S úlitsy Basséinoi!
>
> (99)

(On Baisin Street there lived / an absent-minded man. // He sat down on the bed in the morning / and started putting on his shirt. / Into the sleeves he stuck his arms— / It turned out to be his pants. // That's how absent-minded is / the man from Baisin Street!)

One stanza offers spoonerisms, a kind of linguistic play at which Kharms later excelled.[44]

> —Glubókouvazháemyi
> Vagónouvazhátyi!
> Vagónouvazháemyi
> Glubókouvazhátyi!

> Vo chtó by to ni stálo
> Mne nádo vykhodít'.
> Nel'ziá li u tramvála
> Vokzái ostanovít'?

(Deeply respected / tramdriver! / Tramly respected / deepdriver! / No matter what the cost, / I must get off. / Can't you stop the tration / at the stam?)

This poem is Marshak's tour de force in the topsy-turvy genre, giving children a wonderful opportunity to identify all the mistakes. And as with some of Chukovskii's lines, the refrain has entered popular speech.

Another of Marshak's best-known poems, "Baggage" ("Bagazh," 1926), involves a linear story line enhanced by a refrain-line repetition.

> Dáma sdavála v bagázh
>   Diván,
>   Chemodán,
>   Sakvoiázh,
>   Kartínu,
>   Korzínu,
>   Kartónku
> I málen'kuiu sobachónku.
>
> Výdali dáme na stántsii
> Chetýre zelénykh kvitántsii
> O tóm, chto polúchen bagázh:
>   Diván,
>   Chemodán,
>   Sakvoiázh,
>   Kartína,
>   Korzína,
>   Kartónka
> I málen'kaia sobachónka.
>                            (80)

(A lady checked as baggage / a sofa, / a suitcase, / a handbag, / a picture, / a basket, / a hatbox, / and a very small dog. // At the station the lady received / four green receipts / for checking as baggage / a sofa, / a suitcase, / a handbag, / a picture, / a basket, / a hatbox, / and a very small dog.)

Each subsequent action is followed by a list of the baggage, twice varied by the omission or rearrangement of some of the items. At the end of the trip the lady is given not her small dog, but a big dog.

The conductor's response in the final stanza is reminiscent of a children's joke.

> Odnáko
> Za vrémia putí
> Sobáka
> Moglá podrastí!
>
> (82)

(However / during the time of the journey / the dog / could have grown up!)

In several of the longer poems the narrative line unfolds directly, with minimal repetition. In contrast to the anecdotal ones, in these poems subject matter takes precedence over manner. To this group belongs "The Fire," the longest of Marshak's early poems. This didactic tale admonishes children to obey their parents and not to play with fire. Despite the seriousness of the theme, Marshak's approach was fanciful—he anthropomorphized the fire.

> Tól'ko mát' soshlá s kryléchka,
> Léna séla pered péchkoi,
> V shchélku krásnuiu gliadít,
> A ogón' poët—gudít:
> "Nýnche v péchke mésta málo,
> Razguliát'sia négde stálo!
> Máma, Lénochke, ne vér'.
> Priotkrói nemnózhko dvér'!"
>
> (341)

(As soon as mother had left the porch, / Lena sat down before the oven; / she looked into the red chink / where the fire was singing and whistling: / "There's not enough room in the oven now, / there's no room left to go on a spree! / Don't believe your mother, Lena, / Open the door a little bit!")

Despite his playful manner, Marshak depicts the situation seriously with special emphasis on the hard-working firemen.

> Na plóshchadi bazárnoi,
> Na kalanché pozhárnoi—
> Dín'-dón, dín'-dón—
> Razdaëtsia grómkii zvón.
> Nachináetsia rabóta.
> Otpiráiutsia voróta,
> Sobiráetsia obóz,
> Tiánut léstnitsu, nasós.
>
> (342)

(On the marketplace square, / on the firetower— / ding-dong, ding-dong— / a loud noise resounds. / Work is beginning, / the gates are opened, / a string of carts is gathered, / they pull the ladder and the pump.)

The hero Kuz'ma is a fearless veteran fire fighter who endangers his life to save the girl's cat. His daring labor is underscored in the last stanza.

> Vot Kuz'má sidít na drógakh.
> U negó litsó v ozhógakh,
> Lob v kroví, podbítyi gláz.
> Da emú ne v pérvyi ráz!
> Porabótal on nedárom—
> Slavno správilsia s pozhárom!
>
> (345)

(There sits Kuz'ma on the wagon. / His face is covered with burns, / his forehead is bleeding, / he had a black eye. / But he's used to this! / He didn't work in vain— / He handled the fire famously!)

How surprising it is to learn, therefore, that "The Fire" is one of Marshak's works that came under proletarian attack. As late as 1932 the ninth edition of the work was reviewed critically.

> It is puzzling, first of all, that the author did not introduce the image of Kuz'ma as a shock-worker, and second, that he did not show in somewhat stronger colors the firemen's communal relationship toward labor and its responsibilities, their discipline and consciousness of responsibility for the task entrusted them.
>
> Marshak should try to write a book that would teach children what a great harm fires cause the socialist economy, how much strength and what enormous quantities of human labor is sometimes lost in a fire. That kind of book would teach children to have a conscious, careful attitude toward fire, to strive to save the colossal labor losses of the whole collective building socialism.[45]

Marshak did publish a revised version into which he introduced at the beginning several stanzas extolling the vigilant firemen and removed most anthropomorphic references to the fire. Needless to say, much of the spirit is lost in the second version.

In most of Marshak's poems the narrator is an omniscient adult storyteller who has retained an excellent sense of what it means to be a child. The narration is straightforward, sincere, often humorous and playful, never condescending. In several poems the child's voice is clearly heard. "The Ball" ("Miach," 1926) echoes a young child's chant that might spontaneously arise during play.

Mói
Vesëlyi
Zvónkii
Miách,
Ty kudá
Pomchálsia
Vskách'?
(21)

(My / merry, / singing / ball, / where did you / bound off / with a bounce?)

In rhythm, rhyme, and lexicon, Marshak's poetry conforms well to the abilities and needs of children. His practice compares favorably with that of Chukovskii. As his poems clearly demonstrate, he was keenly aware of the central role of rhythm. On that subject he once said, "Without even penetrating the meaning of the verses, children often love them for their rhythm. In that way, for example, they love playful counting-out rhymes at times without understanding the words."[46] His own retention of a certain childlike appreciation of rhythm could only add to his poetry's success. Chukovskii delighted in recalling the quality of Marshak's knock at the door the first time he was visited by the younger poet. The two strokes of the knock seemingly beat the rhythm of the two syllables in Marshak's name: Mar-shak![47] Children, too, perceived the intrinsic bond between Marshak and his name. One of his young readers is reported to have said, "Isn't it true, Comrade Marshak, that you got your name because you write everything as in a march."[48] Marshak's special sensitivity to rhythm was one reason for his great fondness for children's incantations, which in turn permeated his own poetry. "From childhood I have loved passionately those little folk songs where man commands the rain, thunder, fire. Everything is in the imperative mood."[49] "The Rainbow" ("Raduga," 1926), for example, strikingly echoes the rhythms of children's folklore.

V nébe gróm, grozá.
Zakryvái glazá!

Dózhd' proshël. Travá blestít.
V nébe ráduga stoít.

Poskoréi, poskoréi,
Vybegái iz veréi,
Po travé
Bosikóm,
Priámo v nébo
Pryzhkóm.

Ládushki, ládushki!
Po ráduge, po ráduzhke,
Po tsvetnói
Dugé
Na odnói
Nogé.
Vniz po ráduge verkhóm
I na zémliu kuvyrkóm!
(123)

(In the sky there's thunder, a storm. / Close your eyes! // The rain has
stopped. The grass is shining. / There's a rainbow in the sky. //
Quickly, quickly / run outdoors, / on the grass / barefoot, / right into
the sky / with a jump. // Clap hands, clap hands! / On the rainbow, on
the little rainbow, / on the flowered / bow / on one / leg. / Down
astride the rainbow / and topsy-turvy to the ground!)

The rhythm and intonation of the initial couplet is that of a child's
incantation such as "Rain, rain, go away!" The last stanza, beginning with "clap hands," can be compared with an entertaining song.
Children's love of imaginative play—here the ride on the rainbow
—is especially well captured in this poem.

If, as Chukovskii established, a basically trochaic meter is the
rhythm most natural to children's movement and verbal creativity,
one would expect to find it in Marshak's work. Indeed, a computer-
aided study of all his children's poetry has shown that two-thirds of
his lines are trochaic.[50] In the early poems, which are aimed more
exclusively toward a younger audience than many of the later ones,
the percentage is slightly higher. Several poems use a mixture of
trochaic and iambic stanzas, but most are entirely in trochaic meter.

While Marshak can hardly be accused of using dull rhythms, he
rarely played with shifting metrical patterns in the manner of
Chukovskii. Instead, he achieved rhythmic variety largely through
other means. Some was introduced through variation in the length
of stanzas and the order of rhyme. His placement of lines on the page
was also important. However, his primary means of rhythmic variation were syntactic devices. In accordance with children's abilities,
syntactic units in his poems almost invariably coincide with verse
lines; sentences are either short or divided into compound, not
complex clauses. In such verses, rhythm most obviously derives
from frequent repetition and parallel construction. A good example
of this is the poem "Baggage" (quoted above), structured entirely on
repetition. In each seemingly repetitious stanza, subtle and not-so-
subtle changes occur. There are usually changes in the last line,

which completes the repetitious catalogue of objects. Also pertinent are "The Tale of Little Baby Mouse" and "That's How Absent-minded." The tauntlike refrain of the latter occurs six times, yet the stanzas it follows vary in length, eschewing monotony.

Although its overall structure is less regular than that of "Baggage," "Ice Cream" employs a similar catalogue of single words, repeated in various ways.

> —Otlíchnoe
> Zemlianíchnoe
> Morózhenoe! . . .
>
> . . . I klubníchnoe,
> Zemlianíchnoe
> Morózhenoe! . . .
>
> . . . Imenínnoe
> Apel'sínnoe
> Morózhenoe! . . .
>
> . . . Prekrásnoe
> Ananásnoe
> Morózhenoe! . . .

(Excellent / wild strawberry / ice cream! // And garden strawberry, / wild strawberry / ice cream! // Name day / orange / ice cream! // Fine / pineapple / ice cream!)

These all come together in the final, extended refrain.

> . . . klubníchnoe
> Zemlianíchnoe,
> Imenínnoe
> Apel'sínnoe,
> Prekrásnoe
> Ananásnoe
> Morózhenoe!
>               (140–43)

(Garden strawberry / wild strawberry / name day / orange, / fine / pineapple / ice cream!)

The frequent parallel constructions found in Chukovskii's *skazki* and reminiscent of folk poetry are on the whole absent from Marshak's poems. That absence can in part be explained by the fact that many of Marshak's poems are relatively short, with little opportunity for developed parallelisms. The longer ones are usually juxtaposed or developed anecdotes. Not surprisingly, parallel syntactic construction occurs most conspicuously in those poems closest to the folk tradition, that is, in the freely adapted nursery rhymes.

As is the case with meter, the rhyme patterns of Marshak's poems are largely in accordance with Chukovskii's practice. The poems abound in exact, often grammatical rhyme—always close, usually paired, sometimes crossed or enclosed. Internal rhyme occurs frequently and is likely to be accentuated by the typographic arrangement on the page. An outstanding example comes from "Baggage."

| | |
|---|---|
| Dáma sdavála v bagázh | a |
| Diván, | b |
| Chemodán, | b |
| Sakvoiázh, | a |
| Kartínu, | C |
| Korzínu, | C |
| Kartónku | D |
| I málen'kuiu sobachónku. | D |

(80)

The b and C rhymes would be located inside the regular dactylic metrical scheme of the stanza if it were arranged in the traditional manner. Along with rhyme, assonance and alliteration are prominent acoustic features of Marshak's poetry. However, despite the considerable role sound plays in these poems, it does not carry the overall force found in Chukovskii's poetry. Here, sound rarely operates in and of itself. Unlike that of Chukovskii, Marshak's poetry tends not to acquire meaning through sound. Instead, sound in many cases is subordinate to subject matter.

Among poets whose works aim to reach young children, the basic vocabulary used to build poems is inevitably similar. To communicate, children's poets must work creatively under what otherwise would be considered a severe handicap. Marshak enables children to participate in his poetry by limiting its range to words familiar to them from their daily experience. His lexicon consists of short, often monosyllabic words.

As Chukovskii emphasized, verbs typically play an obvious and vital role in such poetry. Most of Marshak's frequent verbs explicitly or implicitly convey motion.

> *Priotkrýla* dvériu Léna.
> *Soskochíl* ogón' s poléna
> Pered péchkoi *výzheg* pol,
> *Vlez* po skáterti na stól,
> *Pobezhál* po stúl'iam s tréskom,

Vverkh *popólz* po zanavéskam,
Stény dýmom *zavolók*,
*Lízhet* pól i potolók.

(342)

(Lena opened the door slightly, / the fire jumped down from the log. / It scorched the floor in front of the oven, / it climbed up the table-cloth onto the table, / it ran along the chairs with a crackle, / it crept up the curtains, / it clouded the walls with smoke, / it licked the floor and the ceiling.)

Occasionally verbs may gain additional emphasis by their initial position in a line, as in "That's How Absent-minded."

*Pobezhál* on na perrón,
*Vlez* v ottséplennyi vagón,
*Vnës* uzlý i chemodány,
*Rassovál* ikh pod divány.
*Sel* v uglú pered oknóm
I *zasnúl* spokóinym snóm. . . .

(100)

(He ran on to the platform, / crawled into an uncoupled car, / carried in his bundles and suitcases, / shoved them under the seats, / sat down in the corner by the window / and tranquilly fell asleep.)

End position in a sentence also emphasizes verbs, though it is rare for more than two verbs to occur together in that construction, due to the limitations imposed by rhyme. Sometimes Marshak's use of verbs suggests a lesson in morphology. The above example with verbs in initial position focuses on prefixed verbs of motion. Other stanzas drill the reflexive particle, as does this one from "The Fire":

Razdaëtskia grómkii zvón.
Nachináetsia rabóta,
Otpiráiutsia voróta,
Sobiráetsia obóz . . .

(342)

Some emphasize verbal aspect.

Nouns in this poetry are usually concrete and familiar—animals, children, parts of the body, everyday objects. Sometimes they occur in diminutive forms, but not predominantly. Diminutives arise above all in two situations—when there is a strong folk tone, as in this stanza from "Yesterday and Today" ("Vchera i segodnia," 1925), a poem contrasting old methods with new technology:

> Podkhodíli k réchke blízko,
> Rechke klánialisia nízko:
> —Zdrávstvui, réchka, násha mát',
> Dai vodítsy nam nabrát'!
>                                    (97)

(They walked up to the little river, / they bowed down low before the little river: / "Hello, little river, our mother, / let us take some water!")

Or when the point of view is indisputably a child's, as in "Ice Cream":

> Dali kázhdomu iz nás
> Úzen'kuiu lózhechku,
> I edím my tsélyi chás,
> Nabiráia vsiákii ráz
> S kraiú ponemnózheckhu.
>                                    (140)

(They gave each of us / a narrow little spoon, / and we ate for a whole hour, / each time taking / a tiny little bit from the edge.)

Marshak used adjectives with moderation. Like his nouns, they are on the whole simple, concrete, and from everyday experience. Often they are derived from nouns, as in "The Fire."

> Na plóshchadi bazárnoi,
> Na kalanché pozhárnoi . . .
>                                    (341)

Sometimes adjectives are used repeatedly within a poem and thus acquire characteristics of the fixed epithet. *Glupyi malen'kii myshonok* occurs seven times in "The Tale of the Silly Baby Mouse." *Rasseiannyi* is used similarly in "That's How Absent-minded." In "The Fire" there is *bednaia Lena*. More intricate folk expressions are absent from Marshak's poetry. The only fixed phrase he borrowed is an occasional *zhili-byli* (once upon a time). However, he did occasionally create compound nouns in the folk manner: *myshka-mat'* (mouse-mother), *knizhki-kaleki* (books-cripples), *atlety-silachi* (athletes-strongmen).

Recognizing children's fascination with counting, Marshak delighted in including numbers in his poems whenever possible. This example is from "Two Tomcats" ("Dva kota," 1927).

> Zhíli-býli dvá kotá—
> Vósem' lápok, dvá khvostá.
>                                    (273)

(Once upon a time there lived two tomcats— / eight paws, two tails.)

At times Marshak's use of numbers imitates the counting-out rhymes of children's folklore. The following stanza is from "Maker-Breaker" ("Master-lomaster," 1927), who here is struggling with an ax.

> Raz, dvá—
> Po polénu.
> Tri, chetýre—
> Po kolénu.
> Po polénu,
> Po kolénu,
> A potóm
> Vrubílsia v sténu.
> (214–15)

(One, two— / against the log. / Three, four— / against the knee. / Against the log, / against the knee, / and then he cut into the wall.)

As one would expect, Marshak essentially limited his figurative language in these poems to concrete similes. Referents are typically animals and objects, used to elucidate verbal action: *ubegaia, kak lisitsa* (running away like a fox), *zazhuzhzhala, kak pchela* (began to buzz like a bee), *topaet, kak slon* (stamps like an elephant). Nouns are less commonly the subject of such similes: *shchëki, kak podushki* (cheeks like pillows). Although Marshak generally avoided hyperbolic imagery, he created a definite sense of hyperbole through structural repetition leading to playful exaggeration, as in "The Tale of the Silly Baby Mouse," "Look How Absent-minded," and "Baggage." In "Ice Cream" the development of the narrative line is itself hyperbolic. Most strikingly, this poem, which begins as a simple, realistic description of an ice cream man and his cart surrounded by children, culminates in a fantastic image bordering on the grotesque. A fat man who gluttonously persists in eating more and more ice cream slowly turns into an enormous snowdrift in a wintry setting.

> A tolstiák molchít—ne slýshit,
> Ananásnym párom dýshit.
>
> Na spiné ego sugrób.
> Pobelél bagróvyi lób.
>
> Posinéli óba úkha.
> Borodá belée púkha.

Na zatýlke—snézhnyi kóm.
Sneg na shliápe kolpakóm.

On stoít i ne shevélitsia,
A krugóm shumít metélitsa. . . .
(142–43)

(But the fat man is silent—he doesn't hear, / he is breathing out pineapple steam. // On his back there is a snowdrift. / His crimson forehead has turned white. // Both his ears have turned blue. / His beard is whiter than goose down. // At the back of his head there's a snowball. / The snow on his hat is like a hood. // He is standing still, he doesn't stir, / roundabout a snowstorm howls.)

Marshak's portrayal of gluttony is a subtle parallel of the mode of Hoffmann's *Struwwelpeter*. Marshak simply describes, with no moral implied, and the subject is an adult, not a child.

The unique example of a neologism in this poetry comes from a child's point of view in "Maker-Breaker."

Tý u nás ne máster,
Tý u nás lomáster!
(213)

(You are not our maker, / you are our breaker!)

By joining the noun *master* (literally, expert) with the verb *lomat'* (to break), Marshak devised an amusing hybrid, which children themselves might easily have created.

Although his approach to subject matter varied from poem to poem, an underlying unity is discernible in Marshak's work of the 1920s. In strong contrast to Chukovskii's *skazki*, these poems focus, directly or indirectly, on the concrete, tangible reality of daily experience. In the poems where setting is delineated, the action takes place in an urban environment, sometimes specifically Petrograd, later (after 1924) Leningrad.

Poshél Antósha v Létnii sád
Odnázhdy v voskresén'e
I uvidál, chto Petrográd
V trevóge i smiatén'e.[51]

(Tony went to the Summer Garden / one Sunday / and saw that Petrograd / was alarmed and confused.)

Èto ón.,
Èto ón,
Leningrádskii pochtal'ón.
(88)

(It's he, / it's he, / the Leningrad postman.)

There are no excursions in these lines to distant, exotic, or fantastic lands. In "Kids in a Cage" Africa is merely mentioned a few times in passing as the original homeland of some of the animals. Nowhere in these poems are there cannibalistic giants or trees that grow shoes. Beyond the anthropomorphism of animals and objects, there is little distortion of reality. The creation of a man who turns into a mound of ice cream is Marshak's only excursion into delightful whimsy.

In addition to the anthropomorphized animals and objects, important participants in the action of these poems are children. A few are identified by name—Antosha, Grishka, Lena. Most are anonymous—*my* (we), *rebiata* (children). When adults appear, they are usually working—on the train, for the postal service, in the circus, behind an ice cream cart. Kuz'ma the fireman in "The Fire" receives the most attention. (See the stanza cited above.) Although details are scant, these portraits are largely realistic.

In Marshak's poems there is a high correlation between his essentially realistic approach and his intent. In many of them an obvious cognitive lesson stands out. Thus, for example, modern technology receives special attention. "Yesterday and Today" describes the new—an electric light bulb, typewriter, and running water—in contrast to the old—an oil lamp, quill pen, and yoke and water buckets. In simple terms, "The Post" ("Pochta") surveys the efficient methods of the Soviet and international postal service and gives a rudimentary geography lesson as well. "How the Plane Made a Plane" ("Kak rubanok sdelal rubanok") familiarizes children with the process involved in making a carpenter's plane. The last two poems were both published in 1927, the same year Maiakovskii published a poem for children about the operation of a lighthouse. That Marshak and Maiakovskii each wrote his first poem on the theme of labor in the same year is a significant coincidence, indicating the proletarians' success in dictating subject matter.

The following year, 1928, Marshak published "The Troop" ("Otriad") his first obviously ideological poem for children. Through a series of riddles, this poem manages to treat the theme of Pioneers in a relatively playful way.

> Chtó tam za prokhózhii
> Idét po mostovói,
> Chtó za krasnokózhii
> S góloi golovói?
> (364)

(What kind of a passer-by / is that walking there on the street? / What sort of sunburnt one is he / with a bare head?)

A few years later, as his ideological commitment at least outwardly increased, Marshak's poems grew less imaginative. Two exceptions, addressed to a somewhat older audience, stand out.

"War with the Dniepr" ("Voina s Dneprom," 1931) is Marshak's attempt to dedicate a work to the First Five-Year Plan. His subject is the building of the celebrated Dniepr River Power Station, designed by an American engineer and completed in 1932. However one regards the merit of such a theme, Marshak deserves credit for having succeeded in creating a highly spirited poem. It far surpasses innumerable inferior works addressed to production themes.

> I vót v reké postávlena
> Zheléznaia stená.
>
> I vót reké ob'iávlena
> Voiná,
> Voiná,
> Voiná!
>
> Vykhódit v bói
> Pod'émnyi krán,
> Dvadtsatitónnyi
> Velikán,
> Nesét
> V protiánutoi ruké
> Chugúnnyi mólot
> Na kriuké.
>                     (437–38)

(And then an iron wall / was built in the river. // And then they announced to the river: / War, war, war! // A crane / goes into battle, / a twenty-ton / giant; / in his outstretched hand / he carries / a cast-iron hammer / on a hook.)

Marshak's image of the anthropomorphized crane has become a commonplace in subsequent poems on construction topics. Thus, even among the poems of some of the best post-Stalin poets, one inevitably finds the same crane.

Another memorable poem of this period is "Mister Twister" ("Mister Tvister," 1933), a sharply satirical portrayal of a wealthy, racist American visiting the Soviet Union with his wife and spoiled daughter. The poem is a highly imaginative contribution to the Soviet fund of stereotypic, anticapitalist propaganda. The verbal brilliance of this long but fast-paced narrative far outweighs the apparently simple subject. A catchy refrain in different variations rhythmically unifies the work.

> Míster
> Tvíster,
> Bývshii minístr,
> Míster
> Tvíster,
> Millionér . . .
>                (432)

(Mister / Twister / the former Minister, / Mister / Twister / a millionaire . . .)

Marshak's pointed wit is captivating. After refusing to stay in a hotel with dark-skinned guests, Twister and his family are boycotted by all the hotels in Leningrad.

> Ia óchen' ustála!—
> Dóch' prosheptála.—
> Esli nochléga
> Nigdé
> Ne naidëm,
> Mózhet byt',
> Kúpish'
> Kakói-nibud'
> Dóm?
>
> —Kúpish'!—
> Otéts
> Otvecháet,
> Vzdykháia.—
> Tý ne v Chikágo,
> Moiá dorogáia.
> Dóm nad Nevóiu
> Kupít' by ia rád . . .
> Da ne zakhóchet
> Prodát' Leningrád!
>                (431)

("I'm very tired!" / his daughter whispered. / "If we don't find / lodging / anywhere, / maybe you'll buy / some kind of / a house?" //. "Buy!" / her father / answers / with a sigh. / "You're not in Chicago, / my dear. / I'd be happy to buy / a house on the Neva . . . / but Leningrad / won't want to sell!")

Only the like of Twister himself could find this work anything but hilarious.[51]

From the work of Chukovskii and Marshak, and from that of Sasha Chërnyi before them, an important pattern emerges. In order to be able to write good poetry for children, one must love both poetry and children. Marshak is remembered not only as the first Russian lyric poet to write successful poetry for children, but equally importantly as the editorial mentor of the generation of children's writers that included the Oberiu poets and their friends.[52]

**6**

## THE OBERIU POETS

$\mathrm{T}$OLD IN THE broadest strokes, the early history
of Soviet children's poetry emphasizes the work of Chukovskii,
Marshak, and Maiakovskii. The central role of Chukovskii and
Marshak is indisputable. Their ideas and inspiration together gave
the new children's literature in the Soviet Union a vital, highly
imaginative thrust, the impact of which has lasted to the present
day. Maiakovskii's contribution, on the other hand, is much less
significant. If intrinsic worth were truly considered, the place
shared with Chukovskii and Marshak would go not to Maiakovskii
but to a collective of writers centered on Oberiu, an acronym for
Ob'edinenie real'nogo iskusstva (Association for Real Art), a short-
lived avant-garde literary group, which had coalesced in Leningrad

in the second half of the 1920s. Of the declared members of the group, Kharms, Vvedenskii, Vladimirov, and Nikolai Zabolotskii wrote children's poetry; Boris Levin and Igor' Bakhterev wrote prose. The only member who did not write for children was Konstantin Vaginov. Closely associated with this group were Shvarts and Oleinikov, who also wrote for children.[1]

A definitive study of the Oberiuty, as they called themselves, has yet to appear. Through the years of Stalin's terror the evidence of their existence was completely suppressed, and only after the "thaw" did it begin to resurface. Collecting material on the Oberiuty remains a difficult task, since the experimental nature of their work is disapproved of officially even in the post-Stalin period. Kharms, Vvedenskii, and Oleinikov all fell victim to Stalin's terror. With the exception of the work of Zabolotskii, who survived arrest and exile, little of their adult writing has been published in the Soviet Union. Yet, with the appearance of samizdat, some of their work has gained a large underground following, especially that of Kharms. With texts being published abroad, more scholars attempt to unravel the almost forgotten story of the Oberiuty.

The history of Oberiu's connection with children's literature begins indirectly with Evgenii Shvarts (1896–1955).[2] It is little known that before 1930, when he became known as a playwright, he spent an important early phase of his career as a children's writer and editor on Marshak's now famous editorial staff in Leningrad. Shvarts first came to what was then Petrograd in 1921 as a fledgling actor with a theater from Rostov-on-the-Don. While still in Rostov, he had begun writing humorous poetry,[3] only one manifestation of his abundant and highly developed wit. Once in Petrograd, he made numerous literary acquaintances; among them were some of the Serapion Brothers—and Nikolai Chukovskii, Kornei Chukovskii's son. For several months Shvarts worked as a secretary for the elder Chukovskii[4]—then involved primarily in scholarship on Nekrasov—whose fame as a children's poet still lay ahead.

Up to the present the literary and artistic circles of Leningrad and Moscow are tightly knit communities. This means that the paths of Russian intellectuals frequently cross; fates are intertwined oddly, sometimes even "mystically," as in the earlier case of the symbolists Blok and Andrei Belyi. Especially during the physically difficult days of the early 1920s, Russian writers stayed in close contact. In Petrograd this was officially condoned and encouraged under the auspices of such artistic collectives as the House of the Arts. Thus it was that Kornei Chukovskii enthusiastically invited everyone to attend an evening with Samuil Marshak, his new friend and recent arrival from Krasnodar. Shvarts, one of the guests at the reading, "was quickly conquered" by the poet and his poetry.[5] Soon afterward, in 1923, when Shvarts returned to the Don Basin to work for a small newspaper, he wrote his friend Mikhail Slonimskii, one of the Serapions. "I really want to write to Marshak! I have been dreaming about it for two months. At first I was afraid he would not be interested in me, now I'm afraid he's not in Petrograd. You're lucky, you can call him on the telephone and learn where he is, what he's doing; and I'm left in the dark. I feel bad. I like Marshak a lot . . . .[6]

By the time Shvarts returned to Leningrad in 1924, Marshak was the editor of the children's magazine *Sparrow* (soon to be called *New Robinson*). Therefore he was able to turn to his new mentor with the manuscript of his first work for children, "The Story of an Old Balalaika" ("Rasskaz staroi balalaiki"), a tale in rhymed prose familiar from folklore, a style he had used in his newspaper column.[7] In addition to the story, he brought to Marshak his new friend and fellow journalist, Nikolai Oleinikov.

> By nature Oleinikov had a passion for mystification, for ingenious joking. He uttered the most fantastic and absurd things in such a serious way that imperceptive people took them at face value. Oleinikov and Shvarts were brought together above all by humor— with each it was both very different and very close. They loved to laugh and cause laughter; they found something funny where others saw only something solemn and majestic. Sometimes their humor was concrete and ordinary, sometimes it was parodistic and eccentric; together they struck one with their inexhaustible supply of jokes, very simple and merry on the surface; but if one looked more deeply, at times their sad significance was striking."[8]

Soon their humor found its way into children's literature.

Encouraged by Marshak, for several years Shvarts and Oleinikov channeled much of their energy into writing for children. After Marshak's move to the children's division of Gosizdat, they became involved with the new magazines, first *Ëzh* in 1928, and then *Chizh* in 1930. Although Marshak was the editor-in-chief, Shvarts and Oleinikov were the de facto editors, doing most of the work.[9] In their first years of publication, these magazines—full of humor and interesting material—were the most captivating periodicals Russian children had ever been offered. Between 1925 and 1932, in addition to his regular participation in *Ëzh* and *Chizh*, Shvarts published more than fifteen separate little books for chidren. While for adults

Oleinikov wrote poetry, for children (an older audience than the one toward which Shvarts directed his work) he wrote realistic prose. And to many he was first of all the creator of the legendary "Makar the Fierce," a colorful epic hero whose adventures appeared from issue to issue on the pages of *Ëzh*. [10]

When *Ëzh* was still in the planning stages, the Oberiuty were already an established phenomenon. Six writers had coalesced as a group by the spring of 1926 and made frequent public appearances in 1927. [11] Vladimirov joined them later. That year also marked the debut of some of them as children's writers, although the exact sequence of events remains unclear. The story most widely known is Marshak's: "Soon after we began to work I had the idea of attracting the trans-sense poets [Oberiuty]. I thought these people could bring whimsy into children's poetry by creating counting-out rhymes, refrains, humorous sayings. . . ." [12] Bakhterev recalls that after an Oberiu reading in the spring of 1927, Shvarts and Oleinikov came up and invited them all to write for children, [13] very likely upon Marshak's urging.

The new careers of Oberiu poets as children's writers raises the important question of why they accepted Marshak's offer. A factor now easy to overlook is the financial one. The Oberiuty were undoubtedly grateful for an opportunity to earn some money. In the second half of the 1920s the modernist aesthetic they espoused could hardly provide them with a source of income. Kharms, for example, published only three adult poems during his lifetime. Zabolotskii is known to have had trouble finding work until he joined forces with Gosizdat. [14] It is likely that each of them was in similarly desperate material straits.

At the same time, there was a fortuitous coincidence of Weltanschauung. Although the Oberiuty would have been disturbed by Marshak's description of them as trans-sense writers (they took a vehement stand against trans-sense language in their 1928 manifesto), the designation is apt if interpreted more broadly. Khlebnikov was indisputably an important source of inspiration for their early work. [15] But purely verbal experimentation was only a minor aspect of the new, revolutionary, futurist orientation that fascinated the Oberiuty. Ultimately, they were more concerned with expressing a total vision of the world around them, leaving elemental, verbal experimentation behind.

> Who are we? And why do we exist? We, the Oberiuty, are honest workers in art. We are poets of a new world view and of a new art. We are not only creators of a poetic language, but also founders of a new

feeling for life and its objects. Our will to create is universal. It spans all genres of art and penetrates life, grasping it from all sides. The world covered by the rubbish of the tongues of a multitude of fools bogged down in the mire of "experiences" and "emotions" is now being reborn in all the purity of concrete, bold forms. . . . We, people who are real and concrete to the marrow of our bones, are the first enemies of those who castrate the word and make it into a powerless and senseless mongrel. In our work we broaden the meaning of the object and of the word, but we do not destroy it in any way. The concrete object, once its literary and everyday skin is peeled away, becomes a property of art. In poetry the collisions of verbal meanings express that object with the exactness of mechanical technology. . . . Art has a logic of its own, and it does not destroy the object but helps us to know it.[16]

Their vision of the world prominently includes the myriad incongruities that adults are conditioned to overlook, filter out, repress. Through a new mode of "making strange," the Oberiu reality approaches that of children. They accept and even emphasize relationships that from a "classical" adult point of view are absurd, illogical, non sequitur. The Oberiu worldview made them highly sympathetic to children; they came closer than most adults to understanding and communicating with children on their own terms.

The "return" to a child's vision is like a return to spontaneity of perception; between a child and the world there is no, or almost no, curtain of accustomed perceptions, automatic associations, canonized conceptions, which obscure the real outlines of objects. A child's vision is hardly subordinate to that peculiar "self-censorship," which often involuntarily interferes with our perception and rather strictly corrects it according to definite, accepted measures and tastes. A child communicates his impressions of things with no concern as to how one "must" see them and how one "should" talk about them.[17]

Perpetuating the tradition of Russian modernism, the Oberiuty were associated with several leading artists, including Pavel Filonov and Kasimir Malevich.[18] Children's books, with their potential union of the verbal and the graphic, offer an excellent opportunity for collaboration between writers and artists. As the early works of Chukovskii and Marshak show, the best children's literature of the early Soviet period was the result of the joint creative efforts of writers and artists.[19] Yet, as the 1920s wore on and conservative criticism prevailed, the work of such teams was undermined.

Among the Oberiuty, Daniil Iuvachëv (1905–1942), better known

by the pseudonym Kharms, made the most significant contribution
to children's poetry. He entered the Leningrad literary scene in 1925,
when he participated in his first public poetry reading at the age of
twenty.[20] As noted above, he himself witnessed the publication of
only three of his adult poems, while only a few more of his works
appeared posthumously in the Soviet Union in the 1960s. His work
for adults includes poetry, drama, and short prose fantasies.
Kharms's inclination for fantasy was not satisfied by his writing; he
was also known as an incredible prankster whose eccentric, often
daring, behavior was at times frighteningly out of tune with Soviet
reality. For ten years, between 1928 and 1938, Kharms published
verse and prose pieces for children. In 1941 he was arrested and died
in prison half a year later.[21]

With their bold display of his penchant for nonsense, Kharms's
poems and stories for children even today intimidate conservative,
unimaginative Soviet minds. In a huge market for children's literature, only three editions of Kharms's work for children have appeared since the death of Stalin. A first, slim volume was published
in 1962, when the "thaw" finally reached children's literature. The
most complete edition to date appeared in 1967; some excerpts from
it were reprinted in 1972.[22] While it is fortunate that Kharms's work
for children has reappeared, it deserves to be as easily available as
that of Chukovskii, Marshak, Maiakovskii, and innumerable inferior children's poets. Meanwhile, the few recent editions have
become collectors' items, as greatly cherished by some Russians as
out-of-print volumes of Khlebnikov.

Kharms's friend Aleksandr Vvedenskii (1904–1942?) produced a
far greater quantity of works for children, but their quality is highly
uneven. What little is known of his life closely parallels that of
Kharms. He first read his poetry publicly in 1926. In the same year
and the following one a few of his poems were anthologized. After
that, only his children's stories, which began appearing in 1928,
were published. Like Kharms, he was arrested in 1941; shortly
thereafter he perished somewhere in the Ukraine.[23] Only a few
editions of his children's works have been published since 1960.[24]

Iurii Vladimirov (1908–1931), who is often mentioned along with
Kharms and Vvedenskii, tried his hand at poetry at a very young age.
He grew up in a literary milieu—his mother was originally a secre-
tary for *Apollon*, the literary artistic journal published in St.
Petersburg from 1909 to 1917. After the revolution she worked in a
similar capacity for the Theater for Young Spectators. At school

Vladimirov participated both in the student newspaper and in an active drama circle. In the difficult days after finishing school, he took whatever work he could find, sometimes as a bookkeeper. About 1928 an artist friend from school, Iurii Mezernitskii, who worked as an illustrator for the Rainbow Publishing House, first introduced the young poet to the world of children's literature. Until his untimely death from tuberculosis at the age of twenty-three, Vladimirov published poetry both in Ëzh and in individual books. After his death his parents moved to central Asia and are rumored to have taken along a trunk of their son's manuscripts. The trunk and its contents disappeared during the war.[25]

When Nikolai Zabolotskii (1903–1958) met Marshak in 1927 and began working in children's literature, he already had behind him a long "literary" career, reminiscent in some ways of Marshak's own youth. In the third grade Zabolotskii put out a manuscript magazine, in which he included some of his own poems.[26] By the time he finished the Herzen Pedagogical Institute in Leningrad in 1925, he had a "voluminous notebook of bad poetry."[27] Before his military service (1926–1927), also spent in Leningrad, he read his poetry in the House of the Press, where the Oberiuty sometimes "performed."[28] Thus it was along with his fellow Oberiuty that Zabolotskii was discovered by children's literature. During 1929–1931 Zabolotskii served on the editorial boards of Ëzh and Chizh. "In ten years of work I published a series of poems and stories in the magazines Ëzh, Chizh, Pioneer, Campfire, and also published several separate books for children. I consider the most substantial of them my re-workings of Rabelais's Gargantua and Pantagruel and de Coster's Til Eulenspiegel. Children's literature, however, did not exhaust my interests and I continued to write lyric verse."[29]

As it turned out, the playful spirit of that group of poets who worked together on a top floor in the former Singer Building on Nevskii prospekt was incompatible with the larger cultural trends in the Soviet Union then—and now. The original association—Oberiu—that brought them together was effectively stifled by 1930, and their creative attempts in the field of children's literature did not last much longer. By his premature death, Vladimirov was spared the tragic fate of Kharms, Vvedenskii, Oleinikov, and Zabolotskii. At least the latter was lucky enough to come out of his ordeal alive. Shvarts alone survived the war years in "freedom." The posthumous rehabilitation of Kharms and Vvedenskii was largely an empty gesture, since most Russians remain unfamiliar with their work.

Evgenii Shvarts was one of Marshak's early disciples. From the time of his return to Leningrad in 1924 until the early 1930s, when he devoted himself to drama, Shvarts regularly published short works for children, several of them at Kliachko's Rainbow Publishing House. His books, which appeared between 1925 and 1932, are distinguished above all by their dynamic thematics. They actively involve children's imaginations, forcing them to participate in the story and not just to listen passively.

In his very first work, "The Story of an Old Balalaika" (1925), a relatively long narrative about the celebrated St. Petersburg flood is told from a balalaika's point of view. Shvarts immediately captures the attention of his young audience by constructing a nonsense puzzle for them to solve. "Nachináetsia rasskáz moi prósto, otshchitáite godóv ètak dó sta, a kogdá podvedéte shchët, ugadáite, kakói byl gód."[30] (My story begins simply. Count the years more or less to one hundred, and when you arrive at the sum, guess what year it was.) Shvarts attempts and usually succeeds in engaging children's minds, no matter what the thematic orientation of his material. A purely playful poem like "Balloons" ("Shariki," 1926) ends on a challenging note.

> I ponës ikh véter
> Po chuzhím kraiám.
> Ésli kto ikh vstrétit,
> Púst' rasskázhet nám.[31]

(And the wind carried them off / to foreign lands. / If somebody meets them, / let him tell us about them.)

In this way children are encouraged to take over where Shvarts the storyteller leaves off.

About half of these works are aimed at nothing more than satisfying children's emotional needs. They narrate stories; many describe games or other play activities. Ideology is largely absent. Morality tales are also few. "The War between Punch and Struwwelpeter" ("Voina Petrushki i Stëpki-Rastrëpki," 1925), is a new variation on the old cleanliness theme, most recently treated by Chukovskii in "Wash'em Clean." Shvarts joins in adventure the folk character Petrushka, the Russian Punch, with Stëpka-Rastrëpa, the Russian Struwwelpeter. Struwwelpeter seeks to marry Punch's winsome daughter, who at first spurns him because he is slovenly. The heroes proceed to cavort in a fashion reminiscent of Chukovskii through a battle scene with chocolate cannon balls (Struwwelpeter is captured because he swallows them!) and, after a purifying scrub for the bridegroom, there is a wedding feast and dance at the end.

> Dvádtsat' tri tórta ráznogo sórta, iábloki s arbúz, kak sákhar na vkús, tashkéntskii vinográd, konfékty, shokolád—gósti éle-éle vsë èto poéli! A poshlí pliasát', priamo nóg ne vidát'—tak vysokó prýgali, tak nogámi drýgali.[32]

> (Twenty-three cakes of various kinds, apples as big as watermelons, sweet as sugar, Tashkent grapes, candy, chocolate—the guests just barely ate it all up! And when they went to dance, you couldn't see their legs—they jumped so high and kicked their feet.)

As in Chukovskii, the didactic point is conveyed painlessly.

However, morality lessons, even sugar-coated ones, seem not to have greatly interested Shvarts. There are no more until his last works in the early 1930s. "Stop! Learn the Traffic Rules like Multiplication Tables" ("Stop! Pravila ulichnogo dvizheniia znai, kak tablitsu umnozheniia," 1931) combines information about traffic regulations with simple warnings about conduct on the street.

> Ne khodí po mostovói!

> Panél'—dlia liudéi,          A poidésh' po mostovói—
> Mostováia dlia loshadéi,   Otshtrafúet postovói![33]

> (Don't walk on the street! / The sidewalk is for people, / the street is for horses. / If you walk on the street, / the policeman will fine you!)

Ideology merges with morality in "Vasia Shelaev" (1932), where the point is made that everyone must work during the summer. The stridently moralizing end is unlike any of Shvarts's early works and reeks, it seems, of unnecessary editorial interference: "Vsiúdu i vsiúdu rabóta kipít, a otstaiúshchim pozór i stýd!"[34] (Everywhere, everywhere, work is in full swing; shame and disgrace to the laggards!) Here the word *styd* (shame) communicates a far more authoritarian tone than when Chukovskii used it in a childlike taunting way in "Wash'em Clean."

Some of these poems have a basically cognitive orientation, acquainting children with such things as modes of transport, markets, and farm animals. Most of the factual material is conveyed through description of activity. Everything is in motion, whether it is simply the local market— "Toropítes', brátsy, v srók nádobno otkrýt, larëk. Èi, prokhózhie s dorógi, a ne tó otdávim nógi!"[35] (Hurry, brothers, the stall must be opened in time. Hey, passers-by, get off the street, or we'll tread on your feet!)—or two Arab brothers racing one another around the world—"Bezháli oní, chto est' móchi, bezháli dva dniá i dve nóchi"[36] (They ran as fast as they could, / they ran two days and two nights).

The structure of Shvarts's poems is distinguished by the frequent use of his favorite rhymed prose style. Through this form he succeeded in combining a regular rhyme scheme (the equivalent of paired rhymes) with great metrical flexibility. Although sentences are written on the page as prose, the rhyme forces them into couplets, some reflecting a more regular metrical pattern than others. This tendency away from a highly organized meter brings Shvarts closer to the oral tradition, where the metrical patterns of poetry are more flexible than in the literary tradition and where prose tends to be organized in a highly rhythmical way. Further echoing the folk tradition, Shvarts's work frequently contains syntactic repetition and parallel construction. Other folk devices, such as fixed epithets, compound words, and concrete similes also occur occasionally.

With the exception of rhyme, the acoustic texture of Shvarts's work is less elaborate than that of the children's poetry of most of his contemporaries; it is, in fact, closer to prose. On the whole, the element of play derives more from content than from abstract combinations of sound. An exception to this rule is "Hide and Seek" ("Priatki," 1927), a poem in which the verbal texture essentially develops as repetition and variation of the sounds in the names of the two protagonists.

> Stëpka-Rastrëpka
> I Miśhka-Strízhka.
> Priáchetsia Stëpka,
> A íshchet Míshka.
>
> Stëpka khitréishii
> Píshet uglëm:
> "Ia tám-to i tám-to,"
> A sám za uglóm![37]

(Stëpka-Rastrëpka / and Mishka-Strizhka. / Stëpka hides / and Mishka seeks. // Very sly Stëpka / writes with coal: / "I'm in such and such a place." / But in fact he's around the corner!)

Play comes inevitably from the constant repetition of the names throughout the poem.

"Hide and Seek" also serves as an excellent example of the possibilities of the interrelationship of text and illustrations. The artist is Vladimir Konashevich, who created some of the best illustrations for children's books in the Soviet Union, including editions of Chukovskii and Marshak. It is impossible to convey verbally the force of Konashevich's drawings. They do not simply duplicate in another medium the meaning of the words. Instead, they add a significant new dimension. All the drawings are marked by cartoon-like simplicity.

> Odín khitér—
> I drugói ne prostói.
> Kostiúm otyskálsia—
> Da tól'ko pustói!
>
> Agá, Stepán!
> Ne nashél, Stepán!
> Stoísh' nad vodói,
> Nu, i stói, kak barán!

(One may be sly— / but the other isn't simple-minded. / He found the suit— / but it was empty! // Aha, Stepan! / You didn't find me, Stepan! / You didn't find me, Stepan! / You're standing above the water; / well, stand there, like a ram!)

To accompany these two stanzas, Konashevich drew one child on the river bank and the other hiding naked in the bushes. The latter's clothes are cleverly depicted as lying on the bank near the first boy—with a stick figure body drawn in! On the next page the first boy discovers the trick and picks up the clothes, leaving a drawing of face, arms, and feet behind. The additional humor which comes from the stick figure is Konashevich's independent graphic creation. With the exception of "The Story of an Old Balalaika," which was illustrated in a realistically detailed and rather dull manner, until 1929 Shvarts's books were strikingly illustrated, often in the constructivist style of the day. The best example is the work of Aleksei Pakhomov, whose bold areas of color approach pure design. Unfortunately, art was as subject to proletarian criticism as literature. For this reason, Pakhomov's later illustrations are traditionally realistic.[38]

By the time Daniil Kharms turned to children's literature, all the adult poetry he managed to publish during his lifetime had already appeared—a total of three poems. Of course there was more, but it remained unpublished.[39] The critic Adrian Makedonov suggests that the Oberiuty gradually disintegrated as a group once some of them channeled much of their energy toward children.[40] It is more likely, however, that their creativity for adults diminished in direct relation to the repression of their activities from above.

Kharms's first small book for children, "The Theater" ("Teatr," 1928), might have led unsuspecting readers to welcome the appear-

ance of another Marshak. As has been inevitably pointed out, this
series of epigrammatic captions for illustrations is reminiscent of
Marshak's "The Circus."[41] But "The Theater" is clearly a fledgling,
derivative piece of work in which Kharms's own voice is difficult to
discern. One detects it, however, in the juxtaposition of traditional
and contemporary thematics. Ten couplets, each accompanying a
drawing, are arranged in conscious thematic symmetry. Two stanzas in the center evoke the caricatures of Maiakovskii's ROSTA windows.

> Rasprokliátogo burzhúia
> V tri minúty ulozhú ia.
>
> Devchónka-komsomólka
> Ne boítsia vólka.[42]

(I'll flatten in three minutes / an accursed bourgeois. // A Young
Communist girl / doesn't fear the wolf.)

These are framed by such popular figures as "Harlequin," "Punch,"
"The Humpbacked Horse," and "Sleeping Beauty." In what perhaps
was an attempt to be topical and relevant, Kharms brought together
a bizarre selection of types. With such a work there is also the
possibility that the artist was a close collaborator and perhaps influenced the choice of thematics, as was the case with Marshak in
"Kids in a Cage" and "The Circus."

After "The Theater," Kharms went on to write excellent poetry
for children that ranks in imaginative quality with that of
Chukovskii and Marshak.[43] His work is permeated and unified by
the all-important concept of play. Play in his poetry falls into two
categories: linguistic play, which helps build and exercise children's
developing language skills, and intellectual play, which more generally facilitates their mental development. In these works he succeeded in channeling toward children his own seemingly boundless
capacity for play.

"Ivan Ivanych Samovar" (1928), Kharms's contribution to the in-
augural issue of Ëzh and one of his best and most beloved poems, is
the epitome of linguistically playful children's poetry. Chukovskii
singled it out, saying that it "remains one of the best monuments"
of Kharms's "verbal play, where the whole narrative is given such a
laughably single-minded (and very childlike) quality."[44] Here and in
other of Kharms's poems for children, the central focus is on the
syntactic structure. Throughout the poem a single basic pattern
undergoes careful manipulation. The first stanza establishes the
fundamental scheme, based on triplet repetitions.

Ivan Iványch Samovár
byl puzátyi samovár,
trěkhvedérnyi samovár.
V něm kachálsia kipiatók,
pykhal párom kipiatók,
raz'iarěnnyi kipiatók,
lilsia v cháshku cherez krán,
cherez dýrku priamo v krán,
priamo v cháshku cherez krán.[45]

(Ivan Ivanych Samovar / was a big-bellied samovar, / a three-gallon
samovar. / In him boiling water was rolling, / boiled water puffed out
steam, / furious boiling water / poured into the cup through the
spigot, / through a hole right in the spigot, / right into the cup through
the spigot.)

While the all-important rhymed word remains intact, other words
in the line change. The process of these changes involves internal
rhyme and assonance, alliteration, and often the repetition of words
in a new position. Using such basic devices, the poem proceeds in
the accumulative fashion of folklore.

Utrom ráno podoshěl,
k samováru podoshěl,
diadia Pétia podoshěl.
Diadia Pétia govorít:
—Dai-ka, výp'iu,—govorít,—
vyp'iu cháiu,—govorít.

(Early in the morning he went, / to the samovar he went, / Uncle
Petia went, / Uncle Petia said, / "I think I'll drink some tea," he
said. / "I'll drink some tea," he said.)

Seven family members—pets included—go to pour themselves a
cup of tea. The orderly progression of six-line stanzas is disturbed
only when the child Serëzha, the seventh would-be tea drinker,
arrives. Suddenly there is an eight-line stanza, conveying a break in
the sequence.

Nakloniáli, nakloniáli,
nakloniáli samovár,
no ottúda, vybiválsia
tol'ko pár, pár, pár.
Nakloniáli samovár,
budto shkáp, shkáp, shkáp,
no ottúda vykhodíli
tol'ko káp, káp, káp.

(They tipped, they tipped, / they tipped the samovar; / but from it came out / only steam, steam, steam. / They tipped the samovar, / like a cupboard, cupboard, cupboard, / but from it came / only drip, drip, drip.)

This is followed by the last stanza, in which Kharms comes closer to didacticism than anywhere else.

> Samovár Ivan Iványch!
> Na stolé Ivan Iványch!
> Zolotói Ivan Iványch!
> Kipiatóchku ne daët,
> opozdávshim ne daët,
> lezhebókam ne daët.

(Samovar Ivan Ivanych! / On the table Ivan Ivanych! / Golden Ivan Ivanych! / It doesn't give boiling water, / it doesn't give it to late-comers, / it doesn't give it to lazybones.)

The gentle moral may have come from Marshak's influence, since this is one of Kharms's early poems, on which he is known to have worked under the close guidance of the older poet.[46]

Similarly structured, the other longer poems—those containing more than three or four stanzas—also emphasize linguistic play. As the title itself betrays, in "Play" ("Igra," 1930) verbal play is enhanced by thematic play. It is a playful poem about play.

> Begal Pét'ka po doróge,
> po doróge,
> po panéli,
> begal Pét'ka
> po panéli
> i krichál on:
> —Ga-ra-rár!
> Ia tepér' uzhe ne Pét'ka,
> razoidítes'!
> Razoidítes'!
> Ia tepér' uzhe ne Pét'ka,
> Ia tepér' avtomobíl'.[47]

(Along the street ran Petia, / along the street, / along the sidewalk; / Petia ran / along the sidewalk / and shouted: / "Vrr-oo-m! / I'm not Petia anymore, / clear the way! / Clear the way! / I'm not Petia anymore: / now I'm an automobile.")

Using the typical triple formula, the poem deals with three boys pretending to be vehicles. As each is introduced, Kharms employs repetition and substitution, as Marshak did in "The Tale of the Silly

Baby Mouse." In a sense, this poem introduces a certain cognitive element through its description of automobile, train, and airplane. But Kharms does it imaginatively, depicting children behaving in ways they naturally do. He avoids static description—whatever knowledge of the surrounding world he communicates comes through movement, involving children directly.

A poem with a more traditional narrative plot, such as "About How Papa Shot Me a Polecat" ("O tom, kak papa zastrelil mne khor'ka," 1929), becomes a nonsense game just the same. Narrated from a child's point of view, the story is replete with repetition. In almost every quatrain the rhymes are in fact the same word. And in the beginning, whole lines are repeated, as internal refrains.

> Kak-to vécherom domói
> Vozvrashchálsia papa mói.
> Vozvrashchálsia papa mói
> Pozdno pó poliu domói.
> Papa smótrit i gliadít—
> Na zemlé khorëk sidít
> Na zemlé khorëk sidít
> I na pápu ne gliadít.[48]

(Once in the evening / Papa was coming home. / Papa was coming home, / late along the field, home. / Papa looked and stared— / on the ground a polecat sat, / on the ground a polecat sat, / and he wasn't staring at Papa at all.)

The series of silly antics the father goes through in order at last to shoot the animal evokes a style typically found in children's own storytelling milieu. In a way it is also reminiscent of animated cartoons. The last stanza is a pleasing example of the integrity of text and illustration.

> Vot pred vámi moi khorëk
> Na stranítse poperëk
> Narisóvan poperëk
> Pered vámi moi khorëk.

(Here before you is my polecat / sideways on the page. / Drawn sideways / before you is my polecat.)

While most of Kharms's poems have reached a relatively limited audience, "Merry Finches" ("Vesëlye chizhi," 1930), designated as a product of collaboration with Marshak, is more widely known, since it has appeared frequently in collections of Marshak's poetry. In fact, during the years that Kharms was suppressed, Marshak was given exclusive credit for the poem. Seven stanzas, each a variation of the first, present children with a wide range of vocabulary practice.

> Zhíli v kvartíre
> Sórok chetýre,
> Sórok chetýre vesëlykh chizhá:
>     Chízh—sudomóika,
>     Chízh—polomóika,
>     Chízh—ogoródnik,
>     Chízh—vodovóz,
>     Chízh—za kukhárku,
>     Chízh—za khoziáiku,
>     Chízh—na posýlkakh,
>     Chízh—trubochíst.[49]

(In an apartment lived / forty-four, / forty-four merry finches: / a dishwasher finch, / a floorwasher finch, / a gardener finch, / a water carrier finch, / a finch for a cook, / a finch for a housekeeper, / a finch for messages, / a chimney sweep finch.)

While each stanza depicts a realistic domestic situation, ultimately the poem is pure fun, abounding in untranslatable sound imitation reminiscent of children's folklore.

> Lëzha v postéli,
> Drúzhno svistéli
> Sórok chetýre vesëlykh chizhá:
>     Chízh—triti-títi,
>     Chízh—tirli-tírli,
>     Chízh—dili-díli,
>     Chízh—ti-ti-tí,
>     Chízh—tiki-tíki,
>     Chízh—tiki-ríki,
>     Chízh—tiuti-liúti,
>     Chízh—tiu-tiu-tiú!

(Lying in bed, / forty-four merry finches / whistled all together.)

In "Ivan Toporyshkin" (1928), the verbal master Kharms created what he himself subtitled a tongue-twister: the situation presented in the first two couplets is twice nonsensically reordered through grammatical and syntactic transposition.

> Iván Toporýshkin poshël na okhótu,
> s nim púdel' poshël pereprýgnuv zabór.
> Iván, kak brevnó, provalílsia v bolóto,
> a púdel' v reké utonúl, kak topór.

Iván Toporýshkin poshél na okhótu,
s nim púdel' vpriprýzhku poshél, kak topór.

Iván provalílsia brevnóm na bolóto,
a púdel' v reké pereprýgnul zabór.

Iván Toporýshkin poshél na okhótu,
s nim púdel' v reké provalílsia v zabór.

Iván, kak brevnó, pereprýgnul bolóto,
a púdel' vpriprýzhku popál na topór.[50]

(Ivan Toporyshkin set off on a hunt, / with him went a poodle, having
jumped over the fence. // Ivan like a log fell into the swamp, / and the
poodle drowned in the river like an ax. // Ivan Topóryshkin set off on a
hunt, / with him went a poodle, with a hop like an ax. // Ivan fell like a
log on the swamp, / and the poodle in the river jumped over the
fence. // Ivan Toporyshkin set off on a hunt, / with him the poodle in
the river fell into the fence. // Ivan like a log jumped over the
swamp, / and the poodle with a hop fell on the ax.)

Beyond the obvious verbal play, there is an additional level of meaning in this poem. Ivan Toporyshkin was one of Kharms's many
pseudonyms, and so the poet places himself in a most irrational
world. Kharms played similar self-parodistic tricks in several of his
prose pieces, where he used the name Karl Ivanovich Shusterling.[51]

In "Million" (1930), using a stanzaic form similar to that of
"Merry Finches," Kharms turned the ideological subject of a
Pioneer troop into a creative counting-out rhyme and an arithmetic
problem.

Shél po úlitse otriád—
sórok mál'chikov podriád:
ráz,
dvá,
trí,
chetýre,
i chetýre
na chetýre,
i chetýrezhdy
chetýre,
i eshché potóm chetýre.[52]

(Down the street went the troop— / forty boys in a row: / one, / two, /
three, / four, / and four / times four / and four times / four, / and then four
more.)

This counting refrain with variation runs through five stanzas. The
point is not ideology, but verbal play in children's own way. Under-

standably, editors have placed "Million" at the beginning of the three recent collections of Kharms's work for children, attempting to exploit what little ideological potential the poem might have.

Verbal play is present to a degree in all of Kharms's poems, but some also involve special types of semantic or intellectual play as well. In the tradition of Chukovskii's topsy-turvy rhymes, "Liar" ("Vrun," 1930) tests children's knowledge of reality. In rhythmic stanzas built on repetition and syntactic parallelism, impossible situations are presented by one child and exposed by the others.

> —A vy znáete, chto Ú?
> A vy znáete, chto PÁ?
> A vy znáete, chto PÝ?
> Chto u pápy moegó
> Bylo sórok synovéi?
> Bylo sórok zdorovénnykh—
> I ne dvádtsat',
> I ne trídtsat',—
> Rovno sórok synovéi!
>
> —Nú! Nú! Nú! Nú!
> Vrésh'! Vrésh'! Vrésh'! Vrésh'!
> Eshchë dvádtsat',
> Eshchë trídtsat',
> Nu, eshchë tudá-siudá,
> A uzh sórok,
> Rovno sórok,—
> Èto prósto erundá!⁵³

("And do you know that PA? / and do you know that PA HAD? / That Papa / had forty sons? / Had forty robust— / and not twenty / and not thirty— / an even forty sons!.//.Well! Well! Well! Well! / Liar! Liar! Liar! Liar! / Maybe twenty, / maybe thirty, / well, maybe that's still possible. / But forty, / an even forty— / that is simply nonsense!")

The intonation evokes the taunting rhymes of Chukovskii's own folklore and specifically echoes his short poem "The Turtle" ("Cherepakha"), which incorporates syllabic repetition. In "Liar" both the question and the group response emanate from a child's point of view. The idea of challenging children's understanding of reality from the viewpoint of peers is an interesting one. There is no adult authority figure here. One child fantasizes and the others identify or expose the fantasy. Kharms's shorter poems often present children with a small problem-solving situation, such as an extended riddle or an implied question. In these poems where children are invited to participate actively the educational value derives especially from the stimulation of children's imaginations.

The notion of the absurd that permeates Kharms's writing both for children and for adults has a different significance in the two literary spheres. Depending on the stage of his development, a child will react variously to such works. "The three-year-old cannot order events sequentially, and juxtaposes ideas instead of forming coherent concepts because of his 'egocentrism.' After the age of four, the child becomes progressively more capable of orderly sequences in recalling events and telling stories. Make-believe games similarly become more coherent and consistent."[54] Thus to a three-year-old child a work by Kharms in all likelihood is acceptable as "real." In it the child finds no contradiction of his or her own perception of reality. A slightly older child, however, is able to recognize the absurd relationships. The situation is the one Chukovskii referred to in his discussion of topsy-turvy rhymes. After a certain point in their development children are able to perceive nonsensical or distorted relationships as such, and they proceed to derive a certain emotional and intellectual satisfaction from identifying them. For children these stories are above all humorous.

For adults, on the other hand, the absurd juxtapositions and nonsensical sequences in Kharms's work acquire abstract, philosophical, existential significance. While children appreciate many of his short adult pieces as purely humorous play, adults, although they cannot help laughing, are ultimately struck by the seriousness, which constantly questions the meaning of life, the direction of the modern world. In just this way does one of Kharms's last poems, "A Man Left Home" ("Iz doma vyshel chelovek," 1938), strike a somber, prophetic chord.

Iz dóma výshel chelovék
S dubínkoi i meshkóm
I v dál'nii pút',
I v dál'nii pút'
Otprávilsia peshkóm.

On shël vsë priámo i vperéd
I vsë vperéd gliadél.
    Ne spál, ne píl,
    Ne píl, ne spál,
Ne spál, ne píl, ne él.

I vot odnázhdy na zaré
Voshél on v tëmny lés.

I s tói porý,
I s tói porý,
I s tói porý ischéz.

No ésli kák-nibud' egó
Sluchítsia vstrétit' vám,
Togdá skoréi,
Togdá skoréi,
Skoréi skazhíte nám.[55]

(A man left home / with a stout stick and sack, / and on a distant journey, / and on a distant journey / he set off on foot. // He kept going straight and forward / and kept staring straight ahead. / He didn't sleep, he didn't drink, / he didn't drink, he didn't sleep, / he didn't sleep, didn't drink, didn't eat. // And then once at sunset / he entered a dark forest. / And from that time, / and from that time / and from that time he disappeared. // But if somehow / you happen to meet him, / then as quickly as possible / then as quickly as possible, / tell us as quickly as possible.)

Fortunately for later generations, someone eventually did meet Kharms. His works for children were rediscovered after the death of Stalin, and his verbal brilliance noticeably influenced the style of younger poets.

An addiction to play similar to Kharms's is found in the few poems Iurii Vladimirov wrote for children. His poem "The Drum" ("Baraban"), more than any single poem by Kharms, is based entirely on incantatory verbal play, which delights children no end, and of which they themselves are masters.

Któ prodyriávil barabán, barabán?
Któ prodyriávil stáryi barabán?
Barabánil v barabán barabánshchik naś,
Barabánil v barabán tarabárskii mársh.
Barabánil v barabán barabánshchik Adrián.
Barabánil, barabánil, brósil barabán.
Prishél barán, pribezhál barán,
Probodál barabán, i propál barabán.[56]

(Who made a hole in the drum, in the drum? / Who made a hole in the old drum? / On the drum our drummer drummed. / He drummed a mysterious march on the drum. / Drummer Adrian drummed on the drum. / He drummed and drummed, / he threw down the drum. / There came a ram, the ram ran up, / he butted a hole in the drum, the drum was done for.)

In the course of thirty-one lines (twenty-one of them rhyming with *baraban*), the poem conveys the simplest of anecdotes. After the drum is damaged, the drummer takes it to Leningrad to be repaired. Vladimirov manages to sustain the tightly structured acoustic and syntactic repetitions until the end. As a tongue-twister "The Drum" is a tour de force. Although repetition is an important rhythmic feature of all these poems, the others depend less directly on it for their total effect.

Vladimirov's first published poem, "Little Nina's Purchases" ("Ninochkiny pokupki," 1928), is based on verbal confusion, as in Marshak's "That's How Absent-minded." Having memorized the shopping list, Nina forgets it during her long wait in line and amusingly mixes it up it when her turn finally comes.

> "Daíte funt kvása,
> Butýlku miása,
> Spíchechnyi pesók,
> Sákharnyi koróbok,
> Máslo i kompót.
> Dén'gi—vót."[57]

("I'll take a pound of kvass, / a bottle of meat, / granulated matches, / a sugar box, / butter, and fruit compote. / Here is the money.")

The topsy-turvy situation is one of those where children, having heard the correct list three times, can immediately catch the mistakes. Beyond the childlike humor, Vladimirov adds sarcastic jibes not only at the long lines in Soviet stores, but also at the literal-minded, humorless mentality of some adults. The cashier announces:

> A pro sákharnyi koróbok
> I spíchechnyi pesók
> Nikogdá ne slykhál ia líchno,—
> Vérno, továr zagraníchnyi. . . .

(And personally I've never heard / of a sugar box / and granulated matches— / I suppose they're foreign goods.)

Two of Vladimirov's poems narrate simple, child-centered anecdotes that reach hilarious, hyperbolic proportions. "The Orchestra" ("Orkestr," 1929) develops the childish pastime of a kitchen band, performing in the parents' absence.

> Vália—na roiále,
> Iúlia—na kastriúle,

> Lёshka—na lózhkakh,
> Sásha—na trubé,—
> Predstavliáete sebé?[58]

(Val plays the piano, / Julie plays a saucepan, / Leo plays the spoons, / Sasha plays the trumpet— / Can you just imagine that?)

In a typically exaggerated, childlike style, the noise wreaks incredible havoc.

> A na úlitse, gde dóm,
>   Razgróm:
> Óchen' stráshno, óchen' zhútko,
> Svorotíla lóshad' búdku,
> Stráshnyi shúm, stráshnyi krík,—
> V lávku v'éxal gruzovík. . . .

(On the street with that house / there's havoc: / How frightening, how terrible, / a horse ran into a stand. / A terrible noise, a terrible cry, / a truck smashed into a shop. . . .)

Despite the uproar, the children are triumphant in the end. Addressed to them directly, the poem is supportive of their playful ways. Their world here takes precedence over that of adults.

Once again in humorous hyperbole, "Evsei" (1930) further demonstrates Vladimirov's definite appreciation of childhood. No amount of determined disturbance can awaken little Evsei.

> . . . zasnúl Evséi.
> Výzvali dvádtsat' pozhárnykh chastéi:
> Priéxal brandméister s bol'shói borodói.
> Prikazál polivát' Evséia vodói.
>
> Poliváli iz stá odnogó rukavá.
> Obmeléla Fontánka, obmeléla Nevá,
> Peresókhla Móika i Kriúkov kanál,
> I tól'ko Evséi popréznhnemu spál.[59]

(Evsei fell asleep. / They called up twenty fire stations, / the long-bearded firechief came. / He ordered them to pour water on Evsei. // They poured from one hundred and one hoses, / they drained the Fontanka River, they drained the Neva River, / the Moika and the Kriukov Canal dried up, / But Evsei just slept on as before.)

The ritual attempt proceeds from firemen to musicians, to circus strongmen, to a Red Army regiment! Only mother does the trick with her gentle suggestion of a favorite treat.

> —Khóches', Evséiushka, miátnogo priánika?
> Kak prosnúlsia Evséi,
> Potianúlsia Evséi, gárknul Evséi
> Grúd'iu vséi! Davái!

("Little Evsei, would you like a fancy gingerbread?" / Evsei woke up in a flash. / Evsei stretched himself, Evsei shouted / with all his might! "I want it!")

To a greater extent than Vladimirov's other poems, this one relies on actual devices from folklore. With its repeated verbal prefixes and inverted syntax, the first stanza immediately echoes folk poetry.

> Zasnúl Evséi.
> Zakhrapél Evséi.
> Tol'ko slýshen khráp
> Po kvartíre vséi.

(Evsei fell asleep. / Evsei began to snore. / All over the apartment / only his snoring was heard.)

Although they are not consistently developed, certain folk motifs, in addition to parallel construction, persist. The triple formula is present in two ways. Three separate attempts to awaken Evsei are organized. One of those itself repeats the triple formula.

> Pozváli k Evséiu stó silachéi:
> Stó trubachéi i stó skripachéi.

(They called to Evsei one hundred strongmen, / one hundred trumpeters, one hundred fiddlers.)

Finally, there is the thrice-repeated refrain, "But Evsei just slept on as before."

Vladimirov's metrical patterns are less regular than those of his fellow poets Chukovskii, Marshak, and Kharms, bringing his poems closer to a conversational norm. Yet the underlying rhythms, deriving mostly from sound repetition and syntactic parallelism, are distinct and especially appealing to children.

Since their adult literary orientation was similar, there is a tendency to link Aleksandr Vvedenskii's work for children with that of Kharms. However, there is in fact little in Vvedenskii's poetry for children that betrays his avant-garde Oberiu affiliation.[60] Except for a very few poems, his work is more properly compared with the less imaginative work of Marshak, as well as to that of Maiakovskii. Much of the time he was simply performing a remunerative task, churning out uninspired verses on stereotypic cognitive and ideological themes.

The visible gap between Kharms and Vladimirov on the one hand and Vvedenskii on the other becomes immediately clear in a comparison of the first poems they each wrote for children. Vladimirov wrote nothing but verbal play; after his first poem, "The Theater," Kharms pursued a similar direction. In contrast, Vvedenskii in one of his early poems, "Many Beasts" ("Mnogo zverei," 1928), followed the established direction of Marshak's "Kids in a Cage" and Maiakovskii's "No Matter What the Page, There's an Elephant or a Lion on It." And it is not only the genre that derives from his predecessors. The emotional tone closely resembles that of Marshak as well.

> Vozvysháetsia verbliúd;
> Nedovólen, ogorchён,
> Chto s pustýnei razluchён.[61]

(The camel stands tall; / he is grieved, displeased / that he's been separated from the desert.)

The end is a developed echo of Maiakovskii's closing line—"Do svidan'ia, zveriki . . ." (Good-bye little beasts): "Do svidán'ia, / Do svidán'ia, / I lisítsy, / I kunítsy,? I tiuléni, / I morzhí, / I medvédi, / I oléni, / I gadiúki, / I uzhí." ("Good-bye, / good-bye, / lions / and martens, / seals / and walruses, / bears / and deer, / vipers / and snakes.) Vvedenskii deserves some credit for his appreciation of a child's point of view as displayed in that closing. It is just like a child to insist on waving good-bye to every animal at the zoo.

With that beginning, Vvedenskii embarked on a rather more acceptable career in children's literature than his friend Kharms, publishing poetry and prose through the end of the 1930s. Ironically, a collection of his works excluding the more inventive ones appeared in 1941,[62] the year of his arrest.

While many of Vvedenskii's poems are unimaginative, there are several in which he shows a sensitivity to children not unlike that of Kharms or Vladimirov. In "Who?" ("Kto?" 1930) Vvedenskii took a playful approach to the old didactic theme of caring for one's possessions, turning complex syntax into a game.

> Diada Bória govorít,
> Chtó
> Ottogó on tak serdít,
> Chtó

Któ-to ná pol uroníl
Bánku, pólnuiu cherníl,
I ostávil na stolé
Dereviánnyi pistolét,
Zhestianúiu dúdochku
I skladnúiu údochku.

(Uncle Boris says / that / he is very angry / that / someone spilled on
the floor / a bottle full of ink, / and left a wooden pistol, / a tin fife, /
and a collapsible fishing pole / on the table.)

The poem is structured as a series of questions and answers, involving repetition of the original situation.

Ili tólstyi, kak sundúk,
Prikhodíl siuda indiúk,
Bánku, pólnuiu cherníl,
Na tetrádku uroníl
I ostávil na stolé
Dereviánnyi pistolét,
Zhestianúiu dúdochku
I skladnúiu údochku?[63]

(Or did a turkey fat as a trunk / come here and spill / a bottle full of ink
on the notebook / and leave a wooden pistol, / a tin fife, / and a collapsible fishing pole / on the table?)

Five years later Vvedenskii published "Volodia Ermakov" (1935),
in which he turned into a playful situation the then-current topic of
the importance of physical fitness.

Stáli piátero rebiát,
stáli riádom, govoriát:
  —Za zabórom est' dorózhka,
  I vedét dorózhka v bór.
  Któ zhe, lóvko, slóvno kóshka,
  pereprýgnet tot zabór.
Iá—nét!
Iá—nét!
Iá—nét!
Iá—nét!
  A Volódia Ermakóv
  govorít:—ia gotóv.
  Vízhu, vízhu ia dorózhku,
  vizhu bór.
Pereprýgnu ia, kak kóshka,
tot zabór.[64]

(Five children were standing, / standing in a row. They said: / "Beyond the fence there is a path, / the path leads to a big pine woods. / Now who as lithely as a cat / can jump across that fence?" / "I can't!" / "I can't!" / "I can't!" / "I can't!" / But Volodia Ermakov / said: "I am ready. / I see the path, / I see the old pine woods. / I'll jump across that fence / like a cat.")

Although nowhere does he approach the fanciful creativity of Kharms and Vladimirov, or Chukovskii before them, a poem like this one suggests that in the other poems Vvedenskii subordinated his spirit of play to economic expediency.

At the time he entered the realm of children's literature, Nikolai Zabolotskii's career as an adult poet had barely begun. More than half the poems he included in his first volume, *Columns* (*Stolbtsy,* 1929), were written after he joined Marshak's editorial staff, following the invitation extended the Oberiuty in the spring of 1927. In his subsequent adult poetry of the late 1920s and early 1930s, one finds both thematic and structural elements that could be attributed to his new experience in children's literature. Especially striking is a childlike point of view.[65]

Many of Zabolotskii's poems for children appeared on the pages of *Ëzh* and *Chizh,* unsigned, or under the pseudonym Ia. Miller, or signed with his real name. According to his widow, E.V. Zabolotskaia, the anonymous ones were largely advertising jingles for *Ëzh.* The poems signed Ia. Miller tend to emphasize ideological thematics,[66] most likely written on command, reason enough for Zabolotskii to have chosen not to sign them. Most of the poems he published under his own name appeared in 1933. The best are those he addressed to the youngest children. They reveal that he, too, along with his fellow Oberiuty, was sensitive to the concept of play.

An early poem, "Good Boots" ("Khoroshie sapogi"), was published as a separate book in 1928. To a certain extent it deals with the theme of labor. In need of shoes, the little boy Karl eventually succeeds in having them made by a shoemaker. The poem opens with a description of the shoemaker at work.

> V nemétskoi derévne sapózhnik zhivët,
> Stuchít molotóchkom i vzád i vperéd,
> Vo rtú u negó poldesiátka gvozdéi
> Razlíchnykh fasónov, razlíchnykh mastéi.
> On výpliunet gvózdik, pribe'ët na sapóg,
> A novýi gvózdik v ladóshku—skók![67]

(In a German village there lives a shoemaker, / he pounds with his hammer up and down; / in his mouth there are a half-dozen nails / of various shapes and kinds. / He spits out a nail, he pounds on the boot, / then a new nail jumps into his hand!)

Such a description is in all probability an attempt to satisfy the prevailing proletarian demands for production-oriented literature. The concession, however, is a minor one, for the poem on the whole is concerned not with labor but with play. Throughout the poem, little Karl's legs lead a fantastic, anthropomorphized existence all their own.

> —Nu, chtó zhe vy, nógi?—Karlúsha skazál—
> Begíte skorée—ia vám prikazál!
> Otvétili nógi:
> —Bez nás probegí!
> My, bédnye nógi, sovsém bosonógi,
> Dovól'no! Zheláem imét' sapogí!—

("Why feet, what are you doing?" said Karl. / "Run faster, as I ordered you!" / His feet replied: / "Run without us! / We, poor feet, are all barefoot / and had enough! We want to have boots!")

From a child's point of view, limbs and other parts of the body often do seem to exist independently, not under the child's direct control. Furthermore, the fantasy is not the only element that appeals to children. This short narrative involves a degree of adventure and suspense—without shoes, little Karl's legs cannot escape the dangers of the road.

> Krichát drovoséki:
> —Shutít' my ne liúbim,
> Seichás toporámi mal'chíshku zarúbim.
> My dróv narubíli, porá nam domói,
> Seichás zhe, seichás zhe s dorógi dolói!

(The woodcutters shout: / "We don't like to joke, / we'll cut down the little boy with our axes. / We chopped up the wood, it's time to go home, / get out of the road right away!")

The structure of "Good Boots," like Zabolotskii's other poems for children, depends largely on those elements found in the best of Russian children's poetry—regular meter, close rhyme, syntactic repetition.

While sounds and rhythms are important, nowhere in this poetry does verbal play take precedence. Zabolotskii's tendency is, rather, to use play as theme. One tale, however, successfully unites the theme and structure of play. "How the Mice Fought with the Tom-cat" ("Kak myshi s kotom voevali"), written in irregular, rhymed verse similar to Shvarts's, uses many folk devices.

> Zhíl-býl kót,
> Róstom on býl s komód,
> Usíshchi—s arshín,
> Glazíshchi—s kovshín,
> Khvóst trubói,
> Sám riabói.
> Aí dá kót!
>
> Prishél tot kót
> K nám v ogoród,
> Zaléz kót na lukóshko,
> S lukóshka prýgnul v okóshko,
> Úgly v kúkhne obniúkhal,
> Khvostóm pó polu postúkal.
> —Egé,—govorít,—pákhnet myshámi!
> Pozhivú-ka ia s nedél'ku s vámi!⁶⁸

(Once upon a time there lived a tomcat, / as big as a chest of drawers, / with whiskers two feet long, / eyes as big as jugs, / a tail like a trumpet, / all speckled. / What a cat! // That tomcat came / into our garden. / He climbed up onto a bast basket, / from the basket / he jumped through the window, / he smelled all the corners in the kitchen, / he knocked on the floor with his tail. / "Aha," he said, "it smells of mice! / I think I'll spend a week with you!")

The tale is largely for fun. In it Zabolotskii creates some of the liveliest acoustic patterns found anywhere in his children's poetry.

> Vperedí generál Kul'tiápka,
> Na Kul'tiápke zheléznaia shliápka,
> Za Kul'tiápkoi—séryi Tushkánchik,
> Barabánit Tushkánchik v barabánchik.
> Za Tushkánchikom—tsélyi otriád—
> Sto piatnádtsat' myshínykh soldát.
>
>                                      (354)

(General Stumpleg is out in front, / Stumpleg is wearing an iron hat; / behind Stumpleg is gray Jerboa, / Jerboa is drumming on a drum; / behind Jerboa comes the whole detachment— / one hundred fifteen soldier mice.

Hyperbole abounds from beginning to end, accompanied by an appropriately exclamatory intonation. The mood suddenly changes, however, in the middle of the last stanza; the end of the *skazka* acquires overtones of a lullaby.

> Ne lázaite, mýshi, po pólochkam,
> Ne vorúite, krýsy, sukháriki,
> Ne skrebítes' pod pólom, pod léstnitsei,
> Ne mesháite Nikítushke spát'-pochivát'!
>
> (355)

(Mice, don't climb onto the shelves, / rats, don't steal the rusks, / don't scrape under the floor and the stairs, / don't keep little Nikita from sleeping.)

"The Tale of a Crooked Man" ("Skazka o krivom cheloveke") reflects a preoccupation of Zabolotskii's—the world of nature and its relationship to man. Mingling little people and animals in a fairy tale–like setting, the poem conveys a simple moral, urging the preservation of nature. Following the repentance of the crooked man who destroyed a bird's nest, there is general merriment, as in Chukovskii's *skazki*.

> I vót nachináetsia múzyka tút,
> Zhukí v barabánchiki pálkami b'iút,
> A násh chelovéchek, kak búdto ispánets,
> Tantsúet s grachíkhoiu tánets.
>
> (352)

(And then the music starts, / the beetles beat drums with sticks, / and our little man, just like a Spaniard, / dances a dance with a lady crow.)

The seriousness of the poet's concern is conveyed in the epilogue, where he turns directly to the child.

> Pust' máiatnik khódit, pust' strélka kruzhít—
> Smeshnói starichók iz chasóv ne sbezhít.
> No vsé zhe, moi mál'chik, kto ptítsu obídit—
> Tot mnógo neschástii uvídit.
>
> (353)

(Let the pendulum swing, let the hand go round— / the funny little man won't run away from the clock. / But still, my boy, whoever offends a bird, / will see much unhappiness.)

Many years later, Zabolotskii's poems for children are not outdated. One wonders, therefore, why they are rarely republished in the Soviet Union today. Although they are hardly controversial, Russian children are not given the proper opportunity to become acquainted with them.[69]

The Oberiuty came into the new world of Russian children's literature after its rapid early development. The pioneering efforts of Chukovskii and Marshak had already established strong trends, which even the harsh criticism of the proletarian pedologists could not ultimately destroy. Yet during their lifetime, odds were against the Oberiuty. Even after Stalin's death, when the work of many of his victims was posthumously rehabilitated, the children's poetry of the Oberiuty remained largely unknown. Kharms's fanciful creations, above all, should have become as popular and easily available as those of Chukovskii and Marshak, but they were not permitted to do so. Fortunately, the spirit of Kharms did live on in a significant, if indirect, way. Once introduced to the young writers of the "thaw" generation, his poetry was to become a significant influence upon several poets of that new generation.

**7**

# VLADIMIR MAIAKOVSKII AND OTHERS

Among the best known early Soviet children's poems in the Soviet Union today, several of the works of Vladimir Maiakovskii (1892–1930) rank second in "official" popularity only to those of Chukovskii and Marshak. Yet in the West, where the names of Chukovskii and Marshak are more likely to be linked with children, Maiakovskii's contribution to that field is largely unknown or ignored.[1] And perhaps rightfully so, for as aesthetic objects his poems fall short of the achievement of Chukovskii and Marshak. As in much of his postrevolutionary adult poetry, Maiakovskii as a children's poet was above all an ideological propagandist for the new Soviet state. While poet-fathers like Chukovskii and Marshak always had immediately before them the demanding audience of their own children, and later their grandchildren, Maiakovskii addressed the vast collective of all Soviet children. Roman Jakobson has gone so far as to suggest that Maiakovskii had a profound dislike for children, explaining this dislike in terms of the poet's "abstract faith in the coming transformation of the world" and his "hatred for the evil continuum of specific tomorrows that only prolong today."[2] Or as Lawrence Stahlberger more concisely put it, for Maiakovskii the "child represents or indicates man's subjugation to time."[3]

On the subject of time, Petrovskii has made an interesting comparison of the differing approaches found in the children's poetry of Chukovskii, Marshak, and Maiakovskii. Chukovskii, who values childhood as such, conveys time in his works from a child's point of view. He uses the "present child tense" (nastoiashchee detskoe vremia). Marshak, for whom the child's world flows into the adult's, canonizes the child's view; he hopes he will not lose it as he grows up. This is the "child continued tense" (detskoe prodolzhennoe vremia). Maiakovskii, who has a negative attitude toward childhood, emphasizes growing up. Things in childhood are good only if they are useful for one's future adult life. His poetry for children uses the "future adult tense" (budushchee vzrosloe vremia).[4] Despite the philosophical odds against him, Maiakovskii did try his hand at creating for children. At times the results were less than inspired. Some of his difficulties in that genre might be attributed to his future-centered Weltanschauung. At the same time, less personal forces also influenced his career as a children's poet.

From available sources it is difficult to chronicle in any detail Maiakovskii's development as a children's poet. Besides the date of the major events connected with the publication of the poetry, there is little evidence to fill in the gaps, to provide a cohesive narrative. One is left to speculate, to deduce from what is known of his larger career and of his life as a whole. The story has its roots in the very origin of the new literature for children, burgeoning on the eve of the revolution under the pioneering guidance of Chukovskii, who had become personally acquainted with Maiakovskii in 1913.[5] Three years later, in 1916, Chukovskii and Gor'kii were planning their almanac for children. Chukovskii invited Maiakovskii to contribute. "The collection is intended for very young children. We would like fantastic, more fairy tale–like material."[6] Maiakovskii's response is unknown, although his biographical chronicler Vasilii Katanian speculates that the poem "Cloudlet Pieces" ("Tuchkiny shtuchki," dated only approximately: 1917–1918) might have been connected with Chukovskii's offer.

"Cloudlet Pieces" stands apart both in time and in essence from the thirteen children's poems Maiakovskii wrote in the second half of the 1920s. In this early poem his predominantly lyric orientation is as yet untouched by ideological considerations. Although the poem is far from being a masterpiece, it attempts to approach a child's point of view. In six rhymed couplets, each of which could easily be accompanied by an illustration, natural phenomena—sky, clouds, sun—are perceived and described in a playful, childlike way.

> Plýli pó nebu túchki
> Túchek—chetýre shtúchki:
>
> ot pérvoi do trét'ei—liúdi,
> chetvértaia bylá verbliúdik.[7]

(Across the sky swam cloudlets. / Cloudlets—four little pieces; // the first three were people, / the fourth was a little camel.)

The poem continues in this vein, ending with the sun—a yellow giraffe. For young children the accentual metrical pattern may be an obstacle, as may some potentially difficult diction and grammar. On the whole, however, the poem bodes well as a first try in an unfamiliar genre.

On 5 December 1918, at a meeting of the literary publishing division of the Commissariat of Education, Maiakovskii presented a proposal for a collection of poetry for children, For Kids (Dlia detkov), in which he intended to include "Cloudlet Pieces." Under a political heading he also wished to incorporate the adult poems "The Tale of Little Red Riding Hood" ("Skazka o krasnoi shapochke") and "International Fable" ("Internatsional'naia basnia").[8] A stenographic report of the meeting quotes Maiakovskii's defense of his proposal: "This book is highly desirable for the division because the new literature has no children's books, no poetry."[9] Since the edition was never issued, it is not known whether Maiakovskii at that early date planned to create any new poems especially for children. One is left, at best, with an early expression of some concern on his part for the literary and political education of the new Soviet child.

Not until five years later is there another hint of Maiakovskii's interest in writing for children. During the intervening years much of his creative energy had been channeled into propaganda, of which his ROSTA window posters are among the most famous. Then, in the middle of 1923, in a list of works in progress that appeared in a foreword to the collection of poems This Year's Things (Veshchi ètogo goda), Maiakovskii included "About Sena and Petia (a children's poem)."[10] After that note, almost two more years passed before Maiakovskii, in March 1925, actually submitted his completed manuscript, retitled "A Tale about Petia, a Fat Child, and about Sima, Who Is Thin" ("Skazka o Pete, tolstom rebënke, i o Sime, kotoryi tonkii," echoing the title of Chekhov's story "Fat and Thin"). Two months later the poem was published as an illustrated book for children.[11] With the appearance of "A Tale about Petia" Maiakovskii entered his prolific period as a children's poet. Between 1925 and 1929 he wrote twelve more poems for children, bringing his total work for children to more than 1,800 lines. (These are unusually short lines, distributed typographically across the page.)

A study of these poems reveals a distinct shift after "A Tale about Petia." Although in all of them, "A Tale about Petia" included, Maiakovskii's primary thematic orientation was ideological, the manner he used to convey his ideas in "A Tale about Petia" was not to be repeated in the later poems.

Maiakovskii's proclaimed futurist orientation did not prevent him from turning to the past for inspiration. A basic thematic orientation of the folktale, the struggle between good and evil, was Maiakovskii's strongest link with the original genre. but unlike his predecessors—Pushkin, Ershov, and even Chukovskii—in their *skazki*, Maiakovskii portrayed the struggle between good and evil in a specific, modern political situation. It is true that Chukovskii in "The Crocodile" defined a real, present-day setting—Petrograd, but he created it for an essentially imaginary subject. His use of the African crocodile to portray aggression in the abstract left many literal-minded adults searching unsuccessfully for allegorical interpretations. The political activist Maiakovskii, on the other hand, left no doubt about the identity of the protagonists in his tale.

> Iásno
> > dázhe i ezhú—
> ètot Pétia
> > byl burzhúi. . . .
>
> Ptítsy s pésnei proletáli,
> péli:
> > "Síma—proletárii!"[12]

(It's clear / even to a hedgehog— / this Petia / was a bourgeois. // Birds flew by with a song, / they sang / "Sima is a proletarian!")

The thematic focus of this poem is not on an actual struggle, but rather on the abstract juxtaposition of communist versus capitalist, developed as good against evil. The behavior of Petia and his shopkeeper father is depicted as despicable, while that of Sima and his worker-father is extolled. This basic issue was a vital one in the Soviet Union during the era of the New Economic Policy, when the revival of small capitalists threatened to be successful. Maiakovskii's attempt to acquaint young children with serious political topics was an innovative step other children's poets had not yet pursued. However, he did not really exploit this direction in his subsequent poems. Although an ideological current runs through them, it is not strongly developed.

Maiakovskii used to his own ends the set formulas of the oral tradition—the prologue (*zachin*) and the epilogue (*kontsovka*). The opening of the poem is striking.

> Zhíli-býli
> > Síma s Pétei.
> Síma s Pétei
> > býli déti.
> Péte 5,
> > a Síme 7—
> i 12 vméste vsém.
> > (217)

(Once upon a time there lived / Sima and Petia. / Sima and Petia were children. / Petia was 5, / and Sima was 7— / and together they were 12.)

Through its non sequitur of categories (the boys' ages combined in an arithmetic problem), the introductory stanza parodies a children's counting-out rhyme[13] and approaches a tongue-twister with its emphasis on verbal play. Even the choice of names seems largely governed by acoustic considerations. The ending allows Maiakovskii's unwavering political stance to culminate in an ideologically based moral.

> Skázka skázkoiu,
> > a vý vot
> sdélaite iz skázki vývod.
> poliubíte, déti, trúd—
> kak napísano tút.
> Zashchishcháite
> > vsékh, kto sláb,
> ot burzhúevykh láp.
> Vot i výrastete—
> > ístymi
> silachámi-kommunístami.
> > (231)

(A tale's a tale, / and as for you— / draw a conclusion from this tale. / Children, learn to love work— / as is written here. / Defend / all who are weak / from the clutches of the bourgeoisie. / Then you'll grow up to be / true / strongmen-communists.)

The body of "A Tale about Petia" is characterized by simple parallelism—a type of parallelism basically alien not only to the oral tradition, but to Chukovskii in the twentieth century as well. Three scenes in the life of the bourgeois Petia alternate with three in the life of the proletarian Sima. This manner is reminiscent of the early cinematic cross-cutting of D.W. Griffith and adopted by Eisenstein, with whom Maiakovskii, who also worked in film, was associated.[14] By means of parallel development culminating in coincidence, Maiakovskii succeeds both in driving home his ideological lesson (the ultimate triumph of communism over capitalism) through stark, graphic comparisons and in maintaining a degree of narrative suspense through shifting plot lines.

From the nineteenth-century tradition Maiakovskii derives the underlying metrical pattern and rhyme scheme of "A Tale about Petia." Rarely does the meter depart from trochaic tetrameter (the meter of Ershov's "The Little Humpbacked Horse" and several of Pushkin's *skazki*). Two of these departures evoke folk dictums that deserve to be set apart.

> Liubí bedniakóv,
>           bogátykh krushí! . . .
>
> Zhivótnye domáshnie—
> tebé
>           druz'iá vsegdáshnie.—
>                     (224)

(Love the poor, / crush the rich! // Domestic animals / are always your friends.)

These lines echo the advertising jingles Maiakovskii wrote for "Mossel'prom," the Moscow food stores (1923–1925): "Nigde krome kak v Mossel'prome" ("Only at Mossleprom's").[15] While maintaining the meter typical of Ershov, Maiakovskii consistently avoids the monotonous rhythms of "The Little Humpbacked Horse" by typographically dividing some of the lines. Occasional dactylic rhymes further vary the rhythm, departing from Ershov's almost invariable masculine-feminine alternation. While Maiakovskii respects children's delight in close rhymes by not deviating from an exclusively paired rhyme scheme, he intersperses the regular and rich, often grammatical rhymes (all more frequent than in his adult poetry)—*torgoval / daval, spit / sopit, slast' / past'*—with more striking combined or inexact rhymes—*po-moemu / pomaiami, proletali / proletarii, za shcheku / iashchiku.*[16] End and internal rhyme is only the most obvious component of the sound texture here. Assonance, alliteration, and sound repetition in general are also prominent features. Lines often begin with the same consonant.

> Plókho Péte.
> > Péte ból'no.
> Pétia mchít,
> > kak miách futból'nyi.
> > > (222)

(Petia feels bad. / Petia is sick. / Petia goes flying like a football.)

In one instance the sound orchestration creates the effect of a tongue-twister.

> Síma chístyi,
> > chíshche mýla.
> Mýlsia sám, i máma mýla.
> > (219)

(Sima is clean, / cleaner than soap. / He washed himself, / and Mama washed him.)

Some of Maiakovskii's images and thematic devices come close to Chukovskii's. The proletarian child-hero has its obvious antecedent in Chukovskii's unvanquishable Vania Vasil'chikov, the Lilliputian defender of besieged Petrograd in "The Crocodile." A phrase like "well-known Sima" (*izvestnyi Sima*) recalls Chukovskii's "Valiant Vania" (*doblestnyi Vania*), which in turn echoes the fixed epithet of the oral tradition. Here again Maiakovskii engages his political concern to convey an additional nuance, resulting in a hyperbolic, poster-like portrait, akin to the figures he depicted in the ROSTA windows.

> Tút figúra Símina.
> —Vót kto núzhen ímenno!—
> Khrábryi,
> > dóbryi,
> > > síl'nyi,
> > > > smélyi!
> Vídno—krásnyi,
> > a ne bélyi.
> > > (225)

(Here is the figure of Sima. / "That is exactly who is needed!" / Brave, / good, / strong, / bold! / Obviously he's a red / and not a white.

Seemingly derivative of Chukovskii's "The Crocodile" is the horde of animals that rushes to the defense of a puppy disappointed by selfish, gluttonous Petia. And one of the draft variants actually introduced a hippopotamus (*begemot*), which is practically a Chukovskii trademark. In a general sense, the animal theme, frequent in children's poetry, does not simply hark back to Chukovskii. Maiakovskii's compassionate attitude toward animals (as analogues for human beings) is manifest in some of his adult poetry too, notably in "A Good Attitude toward Horses" ("Khoroshee otnoshenie k loshadiam").

A concern Maiakovskii shared with both Chukovskii and Marshak is the focus on colloquial, child-oriented language. Although the older poets' diction on the whole better anticipates the desires and capabilities of children, Maiakovskii's lexical choice in "A Tale of Petia" reflects no undue insensitivity to the language of children. He selected many words from children's own colloquial speech: *vpergonki* (tag), *vverkh tormashkami* (head over heels), *lopat'* (to gobble), *vzdut'* (to thrash).[17] With one exception, diminutives are infrequent. The exception occurs in a scene with Petia the bourgeois, which parodies the saccharine trend of much prerevolutionary children's poetry.

> Pétia,
>      výidia na balkónchik,
> zhádno lópal sládkii pónchik:
> slóvno dózhdik po trubé,
> l'ét varén'e po gubé.
>
> (220)

(Out on the little balcony / Petia / greedily gobbled a doughnut: / Just like rain down a pipe, / jam ran down his lips.)

In that common ground Maiakovskii shared with Chukovskii, Marshak, and the folk tradition as a whole, a most important element is fantasy. In his portrayal of a real political point of view—the necessity of communist vigilance against the remnants of bourgeois, capitalist society—Maiakovskii does not hesitate to introduce the hyperbolically grotesque. In depicting little bourgeois Petia he creates a wonderful realized metaphor, one of his favorite poetic devices and very much in keeping with children's own literalism. Petia "stuffs his face" until he literally bursts, showering

the impoverished Sima and his fellow October Kids (*Oktiabriaty*)
with a most welcome feast.

> Nét,
>> ne chúdo èto, déti,
> a—iz lópunvshego Péti.
> Vsë, chto lópal Pétia tólstyi,
> rassypáetsia na vërsty.
>> (230)

(No, / it's not a miracle, children, / it's from Petia who has burst
open. / All that fat Petia gobbled up / is showering down for miles
around.)

In the figure of Petia, Maiakovskii combines the features of heroes
of two prerevolutionary stories, both reminiscent of Hoffmann's
*Struwwelpeter.* In "About Gosha—Long Hands" ("Pro Goshu—
dlinnye ruki"), a disobedient boy greedily overeats, blows up into a
balloon, and floats up into the air.[18] "One Who Burst" ("Kotoryi
lopnul") depicts little George, who after drinking seven cups of different beverages—from coffee to seltzer water—finally bursts.[19] Related imagery is familiar to children (and Maiakovskii) from
folktales, not to mention their own imaginations.

Although "A Tale about Petia" is thematically and structurally
more complex than the long poems of Chukovskii and Marshak, in
it Maiakovskii does try to reach out to children. While it is not the
kind of work a child could easily memorize, it nonetheless shows a
certain understanding of children's capabilities. It is all the more
unfortunate, therefore, that Maiakovskii's performance in his subsequent children's poems does not match the expectations aroused
by "A Tale about Petia." In later poems he largely suppresses his
imaginative approach to children and becomes, instead, schematic,
condescending, and often dully didactic. As Tvardovskii noted:
"Maiakovskii's children's poems were one form of his single-
minded agitational poetry; but he spoke too rationally with his little
reader, he spoke with the effort of someone who seemed to be select-
ing words in a language little known to him. Here he fell far short of
his level of mastery."[20] And as Maiakovskii himself confessed in
1926, "Nothing is working out. I'm writing for children on commission to the State Publishing House."[21]

In the majority of the poems direct ideology persists, but the
vehicle of fantasy disappears. In "We Are Strolling" ("Guliaem,"
written in 1925, published in 1926), an adult's simplistic lecture to a
child reiterates in skeletal fashion the anticapitalist theme that first

appeared in "A Tale about Petia." The exaggerated, poster-like quality is again reminiscent of the ROSTA windows.

Èto—burzhúi.
          Na púzo gliád'.
Egó zaniátie—
          ést' i guliát'.
Ot zhíru—
          kak miách tugói.
Liúbit,
          Chtob za negó
                    rabótal drugói.
                              (238)

(This is a bourgeois. / It's clear from his belly. / His occupation— / is eating and strolling. / This fat makes him— / a rubber ball. / He likes / others to work / in his place.)

A similar point of view is expressed in "Read This and Travel to Paris and China" ("Prochti i katai v Parizh i v Kitai," written in 1927, published in 1928).

Nachináetsia zemliá,
kak izvéstno, ot Kremliá.
Za mórem,
          za súsheiu—
kommunístov slúshaiut.
Té, kto rabótaiut,
slúshaiut s okhótoiu.
A burzhúiam ètot gólos
podymáet dýbom vólos.
                              (257)

(The world begins, / as is known, from the Kremlin. / All around the world— / they listen to communists. / Those who work / listen willingly. / But that voice makes / a bourgeois's hair stand on end.)

"Let's Take Our New Rifles" ("Voz'mëm vintovki novye," 1927) betrays a blatantly militaristic attitude, while his last poem for children—"Song-Lightning" ("Pesnia-Molniia," 1929)—was written in honor of a Pioneer gathering in Moscow. Ideology is present even in the poems primarily intended to contribute to a child's knowledge of the world around him. The concept of the worker and the value of labor is a dominant motif.

Of the cognitive poems, the one least tinged with ideology is "No Matter What the Page, There's an Elephant or a Lion on It" ("Chto ni stranitsa,—to slon, to l'vitsa," written in 1925–1926, but not pub-

lished until 1928). Maiakovskii conceived the poem during a visit to
the zoo in New York City in 1925.[22] Addressed to preschool children, it belongs to the genre of animal picture books to which Marshak's "Kids in a Cage" also belongs. Especially interesting is the
direct relationship between the text and illustrations. The elephant's size is conveyed by depicting him as larger than a single
page.

> Dazhe íkhnee ditiá
> rostom s pápu s náshego
> Vsekh proshú postoronít'sia,
> razevái poshíre rót,—
> dlia takíkh malá stranítsa,
> dali tsélyi razvorót.
> (240–41)

(Even their child / is as big as our papa. / I ask everyone to step aside /
and be amazed— / the page is too small for such animals, / they gave
it a full two-page spread.)

Three poems treat various types of occupations and processes of
labor. "This Book of Mine is about the Seas and the Lighthouse"
("Èta knizhechka moia pro moria i pro maiak," 1927) describes the
operation of a lighthouse. In the end, however, the narrator introduces a moral by transforming the lighthouse into a metaphor with
ideological implications.[23]

> —Déti,
>        búd'te kak maiák!
> Vsém,
>        kto nóch'iu plyt' ne mógut,
> osveshchái ognём dorógu.
> Chtob skazát' pro èto vám,
> Ètoi knízhechki slová
> i risúnochkov nabróski
> sdélal
>        diádia
>            Maiakóvskii.
> (245)

(Children, / be like a lighthouse! / For all / who cannot sail at night /
light the way. / To tell you about this, / Uncle / Maiakovskii / made /
the words of this book / and sketches for the drawings.)

The other two cognitive poems are straightforward enough. "The
Fire Horse" ("Kon'–ogon'," 1927), which traces the various types of
labor involved in constructing a rocking horse, is a children's version
of the "production" literature encouraged, even demanded, by the

proletarians at that time. Maiakovskii himself described his motivation for this poem. "Here I am taking advantage of the opportunity to explain to a child how many people must work to prepare such a horse. . . . In this way a child becomes acquainted with the collective nature of labor."[24] "What to Be" ("Kem byt'," 1928), ostensibly from a child's point of view, surveys future career possibilities. Though there is a certain bias toward blue-collar jobs—carpenter, factory worker, trolley conductor, taxi driver—the end sounds unprejudiced.

> Knígu perevoroshív,
> namotái sebé na ús—
> vse rabóty khoroshí,
> vybirái
>         na vkús!
>             (274)

(Having leafed through the book, / don't forget— / all jobs are good, / choose / according to your taste!)

Apparently some Russian girls were disappointed that Maiakovskii addressed the poem solely to boys. Among his papers there is a letter from an irate little girl, who demanded that he hurry up and write a version of "What to Be" for girls.[25] No such poem ever materialized.

Unless they are handled imaginatively, didactic tales for children can be deadly. Twice Maiakovskii wrote poems focusing on questions of proper child behavior; each time his treatment of the subject—so remote from Chukovskii's and Marshak's—is disappointing. "What Is Good and What Is Bad?" ("Chto takoe khorosho i chto takoe plokho?" 1925) is structured as a father's answer to a child's question about good and bad. The father's series of answers are arbitrarily arranged, schematically presented, and hardly developed to capture a child's attention. Nonetheless, despite its didacticism, this poem is a generally accepted success and popular with children.[26] Undoubtedly its most interesting aspect is the interaction between the text and the illustrations. In the original edition one verse was cleverly accompanied by a blank page.[27]

> Ésli b'ët
>         driannói drachún
> slábogo mal'chíshku,
> ia takógo
>             ne khochú
> dázhe
>         vstávit' v knízhku.
>             (233)

(If a big bad bully / hits / a weak little boy, / I don't / even want to put him / in my book.)

Despite their larger shortcomings in the context of children's poetry, some of these poems have occasionally redeeming structural qualities. Maiakovskii's extensive use of a conversation or dialogue with the child was new to Russian children's poetry. The presence of the poet-narrator is strongly felt, bringing the child into a closer, more personal relationship with the adult storyteller or teacher. This approach was motivated in part by Maiakovskii's strong sense of ego, so often manifest in his adult poetry.

> Maiakóvskii,
>         zhdëm otvéta.
> Pochemú sluchílos / èto?—
> A ia emú:
> —Potomú,
> chto zemliá kruglá,
> net na néi uglá—
> vrode miáchika
> v ruké u mál'chika.
>                 (263)

(Maiakovskii, / we're waiting for the answer. / Why did this happen?— / And I answered: / —Because / the world is round, / it has no corners— / it's like a little ball / in the hands of a boy.)

If one discounts their highly programmatic themes, among the most successful of these poems are the marching songs: "Let's Take Our New Rifles," "May Song" (Maiskaia pesenka," 1928), and "Song-Lightning" ("Pesnia-molniia," 1929). They call to mind several of Maiakovskii's well-known adult poems—"Left March" ("Levyi marsh") and "Our March" ("Nash marsh"). The meter is basically iambic, the rhyme is crossed, but lines are rhythmically divided, sometimes individual words are split, creating an authentic staccato marching spirit, as in "Let's Take Our New Rifles."

> Shá-
>         gaí
> krú-
>         ché:
> Tsél'
>         siá
> Lúch-
>         shé!
>                 (264)

(Ste- / p / sharp- / ly! / Ai- / m / bet- / ter!)

"May Song" combines collective social consciousness with exuberant feelings about spring. Especially effective is Maiakovskii's metaphoric personification of nature,

> Vesná sushít' rasvésila
> svoë myt'ë.
> (266)

(Spring hung its laundry / out to dry.)

and his inclusion of a composite rhyme.

> Úlitsa ráda,
> vesnói umýtaia.
> Shagáem otriádom,
> i mý,
>       i tý,
>           i iá.
> (266)

(The street is happy, / washed by spring. / We're marching in a troop, / we / and you / and I.)

Most outstanding in "Song-Lightning" is the metaphor in the title itself. Such metaphors built on compound words, typical in Maiakovskii's adult poetry, occur occasionally in this poetry as well, echoing the compound constructions of folklore.

Although his original motivation for writing "A Tale about Petia" is not known, Maiakovskii's own behavior suggests he was sincerely interested in the work. Soon after he wrote it, he is known to have presented it publicly upon several occasions. On 23 February 1925, before he gave the manuscript to the publishers, he read it at a Moscow literary gathering.[28] On 10 May he read it in Sokolniki Park before an audience of school children celebrating Forest Day.[29] Between those two readings there was yet another one, which produced a vociferously disapproving response. At the end of March, before turning in the manuscript, Maiakovskii read "A Tale about Petia" at a meeting of the Committee for the Creation of New Children's Books, a body connected with the Children's Literature Division of the State Publishing House.[30] From that meeting Maiakovskii recorded in his notebook singularly negative responses on the part of the pedologists, the proletarian educators, who were also ranting against Chukovskii and Marshak. They attacked Maiakovskii's poem as antipedagogical, primitive, modernistic, and schematic. Their final verdict read, "Not recommended for libraries."[31] The conservative puritanical mentality that in the near future would proclaim socialist realism as the only acceptable aesthetic method had established a strong foothold by 1925. Maiakovskii's manuscript reveals that he made some minor changes in an attempt to appease the committee; they, however, remained unappeased. And their mood persisted, despite the poet's apparent concessions in his later poems.

The obvious shift from the fanciful "A Tale about Petia" to the subsequent, less imaginative poems reflects Maiakovskii's struggle to please his intransigent proletarian critics. This small struggle in the microcosm of children's literature parallels the developments in his literary career as a whole. After the hostile reception of "A Tale about Petia" in 1925, Maiakovskii capitulated as a children's poet and three years later altogether ceased writing in that genre. Similarly, he tried to capitulate as a poet in the larger sense, a direction that ultimately contributed to his suicide in 1930. His subordination of imagination to political dictates in his children's poetry led to the extinction of that genre in his poetry. More tragically, his attempt to subordinate his total creative impulse to the Soviet state helped result in his extinction as a human being.

During Maiakovskii's lifetime, his children's poems achieved only notoriety. Ironically, those that have entered the contemporary repertory of Russian children's literature are from among the later ones. Although "A Tale about Petia" is included in Maiakovskii's collected works, children's editors now consider it too historically dated to reissue it for its originally intended audience. And so Maiakovskii is remembered and extolled not for his most imaginative contribution to children's literature, but in his official capacity as a state poet.

During the era of fervent artistic activity in early postrevolutionary Russia, just as Maiakovskii did, many writers tried their hand at children's literature.[32] Some of them were established literary figures. However, since good poetry for children makes special demands upon its creators, artistic success as an adult poet in no way guarantees one success as a children's poet. The Russian symbolists' work for children is proof enough of that, as is much of the poetry Maiakovskii addressed to children. A children's poet must display special qualities, of which the most significant are a desire and ability to communicate with children. Aleksandr Tvardovskii once named several modern Russian poets he felt would have been unlikely prospects for children's poetry—Akhmatova, Tsvetaeva, Pasternak, and Mandel'shtam.[33] Surprisingly enough, in the mid-1920s both Pasternak and Mandel'shtam wrote some poems for children. But neither of them can be considered successful as a children's poet, a fact they themselves must have recognized since they chose not to pursue the genre. Nonetheless, since they are two of Russia's greatest poets, their work for children deserves to be examined in light of the established tradition.

In 1924 Boris Pasternak (1890–1960) published two poems for children in separate slim volumes—"The Carousel" ("Karusel' ") and "The Menagerie" ("Zverinets"). Perhaps he did it upon the encouragement of Chukovskii or Marshak. Most likely it was inspired by his then still very young first child, Evgenii, born in 1923.[34] Although the subjects Pasternak chose are appropriate enough, the manner in which he developed them is largely alien to children.

In a laudatory survey review of the "new Russian children's book," Marina Tsvetaeva spoke of "Pasternak's brilliant 'Menagerie' " in the same breath that she described Marshak's "Kids in a Cage" as her favorite children's book.[35] It is a pity she did not comment in greater detail, for it would be interesting to have her comparison of such two dissimilar works. Instead, one is left to guess what in each work appealed to her. One fact is certain—the two "animal books" she singled out reach vastly different audiences. Marshak's communicated successfully with quite young children. Pasternak's, in contrast, is problematic. Some indicators distinctly point to the child audience the poet must have had in mind. The subject matter—a description of zoo animals—is highly traditional in children's literature, but the mode of execution is not. Although the initial stanza attempts to include children in a first person "we," the point of view is unmistakably that of a highly articulate adult.

> Zverínets raspolózhen v párke.
> Protiágivaem kontramárki.
> Vkhodnúiu árku okruzhá,
> Stoiát u kássy storozhá.
> No vót voróta v fórme gróta.
> Pokázyvaias' s povoróta
> Iz-zá izvestniakóvykh grúd,
> Pod vétrom serebrítsia prúd.[36]

(The menagerie is situated in the park. / We hold out our passes. / Surrounding the entrance arch, / guards stand at the ticket booths. / Now here the gates are shaped like a grotto. / Coming into sight around a bend / from behind a limestone heap, / in the wind is a silvery pond.)

The adult point of view persists throughout the tour from cage to cage. In the final stanza there is a slightly stronger sense of the

presence of children. The diction and intonation of the first half of
the stanza approaches that of conversation. The inverted syntax in
the second half, however, complicates the carefully balanced image
juxtaposing animal and mechanical noise.

> Porá domói. Kakáia zhálost'!
> A skól'ko dív eshché ostálos'!
> My osmotréli razve trét'.
> Vsegó zaráz ne osmotrét'.
> V slédnii ráz v orlínyi klékot
> Vliváetsia tramváinyi rókot,
> V poslédnii ráz tramváinyi shúm
> Sliváetsia s rychán'em púm.
>
> (549–50)

(It's time to go home. What a pity! / There are so many marvels still
left to see! / We barely saw a third of them. / You can't see everything
at once. / For the last time the eagles' screams / mingle with the rum-
ble of the tram, / for the last time the noise of the tram / merges with
the pumas' snarls.)

The many stanzas between these two are predominantly out of the
reach of children. The voice is essentially that of Pasternak, the
adult poet. As Guy de Mallac points out, the poem "underscores
humorous descriptions of animals with sadder comments on the
effects of captivity on them."[37] The diction and imagery are difficult; the syntax is complex. Pasternak himself sensed some of the
problems the poem posed. The draft manuscript shows that he
actually omitted thirteen of the most obscure stanzas, which, if
included, would have made the poem half again as long and unques-
tionably more impenetrable for children.[38] In the shortened version,
problems remain nonetheless. Of all the descriptions, the humorous ones come closest to reaching children.

> Begóm po izraztsóvym skhódniam
> Spuskáiutsia v odnóm ispódnem
> Medvédi bélye vtroém
> V odín seméinyi vodoém.
> Oni revút, pleshchás' i móias'.
> Shtanóv v vodé ne dérzhit póias,
> No v stírke nikakói otvár
> Neimét kosmátykh sharovár.
>
> (547)

(Running along tile gangways, / three polar bears / are going down in
their underwear / into a family reservoir. / They roar while splashing

and washing. / Their belts won't hold their pants up, / but in the laundry no special soap powder / can clean the shaggy trousers.)

In "The Carousel," Pasternak strives more obviously to speak to children in their own language. A few times he succeeds, but the poem as a whole does not. The first two lines of static nature description do little to capture a child'a attention.

> Líst'ia klénov shelestéli,
> Byl chudésnyi létnii dén'.
>
> (544)

(The maple leaves rustled; / it was a wonderful summer day.)

With the introduction of movement and concrete objects in the second stanza, the mood becomes more plausibly child-oriented.

> Buterbródov nasováli,
> Iáblok, khléba karavái.
> Tól'ko stántsiiu nazváli,
> Srázu trónulsia tramvái.
>
> (544)

(They packed sandwiches, / apples, a round loaf of bread. / As soon as they called the next station, / the tram set right off.)

There is even a sense of the motion of the merry-go-round in a stanza that is repeated again at the end.

> S kázhdym krúgom tíshe, tíshe,
> Tíshe, tíshe, tíshe, stóp.
> Èti víkhri skrýty v krýshe,
> Posredíne krýshi—stólb.
>
> (547)

(With every round more quietly, quietly, / quietly, quietly, quietly, stop. / The whirlwinds are hidden in the roof, / in the middle of the roof there's a post.)

Toward the end of the poem the sensation of turning is enhanced by a line concluding three successive stanzas.

> Sléva—róshcha, správa prúd.
>
> (548)

(On the left is a thicket, on the right a pond.)

Despite its weak beginning, "The Carousel" works better as a children's poem than does "The Menagerie." Its four-foot trochaic meter, for example, is much livelier than the iambic tetrameter of "The

Menagerie." And that the adult reader finds less of Pasternak in it definitely makes the poem more accessible to children. Yet, its intended audience still comes upon lexical and syntactic difficulties. The complexity of Pasternak's poetic imagination strongly resisted simplification. Writing children's poetry was not suitable for him even as a part-time métier.

Another great Russian poet, Osip Mandel'shtam (1891–1938), published four small books in verse for children. He also published a number of adaptations of poems by Robert Louis Stevenson.[39] When asked about her husband's children's poems, the poet's widow, Nadazhda Iakovlevna Mandel'shtam, vigorously insisted that he had not written them with children in mind at all, but rather to entertain her and to earn some much-needed money.[40] The poems themselves do not contradict her claim, which is further supported by Tvardovskii's reaction to them.

> It is as though this good and intelligent grown-up, who was left alone with little children for a whole day in a city apartment while the parents were gone, exhausted himself trying to occupy them with verses about the properties and purpose of household objects. . . . It is done out of necessity, without any genuine enthusiasm. There is useful information, humor, and an underlying rhythm. . . . But all of this is more likely to attract adults by the expressiveness of its execution than to be of interest to children. These attempts were in no way reflected in the subsequent work of the poet.[41]

Tvardovskii's description applies above all to *The Primus Stove* (*Primus*, 1925), the first collection of poems Mandel'shtam published for children. Incidentally, the poet included a dedication that suggests Nadezhda Iakovlevna was not his exclusive audience: "à mes petites amies Grèthe et Rutti."[42] Tvardovski's characterization comes close to pinpointing the underlying tone of the ten short poems in *The Primus Stove*. Some moments call forth an even less generous appraisal. At times these sound like poems tailored to a simplistic conception of what children's poetry is all about. On one level, therefore, they suggest a subtle jibe at poets professionally involved with children—especially someone like Marshak, of whom Mandel'shtam was hardly fond.[43] They are condescending, not so much to the child, as to the children's poet (at least to a certain type of children's poet—one who attempts to respond to "social command.") At the same time that Marshak published "Yesterday and Today," with its lesson about the wonders of running water, Mandel'shtam wrote:

—V samováre i v stakáne
I v kuvshíne i v grafíne
Vsiá vodá iz krána.
—Ne razbéi stakána.

—A vodoprovód
Gdé
vódu
berёt?
(274)

(In the samovar and in the glass, / in the pitcher and in the
decanter, / all the water is from the tap. / Don't break the glass. // And
where / do the waterpipes / get / the water?)

This poem is especially reminiscent of lines from Chukovskii's
"Wash'em Clean."

In the brief undated essay "Children's literature," Mandel'shtam
expressed some of his attitudes toward the current situation in that
field. "Children's literature is a difficult thing. On one hand, the
anthropomorphism of animals and objects cannot be tolerated. On
the other hand, it is necessary to play a little with the child; but he,
the little rogue, as soon as he starts to play, immediately botches it
and humanizes something. . . . Here there is needed a scientific
organization of things and well-trained, experienced elderly
women."[44] Mandel'shtam's sarcasm understandably lashes out
against the pedologists. More veiled attacks occur in the poetry
itself. A poem like "The Bootblack" ("Chistil'shchik") in *Balloons*
(*Shary*, 1926), appears to fit the order of the pedologists. It is a simple
description of useful labor.

Podoidí ko mné poblízhe,
Krepche nógu stáv' siudá,
U tebiá botínok rýzhii,
Ne godítsia nikudá.

Ia egó pochíshchu krémom,
Chёrnoi bárkhatkoi natrú,
Chtoby zhёltym stal sovsém on,
Slovno sólntse poutrú.
(281–82)

(Come up closer to me, / put your foot more firmly here; / you have a
faded, worn-out shoe, / that is not at all proper. // I'll clean it up with
shoe polish, / I'll wipe it with black velvet, / so that it will be all
yellow, / just like the morning sunshine.)

Mandel'shtam may have been inwardly laughing at the pedologists as he wrote it.[45] Another poem with possible satirical overtones is "The Floor Polishers" ("Polotëry"), from the same collection.

> Polotër rukámi máshet,
> Budto ón v prisiádku pliáshet.
> Govorít, chto on prishël
> Naterét' mastíkoi pól.
>
> Budet shárkat', budet prýgat',
> Lit' mastíku, mebel' dvígat'.
> I vsegdá pliasát' dolzhný
> Polotëry-sharkuný.
> (282)

(The floor polisher waves his arms, / as if dancing Russian style. / He says that he has come / to polish the floor with wax. // He will shuffle, he will jump, / pour wax and move the furniture. / Floor polisher-shufflers / are always supposed to dance.)

*Skarkun* (a person in whom surface gloss hides an empty or bad interior—originally a "heel-clicker") is a suspiciously strong word for a children's poem. More appropriately it might be addressed to the pedologists and other equally despicable keepers of contemporary culture in the Soviet Union.

One work in which both matter and manner are more convincingly in tune with children is "Two Streetcars Named Click and Tram" ("Dva tramvaia Klik i Tram," 1925). A longer, narrative poem, it describes a small adventure in the life of anthropomorphized streetcars.

> Zhíli v párke dva tramváia:
> Klik i Trám.
> Vykhodíli oní vméste
> Po utrám.
> (276)

(Two streetcars lived in the carbarn: / Click and Tram. / They went out together / every morning.)

In the course of the story of how one tired streetcar dallies on his way home to the garage, a certain human feeling—brotherly love and concern—is conveyed.

> Vy, druz'iá-avtomobíli,
> ochen' vézhlivyi naród
> I vsegdá, vsegdá tramvái
> Propuskáete vperëd,

Rasskazhíte mne o Klíke,
O tramváe-goremýke
O dvoiúrodnom moém
S bledno-rózovym ogném.

(278)

(You, friends-automobiles, / are very polite folks, / and always, always, let streetcars / pass. / Tell me about Click, / about the poor, unfortunate tram, / about my cousin / with the pale pink headlight.)

By 1926 Mandel'shtam ceased experimenting in children's literature. In fact he stopped writing poetry altogether for a period of five years (1925–1930). His children's poems are among the last he wrote after a very difficult period of attempted adjustment to life in Soviet Moscow, so different from his familiar, imperial St. Petersburg.

It is understandable that the poems Pasternak and Mandel'shtam wrote for children have been forgotten, along with the second-rate work of numerous inferior writers. It is less understandable, however, that much of the work of Maiakovskii is readily available, while that of the Oberiu poets is not. Without a doubt, the intrinsic merit of the latter far surpasses that of Maiakovskii's. The poetry of Kharms and Vladimirov is certainly on a par with that of Chukovskii and Marshak.

The cultural bleakness of the Stalinist era is variously reflected in the individual fates of the poets whose work for children in the 1920s made the early postrevolutionary period the golden age of Russian children's poetry. The "illegal repression" of the Oberiuty in the purge years, Chukovskii's virtual silence, and Marshak's impaired inspiration were all manifestations of Stalin's rampant destruction of artistic creativity. From the time of the establishment of socialist realism as the single acceptable "method" of art in 1934 until Stalin's death in 1953, children's literature in the Soviet Union was as strictly regulated from above as its adult counterpart. Although those two decades never saw the polemical fireworks of the earlier proletarian debate, the situation in fact was far worse. There was no room for debate. With few exceptions the cultural scene was stagnant.

Nevertheless, two "classic" writers—Agniia Barto (1906–1981) and Sergei Mikhalkov (b. 1913)—gained prominence as children's poets during this period. Later both became leading members of the well-entrenched conservative literary bureaucracy. Barto, who began publishing in the second half of the 1920s, is well known for her poetic output of more than forty years. Mikhalkov, presently head of the Writers' Union of the Russian Republic, began his career as a children's poet in 1935. He is best remembered for his long poem "Uncle Steve" ("Diadia Stëpa," 1935), a perennial favorite of Soviet children, featuring a larger-than-life friendly policeman.[46] In the broadest sense their poetry strives to convey the point of view of a child destined to become a good productive Soviet citizen. Although neither writer is insensitive to children's abilities, and Mikhalkov definitely succeeded in creating an appealing character in his Uncle Steve, they both treat "serious" themes of objective experience and everyday reality, as the cultural dogmatists would have all artists do. Many of their poems are either subtly or directly didactic, setting acceptable standards of behavior for conscientious Soviet children. In this respect they have successfully developed the direction originally attempted by Maiakovskii. At times individual poems are interesting, but taken as a whole, the work of Barto and Mikhalkov—the socialist realism of Russian children's poetry—is unexciting.[47]

No contemporaries of Barto and Mikhalkov achieved lasting renown, with the possible exception of Elena Blaginina (b. 1903). Raised in a provincial town, Blaginina came to Moscow in the 1920s to study at the Institute of Literature and Art founded by Briusov not long before his death in 1924. She published her first poems in the early 1930s in *Murzilka*, a children's magazine also founded in 1924, still in existence and very popular today. Blaginina's first two books of poetry for children appeared in 1936.[48] In the present context she is noteworthy above all as a poet who came under the obvious influence of Chukovskii. Some of her most typical works reflect her sensitivity to the tradition of children's folklore.

> Prostokvashi dali Klashe—nedovol'na Klasha:
> "Nekhochu ia prostokvashi, daite prosto kashi."[49]

> (Klasha was given yogurt—Klasha is dissatisfied: / "I don't want yogurt, just give me porridge.")

Although not all her poems are as universal in spirit as her tongue-twisters, taunts, and counting-out rhymes, even in poems with pointed thematics and contemporary settings she demonstrates an appreciation of the child's point of view. Her understanding of children notwithstanding, Blaginina is not a major poet. Only after the death of Stalin, with a return to a more tolerant attitude toward art, would poets once again approach the level of creativity attained in the 1920s.

**8**

## THE LEGACY OF THE 1920S

$A$MONG THE IMPORTANT manifestations of the cultural "thaw" that followed Stalin's death was the renaissance of Russian children's literature, demonstrating once again the serious place of that branch of the larger Russian literary scene. In poetry the revival was marked by several phenomena. There was, first of all, renewed interest in the work of Chukovskii and Marshak, the pioneers and proven dons of poetry for children, whose work had suffered alternately from criticism and neglect during the Stalinist era. With the onset of more liberal cultural policies, Chukovskii and Marshak again became actively involved in sharing their poetry with children. Also significant was the role they came to play as the mentors of a new generation of children's poets. In its turn, the rapid emergence of that new generation was the second major phenomenon of the period. After two decades of quietude, children's poetry once again began to flourish. Once more poets began to feel free to enter the spirit of childhood. Once again they emphasized humor and play, familiar from children's folklore and developed in the poetry of Chukovskii, Marshak, and Kharms. The stodgy realism and the ideologically weighted "product" demanded by a generation of party dogmatists was displaced by a fresh wave of creativity. As the process of de-Stalinization permitted a rediscovery of the culture of the 1920s, the tradition of children's poetry in Russia reestablished its connection to a healthier past.

In 1962, at what in retrospect can be seen as the height of the "thaw," there occurred an unprecedented cultural event. The Moscow publishing house Children's World (Detskii mir) published a small volume entitled Play (Igra), a collection of children's poems by the Oberiu writer Daniil Kharms, whose work had been suppressed even before he fell victim to the purge. Needless to say, the appearance of Kharms's unorthodox poetry was a literary sensation,[1] immediately becoming an important influence upon some of the younger poets. In stark contrast to the intellectual excitement created by the rediscovery of Kharms was another response to the publication of Play. According to a caustic reviewer, the printers in the town of Kalinin who had worked on the book sent an irate letter to the satirical weekly Krokodil, begging the editors to "defend little children from the poetic mockery of common sense."[2] Whether or not that opinion actually originated in a Kalinin print shop, it clearly demonstrates that the attitude of the bygone proletarian pedologists was by no means a historically isolated phenomenon.

That mentality was strongly challenged in the first decade following Stalin's death. While the publication of Kharms was a daring move, it was not out of character for Children's World. Under the inspiring leadership of Iurii Timofeev, who became editor-in-chief in 1956, that publishing house, originally specializing in toys and picture books for the very youngest children, became an important center for the revival of children's literature. Just as Kliachko and Marshak had done many years before, Timofeev attracted talented young writers and artists. He invited to work with him such a figure as Vladimir Glotser, a specialist in children's own creativity.[3] Of the eight major poets whose work is treated in this chapter, seven published at least one volume, if not more, under the imprint of Children's World between 1958 and 1963. In addition to encouraging writers, Timofeev drew many outstanding artists, some inspired by contemporary European art, others by Russian folk art.[4]

As might be expected, Timofeev's editorship was highly controversial. It was not only the Kalinin printers who expressed strong dissatisfaction with the policies he pursued. In 1964, when a cultural "freeze" set in, the publishing house was reorganized, renamed Kiddy (Malysh), and assigned a new editor. Fortunately, Timofeev's policies had already made a crucial impact. Once again Russian poetry for children had become a serious artistic endeavor. With Timofeev's encouragement many young writers and artists had at last found opportunities for experimentation, for sincere expression of their creative impulses. And even as more conservative editorial tendencies have prevailed in the 1970s and into the 1980s, the accomplishments of the "thaw" have not been forgotten.[5]

The eldest of the contemporary poets is Boris Zakhoder (b. 1918). Besides poetry, he has written prose, and perhaps most importantly, has achieved broad recognition among Russian children and adults alike as the talented translator of several English classics: *Winnie-the-Pooh, Alice in Wonderland, Peter Pan,* and *Mary Poppins.* He has also translated tales of the Grimm brothers, Karel Čapek, and much Polish children's poetry. His brilliant rendition of Milne provides a good example of the degree to which Zakhoder departs from the original, thereby creating a Russian version that can be praised for its originality.[6] More recently, his retelling of Lewis Carroll's *Alice in Wonderland* has for the first time brought Russian children a text that more than adequately conveys the spirit of Carroll's masterpiece.[7]

Zakhoder displayed an early inclination toward literature, creating riddles and tales as a child. From there he went on to write lyric poetry as a young man. Twelve years passed between the time he finished high school in 1935 and published his first poem for children in 1947. In the same year, he graduated with honors from the Gorky Institute of Literature in Moscow. Although Zakhoder seemed quite ready to embark upon a career as a children's poet in the immediate postwar period, the times were not propitious for such an endeavor. Only after the death of Stalin did he succeed in publishing the playful verbal fantasy "The Letter 'I' " ("Bukva 'Ia' "), which had lain in his drawer for almost a decade. Yet as soon as circumstances were favorable, his career moved apace.[8] In 1955, besides "The Letter 'I' "—which appeared in the prestigious journal *Novyi mir*—Zakhoder also published his first small collection of children's poems, *At the Back of the Classroom* (*Na zadnei parte*), winning the praise of Chukovskii.[9] Soon he joined the collective at Children's World. Since that time his works for children have appeared regularly in new editions. Although he is a generation older than most of his contemporaries in the field, he is among the most vital.

It is natural that Chukovskii should have greeted Zakhoder's work with enthusiasm, for their approach to writing for children has much in common. Zakhoder's poems are permeated by the playful verbal spirit long familiar from Chukovskii's, and many of them deserve the designation "comic epic." Prominently featuring animals of many species, the best of Zakhoder's works betray a lively sense of humor, at times touched with a satirical edge, as in "The Parrot" ("Popugai").

> Esli smózhesh', ugadái,
> Chto nam skázhet POPUGÁI!
> —To i skázhet, polagáiu,
> Chto vdolbíli popugáiu![10]

("Guess, if you can, / what the PARROT will tell us?" / "The parrot will say / what was drummed into him!")

He too makes wide use of elements from the folk tradition, being especially attracted by those aspects of children's folklore that earlier appealed to Chukovskii and Kharms: linguistic and intellectual play. Among his favorites are the topsy-turvy rhymes so staunchly defended by Chukovskii. In fact, he dedicated to the elder poet one of his first and most successful works in this genre, "The Whale and the Tomcat" ("Kit i kot"), originally published in *Youth* (*Iunost'*), a magazine devoted to the work of younger writers.

> V ètoi skázke
> Nét poriádka:
> Chtó ni slóvo—
> Tó zagádka!
> Vót chtó
> Skázka govorít:
> Zhíli-býli
> KÓT
> i
> KÍT.

KÓT—ogrómnyi, prósto stráshnyi!
KÍT byl málen'kii, domáshnii.
KÍT miaúkal.
KÓT pykhtél.
KÍT kupát'sia ne khotél.
Kak ogniá vodý boiálsia.
KÓT vsegdá nad ním smeiálsia!

Vrémia ták provódit
KÍT:
Nóch'iu bródit,
Dněm khrapít.
KÓT
Plyvét po okeánu,
KÍT
Iz bliúdtsa ést smetánu.

(In this tale / there is no order: / Each word / is a riddle! / Here is what / the tale says: / Once upon a time there lived / a TOMCAT / and / a WHALE. / The TOMCAT was huge, simply terrible! / The WHALE was small, a homebody. // The WHALE meowed. / The TOMCAT puffed. / The WHALE didn't want to bathe. / He feared the water like fire. / The TOMCAT always laughed at him! // The WHALE / spent his time this way: / He wandered at night, / he snored during the day. / The TOMCAT / swam in the ocean, / the WHALE / ate sour cream from a saucer.)

Just as Chukovskii resolved the disorder in "The Muddle," so Zakhoder straightens things out in "The Whale and the Tomcat," but he ends on an ironic note.

Nú,
I navelí poriádok:
V skázke ból'she net zagádok.
V okeán
ukhódit KÍT,
KÓT na kúkhne
Mírno spít . . . .
Vsě kak nádo,
Vsě prilíchno.
Skázka stála—na "otlíchno"!
Vsém poniátna i iasná.

Zhál'
Chto kónchilas'
Oná! . . .[11]

(Well, / we brought order: / There are no more riddles in the tale. / The WHALE goes out / into the ocean, / the TOMCAT sleeps peacefully / in the kitchen . . . . / All is as it should be, / all is nice and proper. / The tale is graded "excellent"! / It's clear and understandable to all. // Too bad / that it came / to an end! . . .)

Another of Zakhoder's favorite folk genres is the counting-out rhyme. The sound pattern of the following example—"Little Counting-out Rhyme" ("Schitalochka")—conveys additionally the effect of a tongue-twister.

> Zhíli-býli dvá soséda,
> Dvá soséda-liudoéda.
> Liudoéda
> Liudoéd
> Priglasháet
> Na obéd.
> Liudoéd otvétil:—Nét,
> Ne poidú k tebé, soséd!
> Na obéd popást' ne khúdo,
> No otniúd'
> Ne v víde
> Bliúda! [12]

(Once upon a time there were two neighbors, / two cannibal-neighbors. / One cannibal / invited / the other canibal to dinner. / The cannibal answered, "No, / I won't go to your place, neighbor! / It's not bad to go to dinner, / but certainly / not in the form / of a meal!")

Among Zakhoder's translations there are a few from the English tradition. And not surprisingly, some of his shorter poems, such as "Kitty's Sorrow" ("Kiskino gore"), echo the familiar rhythms of nursery rhymes.

> Pláchet Kíska v koridóre.
> U neë
> Bol'shóe góre:
> Zlýe liúdi
> Bédnoi Kíske
> Ne daiút
> Ukrást'
> Sosíski! [13]

(Kitty is crying in the hall. / She is / very upset: / Mean people / won't let / poor kitty / steal / wieners!)

While it is nigh impossible to match the sustained inventiveness of Chukovskii's poetry, there are moments when Zakhoder reveals a similar talent. In his "Shaggy Alphabet" ("Mokhnataia azbuka"),

accompanied by animal illustrations by Lev Tokmakov (husband of
the poet Irina Tokmakova), he presents the following amusing solu-
tion to a difficult task.

> Otkrovénno priznaiú:
> Zvéria nét
> Na búkvu "IÚ".
> Èto—IÚZHNYI KTOTOTÁM.
> Iá egó
> Pridúmal sám![14]

(I openly admit: / No animal starts / with the letter "iu". / This is a
SOUTHERN SOMEONE'S THERE. / I thought him up / myself!)

The word *ktototam* of course evokes Chukovskii's favorite *gippopotam* (hippopotamus). Furthermore, anyone familiar with his
poem "Zakaliaka," recently rendered into English by Mirra
Ginsburg as "Ookie-Spookie," will undoubtedly hear an echo of
these lines.

> "Èto Biáka—Zabiiáka
> Kusáchaia,
> Ia samá iz golový eë výdumala."[15]

(It is Ookie / He is spooky, / I made him up / out of my head.)[16]

In Zakhoder's poem, one senses his pride in continuing the tradition
of Chukovskii.

A fundamental feature of Zakhoder's work, connecting it not only
with the tradition of Chukovskii and the 1920s but with all good
children's literature, is the dual audience to which it communicates. As his interest in Milne and Carroll indicates, Zakhoder is not
only sensitive to the needs of children but succeeds in creating a
dimension accessible to adults as well.[17] To a great extent this is due
to his masterful talent for verbal play, his frequent use of double
entendre and realized metaphors. Small children, for example, are
incapable of grasping the full intent of "The Parrot." "School for
Birds" ("Ptich'ia shkola"), a poem Chukovskii is reputed especially
to have liked, contains the following.

> No vót vletél uchítel' v kláss,
> I sumatókha ugelás'.
> Sidít smirnée golubéi
> Na vétkakh molodézh'.
> Uchítel'—Stáryi Vorobéi,
> Egó ne provedésh'![18]

(But then the teacher flew into the classroom, / and the uproar died
down. / The young ladies and gentlemen / sat as quietly as doves / on
their branches. / The teacher is an Old Sparrow, / he can't be tricked!)

For children "Staryi vorobei" is just that—an old sparrow, teaching
young birds. But for one who has a more sophisticated command of
Russian, the phrase is in fact a set expression with a metaphorical
connotation—a person who is worldly wise. Thus it takes an adult
to appreciate fully the total intent of much of Zakhoder's poetry.

In a more recent work he not only gives full rein to his imaginative
powers but adds a new emotional undercurrent, expressing very
personal feelings connected with growing old. "Counting-out
Land" ("Schitaliia") is an interesting mixed genre, in which
Zakhoder presents a number of counting-out rhymes collected over
the years, accompanied by his own poetic commentary. As the critic Vladimir Prikhod'ko pointed out, the counting-out rhyme is an
excellent verbal symbol of childhood.[19] Its typical rhythm, derived
from two- to four-foot trochaic lines, is a brisk staccato, readily
evoking the brisk tempo of childhood. Zakhoder's accompaniment
in the more languid rhythm of Pushkin's preferred iambic tetrameter provides a kind of adult counterpoint to childhood. The poet
concludes with a nostalgic view of childhood.

> I iá zdes' pobyvál kogdá-to . . .
> I, povinuiás' schétu let,
> Ia tózhe výshel vón, rebiáta,
> I mné, uvý, vozvráta nét.
>
> Mne vkhód zakrýt bespovorótno,
> Khotiá iz kázhdogo dvorá
> Tak bezzabótno i svobódno
> Siudá vbegáet detvorá.
>
> Khot' nét granítsy, net ogrády,
> Khotiá siudá—rukói podát',
> I mózhet stát'sia, býli b rády
> Meniá zdes' snóva povidát' . . . .[20]

(And I was here once . . . / and obeying the sum of the years, // I also
"went out," my children, / and alas, I cannot return. // The entrance is
irreversibly closed to me, / although from every courtyard / children
run in here / so lightheartedly and freely. // Although there is no
boundary, no fence, / although it's just a step away, / and it is very
possible that they'd be happy / to see me here again. . . .)

One hears in those lines of an aging writer an almost desperate love
for the audience he continues to address, but away from whom time

is inevitably taking him. Although the tone is not as bleak or lonely as in the poems Pushkin wrote toward the end of his life, Zakhoder clearly does not write exclusively for children, but also for adults, including himself.

Èmma Moshkovskaia (1926–1981) came to children's poetry in a more fortuitous way than some. As Prikhod'ko points out, she "began to write for children because she saw the world through the eyes of a child; children's literature turned out to be the most convenient form to express a most serious trait of her soul—childlikeness."[21] The poet herself admitted she began and continued to write first of all for herself. How fortunate for children that she shared with them her poetic response to the world.

Moshkovskaia's first career was in music, an interest that understandably enhanced her poetry. As a mezzo-soprano, she studied voice at the Gnesin Institute in Moscow and after graduation in 1954 embarked on the life of a concert singer. When the career she hoped for did not develop smoothly, her artistic destiny took an unexpected turn. Once while sick in the hospital in the late 1950s she wrote some poetry—children's poetry, as it turned out. Perspicacious friends introduced her to Timofeev at Children's World; he immediately recognized her talent. With his encouragement and that of others (very importantly, Marshak's), she began to write poetry for children. Her first works appeared in 1962. Thus, like that of several others, her debut coincided with the flourishing production of new children's books under Timofeev's direction.

An important preliminary step for Moshkovskaia was her discovery of the already classic writers Chukovskii and Marshak, whose best work was not very familiar to her from childhood, which coincided with the Stalinist 1930s. Next she turned to Kharms, enchanted by his musical quality. Retrospectively she identified an affinity in her poetry with that of Chukovskii and Kharms above all. It comes as no surprise, then, that when the aging Chukovskii was shown her first published poems, he warmly praised them.[22]

Already discernible in her earliest work is the significance Moshkovskaia attached to the formal structure of her poetry, down to its careful graphic arrangement on the page—a factor intended to guide the manner of reading, or, more properly speaking, recitation. By the second half of the twentieth century, interest in the visual side of poetry was, of course, not remarkable in itself. Popularized by the futurists, it had already affected the stanzaic style of Chukovskii, Marshak, and Kharms before her. Nonetheless, Moshkovskaia deserves credit for her new emphasis on the graphic element and its relationship to the sound pattern in children's poetry. An early example of her interest in this area is "Telegram" ("Telegramma"), which appeared in her first collection, *Uncle Balloon* (*Diadia shar*, 1962).

> Telegrámmu—
> 
> grámmu—
> 
> grámmu
> 
> Rano útrom prineslí.
> Razbudíli—
> 
> díli—
> 
> díli—
> Razbudíli i ushlí.[23]

(Early this morning they brought a / telegram— / gram— / gram. / They woke us up— / up— / up— / they woke us up and left.)

The device of syllabic repetition, prominent in the poems of Kharms, in fact originated with Chukovskii. While in some of Moshkovskaia's poetry there are strong indications of her familiarity and fascination with Kharms, she cannot be accused of imitation. The lessons she learned from Kharms, together with those from Chukovskii, Marshak, and the oral tradition, all served to motivate her own creativity.

One of her first poems, and still among her best, "Greedy Gut" ("Zhadina"), is reminiscent of accumulative folktales. The central figure is a dog with a loaf of white bread who encounters in succession five different animals, each of whom asks for a bite. The dog considers, then refuses each request, devouring the whole loaf himself in the process.

> Pës
> Shagál
> Po pereúlku.
> 
> On
> Zheval
> Bol'shúiu
> Búlku.
> 
> Podoshël Shchenóchek,
> Poprosíl kusóchek.
> 
> Shël
> Pës,
> Stál gadát':
> "Dát'
> Ili ne dát'?"

Pogadál-pogadál,
Pozhevál-pozhevál . . .
                    Ne dál![24]

(A dog / was striding / down the alley. // He / was chewing / a loaf / of
bread. // A little puppy went up to him, / and asked him for a
piece. // The dog / was walking, / and began to consider / whether to
give / or not. // He considered and considered, / he chewed a bit and
chewed a bit . . . / he didn't give any!)

The first line, with its motion verb and the preposition *po* recalls
constructions found both in folk songs and in first-generation Soviet
poetry. Five of Chukovskii's *skazki* begin similarly. For Kharms the
number is even higher; of the ten poems in *Play,* seven have motion
verbs in the first sentence. Marshak's poems, in contrast, tend toward more static beginnings. While the regular trochaic meter of
the first two sentences of "Greedy Gut" remind one of the typically
strong beat of Kharms's verse (six of the poems in *Play* are in
trochaic tetrameter), the subsequent rhythmic shifts evoke the
metrical variety of Chukovskii's poetry. Moshkovskaia herself said
that her use of more "conversational intonation" came from
Chukovskii.[25]

Although the rich sound texture of her poetry is also admittedly
indebted to the tradition of Chukovskii, Moshkovskaia sometimes
used a kind of verbal pyrotechnics that was uniquely her own—a
poetic extension of children's own repetition and rhyming, a special
trans-sense language. It recalls the futurists' exotic interest in children and their language. Especially striking is her incorporation of
such verbal experiments into poems treating everyday reality.
Moshkovskaia's ability to transform the mundane world into something approaching the fantastic annoys the more "conscientious"
editor. While she cannot be accused of having avoided the material
of daily life, the manner in which she treated it does raise questions.
Take, for example, the long poem "House Number One" ("Dom
nomer odin"), which from the hyperbolic view of a child describes a
modern Soviet apartment building, with its seemingly endless
facade.

i chasámi shlí my, shlí my,
volosámi obroslí my . . .

Vdrúg, ákh!
PARIKMÁKH . . .
Mákherpákher,
márikpákher
v kréslo-tréslo usadíl,

v ètom zdán'e, zdán'e, zdá . . .
nas postrígli—krasotá!
I postrígli nas krasívo,
i skazáli my "spasíbo",
i skazáli: "Do svidán'ia?
Óchen' vás blagodarím!"
I poshlí my
mímo
         án'ia,
bán'ia,
       ván'ia,
gán'ia
       zdán'ia,
ne zabýt' egó nazván'e:
DÓM
NÓMER
ODÍN.[26]

(and we walked for hours and hours, / our hair grew very, very long . . . //
Suddenly, oh! / HAIRDRESS . . . / Dresserhesser, / hairy hesser / seated
us in the hair-chair, / in this building, building, build . . . / they gave us
haircuts—beautiful! // And they gave us beautiful haircuts, / and we
said: "Thank you," / and they said: "Good-bye! / We thank you very
much!" / And we went / past / the ilding, / gilding, / jilding / zilding, /
building, / don't forget its name: // HOUSE / NUMBER / ONE.)

In her neologisms (*makherpakher, marikpakher*), rhyme play
(*kreslo-treslo,* and the series concluding with *zdan'ia*), and trun-
cated words, Moshkovskaia plays with language just as children do,
using sound association. Yet to conservative adults such "nonsense"
is incomprehensible and unnecessary. The old debate about the
place of fantasy in children's literature continues unresolved.

One poem in which Moshkovskaia's verbal acrobatics reach an
extreme is her variant of the topsy-turvy genre, "The Ram Who Did
Not Know the Traffic Rules" ("Baran, kotoryi ne znal pravil
ulichnogo dvizheniia"). She transforms a dully didactic theme into
a wonderful verbal game, a modern tongue-twister. Her treatment is
incomparably superior to Shvarts's earlier poem on the same subject. Onto the scene of a busy city intersection unexpectedly comes
a ram.

Vstál Barán
kak istukán.

I vsë poperepútalos'!
Pópo-pére-pupútalos'!

Ávto-
        tsitsí-
                pedísty!
Móto-
        bubú-
                tsiklísty!
Vélo-
        tsitsí-
                onéry!
Míli-
        tsitsí
                bilísty!

Barán sharákh-sharákhnulsia
i bákhnulsia,
i trákhnulsia,
i búkhnulsia,
i stúknulsia . . .
I be-e-e-e-e-e-e-zhát'!!!²⁷

(The ram stood / as still as a stone. // And everything got all mixed up! / Got-got-all-all-mixed up! / Auto- / toto / cycles! / Motor- / oror- / biles! / Bicy- / cycy- / men! / Police- / ice-ice- / ists! // The ram jum-jumped to the side / and fell with a bang / and fell with a crash / and bumped on the ground / and smashed himself . . . / and ra-a-a-a-a-a-a-n off!!!)

A further demonstration of the poet's fine understanding of the child psyche is the punishment the ram receives for his bad behavior—he is given a haircut.

While the adult appeal of Moshkovskaia's poetry is comparable to that of Zakhoder's, it comes primarily from a different source. In hers it is less intellectual and more emotional. There are, of course, instances of multileveled semantics, expressions that children understand only in a literal and not a metaphoric way, but they occur less frequently than in Zakhoder. In "The Elephant and His Mood" ("Slon i ego nastroenie"), the central idea of the poem derives from the literalization of a metaphorical expression—"His mood fell." At the same time the poem goes on to develop an important theme of human psychology, that of self-acceptance.

Slón poteriál nastroénie.
V désiat' chasóv v voskresén'e
Upálo egó nastroénie
i popálo v bóchku varén'ia.

(The elephant lost his mood. / On Sunday at ten o'clock. / His mood fell, / it fell into a barrel of jam.)

Several stanzas follow in which the elephant expresses dissatisfaction with his lot. If only he were a rabbit! The rabbit, in turn, laments his own situation, thereby amazing the elephant.

> Slón ne povéril ushám!
> I ot bol'shógo volnén'ia
> slópal bóchku varén'ia
> A v ètoi bóchke varén'ia
> býlo egó nastroénie!
> Varén'e
> býlo klubníchnoe.
> Nastroénie
> býlo otlíchnoe.[28]

(The elephant didn't believe his ears! / And from great excitement / he gobbled up a barrel of jam. / And in that barrel of jam / was his mood! / The jam / was strawberry. / His mood / was excellent.)

In the manner of a fable, this poem, while amusing to children and adults alike, also makes a mature philosophical point.

In Russian society, with its long history of censorship, people often look for hidden meanings in unlikely places. So it was with Chukovskii's "The Crocodile." Although Moshkovskaia can hardly be accused of using children's poetry as a vehicle for political allusion, one possible exception stands out. The poem "Bulldog" ("Bul'dog") describes a young girl in a straw hat walking an ugly bulldog with medals on his collar. When the wind blows off the girl's hat, the dog pulls her farther away from it. At the end of the poem the girl's distress ("Oh what will Mama say?") is juxtaposed to the dog's arrogant indifference.

> Idët bul'dóg,
>     idët bul'dóg,
> Zvenít medáliami bul'dóg,
>     bul'dóg
>     takói uródlivyi,
>     takói nepovorótlivyi!
>
>     Medáli,
>     medáli,
> blestiát ego medáli,
>     medáli,
>     medáli,
> za chtó ikh tól'ko
>     dáli. . . .[29]

(The bulldog walks, / the bulldog walks, / the bulldog's medals are ringing; / the bulldog is / so ugly, / so clumsy! // Medals, / medals, / his medals are shining, / medals, / medals, / Why did he get them. . . .)

The rhythmically emphatic image of the bemedaled bulldog is surely a most unflattering allusion to stodgy, self-satisfied officials, insensitive to the needs of others. "The Bulldog" appeared in Moshkovskaia's first collection in 1962 and again in 1967 but has not been republished since then.

Moshkovskaia's most sustained and complex work is the book-length tale *Once Upon a Time There Was a Little Gray Goat* (*Zhil-byl na svete seren'kii kozlik*, 1971), which is predominantly poetry with some prose interspersed. Based on very diverse rhythms and intonations, *Little Gray Goat* is a series of short tales united by the central figure of a lovable little goat. In a manner that communicates to adults as well as to children, Moshkovskaia brings together her interest in the playful and the serious, treating such universal themes as the child's relationship with his parents, the difficulties of growing up, the development of friendship, and the ability to deal with enemies—in short, the joy and pain of being a human being. The introductory episode, in which Little Goat tries to escape the wolf, provides the basis for the main body of the work, the series of Little Goat's tales. Both figures, of course, are familiar from folklore.

> Skók,
> skók,
> shchëlk,
> shchëlk,
> gnálsi a za Kózlikom
> Vólk,
> Vólk.[30]

(Hop, / hop, / pop, / pop, / Wolf ran after / Little Goat.)

After a long chase the Little Goat finally finds refuge with the bear, who asks him to tell some tales. Little Goat responds with delight.

> Kák èto prósto!
> Éto priiátno!
> Éto priiátno
> neveroiátno![31]

(How easy it is! / It's pleasing! / It's pleasing, / incredibly so!)

The first tale establishes Little Goat's goal—he wants to triumph over Gray Wolf.

In his role as storyteller one cannot help identifying Little Goat with the poet, or more generally the artist. This identity is more firmly established by one of the central images in the work, the friendship of Little Goat with Little Donkey. They are depicted as opposite personality types. Little Goat is an intelligent, gentle dreamer; Little Donkey is a loutish realist. The contrast is epitomized in the tale about Little Goat's building a house. Little Donkey assumes the role of boss and has Little Goat do all the work, leaving himself nothing to do but make sound effects. Later, when Little Goat regrets the dullness of a house with a plain ceiling overhead and suggests making a hole in order to see the stars, Little Donkey's practical response is that a hole is impossible since it would let in the rain. Recognizing the difficulties of planning a house that would suit both of them, Little Goat decides to build a bridge.

Stróil-stróil Kózlik
Stróil-stróil móstik.
Perekínul on doshchéchku
cherez óblachnuiu réchku,
gde lesá
iz légkikh túch,
les dremúchii
ne dremúch,
Séryi Vólk iz ètikh mést
Sérykh Kózlikov ne ést:
óchen' ón stesniáetsia . . . .

No nébo proiasniáetsia,
razmyváet beregá
oblakóvaia reká—
i upál chudésnyi móst,
I Kózlik upál
i razbíl nós![32]

(Little Goat built and built, / he built and built a little bridge. / He threw a small board / across the cloudy river, / where the woods / are light clouds, / the dense forest / is not dense; / in these parts Gray Wolf / doesn't eat Little Gray Goats: / he is very, very shy . . . . // But the sky cleared up, / the cloud river / washed away the banks— / and the marvelous bridge fell down, / and Little Goat fell down / and broke his nose.)

In his search for the ideal, Little Goat continually encounters obstacles. However, after a long series of adventures and misadventures, the goat-child-poet does conquer the wolf—through his art. In the final episode Little Goat again takes shelter with the bear in his attempt to escape Gray Wolf. And again the bear wants to hear tales.

I Kózlik rasskázyval dólgo,
i chás . . .
i chetýre chasá.
I Vólk stoiál pod okóshkom,
stoiál,
stoiál ne dyshá.

I slúshal, i slúshal, i slúshal,
ne él! . .
Ne él i ne píl!

Skazál on:—Kózlik, poslúshai,
TÝ
    MENIÁ
        POBEDÍL![33]

(And Little Goat told stories for a long time, / for an hour . . . / for four
hours. / And Wolf stood under the window, / he stood, / he stood
without stirring. // And he listened and listened and listened, / he
didn't eat! . . . / He didn't eat or drink! // Said he: "Little Goat, listen, /
YOU / HAVE CONQUERED / ME!")

Thus Moshkovskaia imbues tales for children with mature philosophical themes—the difficulty of life (especially for an artist), the
need for courage and persistence, and finally, the important place of
art in the world. The complexity of its manner and the universality
of its message puts *Little Gray Goat* at the apogee of Moshkovskaia's work. That she conceived it as an open form and continued to write episodes for it reveals that she felt similarly about it.
Unfortunately, she did not succeed in publishing an expanded version before her death.

When Moshkovskaia became a member of the Writers' Union in
1967 she had in her support a letter of recommendation from the late
Marshak, who described her as "one of the most gifted young poets
writing for children. She has what is essential for a children's
poet—genuine, not artificial liveliness, poetic imagination, musi-
calness, an ability to play with children without talking down to
them."[34] From a later perspective one can add to Marshak's characterization of Moshkovskaia's talent the important quality once described by Chukovskii.

In my opinion, the goal of a storyteller is to cultivate in a child, at
whatever cost, a sense of humanity—that marvelous ability of man
to be disturbed by another's unhappiness, to rejoice over another's
joys, to experience someone else's fate as one's own. Storytellers take
pains so that from his youngest years a child learns to participate
mentally in the life of imaginary people and animals and by this path

breaks through the frame of self-centered interests and feelings. And therefore, while listening to stories a child naturally takes the side of the good, the brave, the wrongly injured . . . our whole task lies in awakening in the receptive childish soul that priceless ability to experience, suffer, rejoice with others, without which a man is not a human being.[35]

Moshkovskaia became just such a storyteller.

Another of the post-Stalin generation of children's poets, Genrikh Sapgir (b. 1928), began his career in 1960 at Children's World, publishing nine books under Timofeev's editorial guidance. Since then he has continued to write regularly. At its best his poetry is characterized by the verbal play of folklore, especially its acoustic and rhythmic patterns. These qualities are well illustrated by his collection *Counting-out Rhymes* (*Schitalki*, 1965), an alphabet of counting-out rhymes, with a separate rhyme for each letter. The one for the letter *shch* works well as a tongue-twister.

> Shchúka
> V ózere
> Zhilá.
> Cherviaká
> S kriuchká
> Snialá.
> Navaríla
> Shchúka
> Shchéi,
> Ugoshchála
> Dvukh ershéi.
> Rasskazáli
> Vsém
> Ershí:
> —Shchí
> U shchúki
> Khoroshí![36]

(A pike / lived / in the lake. / She snatched / a worm / off a hook. / The pike / cooked up / some cabbage soup; / she entertained two perch. / The perch / told / everyone: / "The pike's / cabbage soup / is good!")

And the rhyme for the letter *ia* evokes the nonsense words traditional to the genre.

> Ókhanty,
> Ákhanty!
> Iábloki—

Iákhonty.
Iábloki
Spélye,
Rúki
Umélye—
Iáshiny,
Dáshiny,
Léshiny,
Pétiny.
Iábloki
Sóbrany,
Iábloki
Slózheny,
Iábloki
S'édeny.[37]

(Ah, / ra, / apples, / rubies. / The apples / are ripe, / the hands / are skillful— / Yasha's, / Dasha's, / Liosha's, / Petia's. / The apples / are picked, / the apples are piled up, the apples are eaten up.)

As is Moshkovskaia's, much of Sapgir's poetry is marked by the special spirit of Kharms, whose work was well known to Timofeev's collective. In the manner of Kharms, Sapgir often uses a regular trochaic tetrameter to accompany his fanciful excursions, as in "I'm Leaving" ("Uezzhaiu").

Do svidániia,
Druz'iá!
Édu, édu,
Édu iá—
Ne v metró,
I ne v tramváe.
Ne v vagóne
Elektríchki,
A v koróbke
Iz-pod cháia,
Ili net—
Verkhóm na spíchke!
Na solóminke
Skachú,
Na pushínke
Ia lechú—[38]

(Good-bye, / friends! / I am going, going, / going— / not on the subway, / and not on the tram, / not in the car / of an electric train, / but in a box / from tea, / or no— / astride a match! / I am hopping / on a straw, / I am flying / on a bit of fluff—)

At times he creates hilarious nonsense tales, such as "About Foma and Erëma" ("Pro Fomu i pro Erëmu"), two who do everything stupidly.

> —Slýsh', Fomá!
> —Nu chtó, Erëma?
> —Skúchno dóma
> Vzapertí.
> Na rabótu, chtó l', poití?
> Fú -ty nú -ty, fú -ty, nú -ty,
> Na rabótu, chtó l', poití?[39]

("Listen, Foma!" / "Well what, Erëma?" / "It's dull to be / locked up at home. / What do you say we go to work? / Drats! / What do you say we go to work?")

After failing at farming and hunting due to their ineptitude, they try fishing, only to go down in worthless leaky boats! As Kharms liked to do, Sapgir sometimes presents children with a totally absurd situation that they must sort out for themselves. In "The Cannibal and the Princess or the Reverse" ("Liudoed i printsessa ili vsë na oborot") he creates a new topsy-turvy situation. The tale is actually two, with the second one being the opposite of the first, shown by the following beginnings.

> Printséssa bylá
> Prekrásnaia,
> Pogóda bylá
> Uzhásnaia. . . .
>
> Pogóda bylá
> Prekrásnaia,
> Printséssa bylá
> Uzhásnaia.[40]

(The princess was / beautiful, / the weather / was terrible. // The weather / was beautiful, / the princess / was terrible.)

In the process of amusing them, Sapgir introduces children to the concept of the relative nature of the world.

One of Sapgir's tales, "The Laughters" ("Smeiantsy," 1967), deserves mention not because of its intrinsic merit, which is not great, but because of the obvious influences upon it. The narrative deals with a town of people who like to laugh and make merry and with how they defeat a dragon who comes to threaten them.

> V strané Khokhotánii
> Zhíli smeiántsy.

Liubíli smeiántsy
Vesél'e i tántsy,
I prósto smeiát'sia
Liubíli smeiántsy. . . .

V stranú Khokhotániiu
Príbyl Drakón.
Na trëkh samolëtakh
Pozháloval ón.

Nad Smekhográdom
Udáril gróm:
Drakón opustílsja
Na smekhodróm.[41]

(In the land of Laughica / the laughters lived. / The laughters loved / to dance and be merry. / and the laughers loved / simply to laugh. // To the land of Laughica / a dragon came. / He arrived / on three airplanes. // Above Laugh City / thunder boomed: / the dragon landed / at the laughoport.)

Sapgir's neologisms based on the word laughter (smekh) call to mind Khlebnikov's poem "Incantation by Laughter." While Sapgir falls far short of Chukovskii and Kharms, whose assimilation of elements from Khlebnikov's poetry was more fruitful, it is nonetheless interesting to see a contemporary Russian children's poet reaching back to a poet whose work has never been republished in the Soviet Union. The roots of the early postrevolutionary avant-garde are tenacious.[42]

From the early 1920s when Chukovskii and Marshak translated from the English tradition for children and Gor'kii conceived his vast project to bring world literature to children as well as adults, many Russian children's writers have done translation in addition to their original work. Zakhoder, of course, is an outstanding example, and typical only in that he turned to translation after gaining recognition as a poet. One who reversed the pattern is Irina Tokmakova (b. 1929), who published translations before she began writing her own poetry. While a graduate student of general and comparative linguistics at Moscow State University, she occasionally interpreted for foreign visitors. Once she was given a volume of Swedish folk songs for her young son, which she then translated for his benefit. But soon her audience grew. In 1958 she published one of her translations in Murzilka; two years later an entire book appeared—The Bees' Ring Dance (Vodiat pchely khorovod, 1960). Then, while ostensibly researching her dissertation (which never materialized) in the Lenin Library, she found a collection of Scottish folk songs, which led to her second volume of translations, *Wee Willie Winky* (*Kroshka Villi Vinki*, 1962). In the same year Children's World published her first book of original poems, *Trees* (*Derev'ia*). With that she left her promising academic career to become a successful professional writer of poetry and prose for young children.[43]

A primary feature of the folk rhymes—laconicism—also typifies Tokmakova's own poetry. With the notable exception of a few verse tales, her poems are short, often no longer than eight lines. Many are devoted to nature themes and all reflect an appreciation of children, of their intellectual and emotional needs. Tokmakova addresses them in a relatively simple and direct manner. Her poems do not contain the overtones or subtext so often found in those of Chukovskii and Kharms, or their recent followers. Yet the catchy rhythms and verbal play, all reminiscent of nursery rhymes, are bound to find appreciative adults.

Underlying much of Tokmakova's poetry and creating its appeal to children is an emphasis on play. At times this comes out thematically; the subject of a poem may be play, as in "Wonder soup!" ("Ai da sup!").

> Glubokó—ne mélko,
> Korablí v tarélkakh:
> Lúku golóvka,
> Krásnaia morkóvka,
> Petrúshka,
> Kartóshka
> I krupkí nemnózhko.
> Vót koráblik plyvët,
> Zaplyváet priámo v rót![44]

(Deep, not shallow, / ships in plates: / an onion head, / a red carrot, / parsley, / potatoes, / a little barley. / See the little ship sailing; / it sails straight into your mouth!)

Here one of life's daily essentials becomes a game, as is often the case in children's folklore. In this poetry, there are also various types of verbal play. In the poem "Plim," for example, the child persona tests reality and triumphs over it.

> Lózhka—èto lózhka.
> Lózhkoi súp ediát.
> Kóshka—èto kóshka.
> U kóshki sém' kotiát.

Triápka—èto triápka,
Triápkoi výtru stól.
Shápka—èto shápka,
Odélsia i poshél.
A iá pridúmal slóvo,
Smeshnóe slóvo—plím.
Ia povtoriáiu snóva—
Plím, plím, plím . . .
Vot prýgaet i skáchet—
Plím, plím, plím,
I nichegó ne znáchit
Plím, plím, plím.[45]

(A spoon is a spoon, / we eat soup with a spoon. / A cat is a cat, / the cat has seven kittens. / A rag is a rag, / I wipe the table with a rag. / A hat is a hat, / I put it on and go out. / You know what? I thought up a word, / a funny word—plim. / I'll say it again— / plim, plim, plim . . . / see it jumping and skipping— / plim, plim, plim, / and it doesn't mean a thing— / plim, plim, plim.)

Such neologistic play is an important part not only of the process of language acquisition, but of children's broader cognitive development. Sometimes Tokmakova's persona is an adult, up to amusing verbal tricks, such as spoonerisms.

Na pómoshch'! V bol'shói vodopád
Upál molodói leopád!
Akh nét! Molodói leopárd
Svalílsia v bol'shói vodopárd.
Chto délat'—opiát' nevpopád.
Derzhís', dorogói leopád,
Vernéi, dorogói leopárd!
Opiát' ne vykhódit vpopárd.[46]

(Help! A young weopard fell / into a big waterfall! / Oh no! A young leopard / fell into a big wallerfall. / What can I do—it's still out of place. / Hang on, dear weopard, / I mean, dear leopard! / Again it's out of prace.)

In such a topsy-turvy rhyme Tokmakova cleverly exploits children's natural proclivity for rhyming. They readily respond to such verbal humor, since it demonstrates one of the obstacles they must overcome in mastering language.

While many of Tokmakova's poems reveal strong links to the oral tradition, some of them come more directly from there than others. In this respect some of her genres are typically folk: tongue-twisters, taunts, lullabies. There are also little songs, such as "Porridge" ("Kasha").

Nú-ka, nú-ka, nú-ka, nú li!
Ne vorchíte vy, kastriúli,
Ne vorchíte, ne shipíte,
Káshu sládkuiu svaríte,
Náshikh détok nakormíte.[47]

(Come on, come on, come on now! / Don't you grumble, pans, / don't you grumble, don't you hiss; / cook sweet porridge, / feed our little children.)

Here the regular trochaic meter, sound repetition, and syntactic parallelism all derive from children's folklore. Tokmakova, however, does not usually borrow so directly. More commonly she makes changes in a traditional genre. Thus a poem like "The Sleepy Elephant" ("Sonnyi slon") uses the popular folk feature of sound imitation but introduces a "foreign" animal and more consciously literary word play.

Dín'-dón. Dín'-dón.
V pereúlke khódit slón,
Stáryi, séryi, sónnyi slón.
Dín'-dón. Dín'-dón.

Stálo v kómnate temnó:
Zasloniáet slon oknó.
Ili èto snítsia són?
Dín'-dón. Dín'-dón.[48]

(Ding-dong. Ding-dong. / An elephant is walking in the alley. / An old, gray, sleepy elephant. // It grew dark in the room: / the elephant is covering the window. / Or is it just a dream? / Ding-dong. Ding-dong.)

With its mysterious shadow, this poem conveys the additional feeling of a riddle. In this and many other poems, Tokmakova achieves a good balance between traditional and new elements. Although by the 1970s she moved away from her original interest in folk rhymes and the accompanying focus on verbal play, her early poems have won a lasting place in contemporary Russian poetry for children. Some evidence of their popularity is the fact that they continue to be reissued in new editions. In 1978, for example, the verse tale "Cock-a-doodle-doo" ("Kukareku," 1965) was printed in an edition of one and a half million copies. Normally, large editions of children's paperbacks in the Soviet Union today average between one hundred to three hundred thousand. One and a half million is equal to the very largest editions of works by such classic writers as Chukovskii and Marshak.

Another important children's poet who began his career with translation is Roman Sef (b. 1931). His first work appeared in 1960—one book for adults, one for children. In 1963, the year he completed his study of journalism at Moscow State University, he published his first book of original poetry for children, with illustrations by Lev Tokmakov, as well as his versions of Yiddish children's verses by Ovsei Driz. Since then he has to his credit several more books of children's poetry, two of them with exceptionally handsome drawings by Viktor Pivovarov.[49] Sef's renown as a writer comes as much from his Russian renditions of foreign poetry by Driz, John Ciardi, and Miroslav Valek, as from his original verse.

Along with his contemporaries, Sef acknowledges the debt of modern children's poetry to folklore and himself occasionally draws upon that rich tradition. Sometimes he creates his own variations of oral genres—folktales, riddles, counting-out rhymes. His first book included "A Counting-out Rhyme" ("Schitalka").

> Ia mogú
> Schitát' do stá—
> Vrémeni
> Ne zhálko:
> —Ráz,
> Dvá,
> Trí,
> Chetýre ...
> Stó—
> Vót i vsiá
> Schitálka.[50]

(I can / count up to one hundred— / I'm not afraid / of wasting time: / One, / two, / three, / four ... // One hundred— / that's the whole counting-out rhyme.)

But the verbal texture of Sef's poetry does not typically evoke folklore. Instead, it has more obvious affinities with the written tradition. Sef is less inclined to play with children than to speak to them directly through poetry.

Just as Chukovskii did, Sef stresses the important place of poetry in the lives of young children, emphasizing the qualities normally found in poetic language as a whole. Especially crucial, according to him, is "making strange," seeing things in new ways. By offering children the opportunity to look at the world from different perspectives, Sef encourages them to do more of what comes to them naturally. From this follows his insistence upon the importance of imagination, as in "If You Don't Believe" ("Esli ty ne verish' ").

> Vagóny—èto stúl'ia.
> A paravóz—krovát'.
> A ésli ty ne vérish',
> A ésli ty ne vérish',
> A ésli ty ne vérish',
> To mózhesh' ne igrát'.[51]

(The chairs are the cars. / The bed is the engine. / And if you don't believe, / and if you don't believe, / and if you don't believe, / then you shouldn't play.)

Or, as in "A Miracle" ("Chudo"), he urges children to discover the exceptional in their everyday world.

> Ty eshché
> Ne vídel
> Chúda?
> Nikogdá
> Ne vídel chúda!
> Tak skhodí
> I posmotrí.
> Ty uvídish'
> Prósto chúdo,
> Udivítel'noe
> Chúdo:
> Tám,
> Gdé magazín
> "POSÚDA",
> Vozle dóma
> Nómer 3,
> Skvoz' asfál't
> U perekréestka
> Probiváetsia
> Berézka.[52]

(Haven't you / seen a / miracle yet? / You've never / seen a miracle? / Then come / and look. / You'll simply / see a miracle, / an amazing miracle. / There, / by the hardware store, / next to building / number 3, / a birch tree / is breaking through / the asphalt / at the crossing.)

Although Sef's poetic achievement here is modest, his intentions are good.

Tokmakova has identified in Sef's renewing vision "a polemic directed against everything boureois, Philistine, indifferent."[53] Although to call his position "polemical" is perhaps overstating the case, Tokmakova is essentially correct. In his poetry Sef does try to challenge routinely accepted themes and encourages children to respond to the world imaginatively. However, in comparison with a poet like Moshkovskaia, his challenge is mild.

Sometimes the persona of Sef's poetry is a child, showing the poet's understanding of that perspective. At other times, when the point of view is that of an adult talking with a child, Sef puts him in the time-honored role of the teacher. His poems of the latter type often conclude with a moral, direct or indirect. Needless to say, the more subtle poems, such as "A Good Person" ("Dobryi chelovek"), are the more successful ones.

> Stoliár guliál v gustóm lesú
> Sredí bol'shíkh stvolóv,
> I, ulybnúvshis', on skazál:
> —Kak mnogo tut stolóv.
> Okhótnik záitsev nastreliál
> Piat' shtúk za shést' minút,
> I, ulybnúvshis', on skazál:
> —Kak mnógo díchi tút.
>
> Shël útrom dóbryi chelovék.
> Striakhnúv s vetvéi rosú,
> On ulybnúlsia i skazál:
> —Kak khoroshó v lesú.[54]

(A carpenter was wandering in a dense forest / among thick tree trunks, / and, smiling, he said: / "How many tables there are here." // A hunter shot some hares— / five within six minutes, / and, smiling, he said: / "How much game there is here." // A good man was walking one morning. / After he shook the dew from a branch, / he smiled and said: / "How fine it is in the forest.")

Tokmakova's above-mentioned comment applies well to this poem. Typical of the more heavy-handed approach is the concluding couplet of "The Sofa" ("Divan").

> Tol'ko prézhde chem posmét',
> Nado dúmat' i umét'.[55]

(But before you dare, / you must think and know how.)

Sef's morales are generally wise: be good, be kind, be intelligent. And his best lessons are always the least strident.

One poet clearly indebted to both the oral and the larger lyric tradition of Russian poetry is Valentin Berestov (b. 1928). A longtime friend of Chukovskii's, Berestov, who was originally trained as an archeologist, turned to children's literature in the late 1950s.[56] Over the next few years he published a number of books at Children's World. Berestov does not stand out among his contemporaries as an innovator, yet he is very much a credit to his mentor Chukovskii, for the quality of his poetry and prose tales is consistently high.

His typically short poems are populated by animals, children, and toys. They are playful in both theme and structure. Often, as in "The Hen and Her Chicks" ("Kuritsa s tsypliatami"), the sounds and rhythms of children's folklore are abundant.

> Kud-kudá? Kud-kudá?
> Nú-ka, nú-ka vse siudá!
> Nú-ka k máme pod kryló!
> Kud-kudá vas ponesló.[57]

(Cluckity, cluck! Cluckity, cluck! / Now, now, all come here! / Now come here under Mama's wing! / Did the wind carry you off?)

Sometimes a wise adult voice prevails, always in an understanding tone. The example here is "Geese" ("Gusi").

> Tót, kto s gusiátami blízko znakóm,
> Znáet: gusiáta guliáiut gus'kóm.
> Tót zhe, kto blízko znakóm
> S gusakóm,
> K ním ne risknët podoití bosikóm.[58]

(Someone well acquainted with goslings / knows: goslings strut in a goosestep. / Likewise, someone well acquainted with the gander / won't dare to come close in bare feet.)

Of the folk genres, the ever-popular counting-out rhyme is one of Berestov's favorites too. In "A Nighttime Counting-out Rhyme" ("Nochnaia schitalka"), he transforms the genre into an unusual lullaby.

> RÁZ—
> DVÁ—
> TRÍ—
> CHETÝRE—
> PIÁT'—
> SHÉST'—
> SÉM'—
> VOSÉM'—
> DÉVIAT'—
> DÉSIAT'.

Nádo, nádo, nádo spát'
I ne nádo kurolésit'.
Kto ne spít, tot výidet
Vón.
Kto usnúl, uvídit
Són.[59]

(ONE— / TWO— / THREE— / FOUR— / FIVE— / SIX— / SEVEN— /
EIGHT— / NINE— / TEN. / You must, must, must sleep / you mustn't
be a wild one. / Who doesn't sleep will be / out. / Who falls asleep will
have / a dream.)

One of Berestov's more recent and imaginative cycles is "Puppet
Theater" ("Kukol'nyi teatr"). The poem "The Theater Travels"
("Teatr puteshestvuet"), for example, works as a riddle.

Na útrennik détskii
Artísty speshát.
U níkh v chemodánakh
Artísty lezhát.[60]

(Actors were hurrying / to the children's matinée. / In their suitcases /
actors lay.)

Tokmakov's clever illustration, showing the puppets within the
suitcases, makes the poem's meaning more clear to children.
Another poem in this cycle, "Jester" ("Shut"), says something important about life in a playful, circular fashion.

Chtóby sdélat'sia
Smeléi,
Núzhno stát'
Poveseléi.
Chtóby stát'
Poveseléi,
Núzhno sdélat'sia
Smeléi.[61]

(In order to be / bolder, / you must be merrier. / In order to be / merrier, /
you must be bolder.)

Like his predecessors, Berestov gives his audience both intellectual
and emotional nourishment.

Undoubtedly the best known of the younger generation is Èduard
Uspenskii (b. 1937), who along with poetry writes drama and prose.
He is celebrated by his story "Crocodile Gena and His Friends"
("Krokodil Gena i ego druz'ia," 1966), by now a well-established

childhood classic. The characters of Crocodile Gena and Che-
burashka are especially familiar as stars of children's animated
films. A lesser known but very deserving poet is Vadim Levin (b.
1933) from Kharkov. In addition to his own verse, he has translated
English rhymes. His poetry is remarkable for his outstanding sense
of rhythm. Both Uspenskii and Levin first published collections in
1965. Less successful but still of interest are poems by Irina
Pivovarova (b. 1937) and Iunna Morits (b. 1937), whose first books for
children appeared in 1968 and 1969, respectively. While they also
rely heavily on folklore for inspiration, the nature of their poetry is
less spontaneous than that of Uspenskii and Levin.[62]

Of all the contemporary children's poets, Morits is the only one
who is a well-established adult poet. Others are known to write
adult poetry that for reasons not of their own making remains
largely unpublished. In this respect their careers bear a definite
resemblance to that of Kharms. Although the future appears more
auspicious for them than it was for him, their creative possibilities
are similarly limited.[63]

This situation brings us to an important aspect of Russian children's poetry—one that was already a consideration for Kharms in
the second half of the 1920s and that is true again in the 1960s, 1970s,
and into the 1980s. The fact is that much recent poetry written for
children has been motivated by more than merely an appreciation of
the child's point of view. To varying degrees it comes also from the
greater opportunity it offers poets to create imaginatively, unin-
hibitedly. Children's literature as a creative refuge is most easily
seen if one considers the graphic side of children's books. Even while
fantasy and experimentation in Soviet art are not officially sanc-
tioned, there is some room for other than realistic illustration in
books for children.

On the practical side, for poets who are unable to publish their
work for adults, children's literature remains a quite reliable way to
earn a living. At the same time, it is not without certain shortcomings. Writers with a conscience resist censorship and the dictates of
dogmatic editors, both forms of interference found in the world of
children's publishing too. Moshkovskaia's original manuscript of
Little Gray Goat, for example, was cut by one-third when it was
published, thanks to an editor who found much of the text too
provocative. Playful verbal experimentation is also difficult to get
past the typically censorious editor. Iurii Timofeev at Children's
World was a fortunate exception and an obvious product of the
"thaw."

After a burst of creativity in the 1960s, the vital spirit of the new children's poetry noticeably diminished in the 1970s. The already older generation of poets who came on the scene at the height of the "thaw" continued to write, but their pace became noticeably slower. New volumes appeared less frequently, and those that did appear often contained many poems reprinted from earlier volumes. The original creative impulse was thwarted as stricter external controls were imposed. A strong sense of lethargy, even despair, grew perceptible as the Soviet Union again began to experience greater cultural repression, which continues until the present. Although a second post-Stalin generation of poets has emerged, their poetry is on the whole less successful than that of the first generation. Especially now after Moshkovskaia's death, one is left with a strong sense of uncertainty about the future. The second flourishing period of Russian children's poetry has clearly come to an end.

However, the uncertainty of the future in no way diminishes the achievements of the past. The vantage point of the late twentieth century shows that a very rich poetic tradition for children has developed in Russia since Chukovskii first expressed his dissatisfaction with the state of affairs in 1907. Several major factors have been responsible for the evolution of that tradition. Of great importance was the recognition of the child as a child in the first decades of the twentieth century. The attention Chukovskii gave to early language acquisition and child psychology has shown that a crucial ingredient in good children's poetry is a proper understanding of the audience. Only poets who truly appreciate the nature of children, who are close to them in spirit, if not also in physical proximity, can succeed at the job. Another important factor was the discovery of English nursery rhymes by Chukovskii and Marshak, which then helped turn their attention to Russian children's folklore. Since the relationship between the nature of children and that of their folk rhymes is intimate, the technical lessons offered by the example of folklore has helped poets create in a manner comprehensible and appealing to children. Also vital to the appearance of imaginative poetry was the larger cultural environment in which it developed. The artistic ferment of the immediate postrevolutionary period, especially the experimental orientation of the futurists, played an important role in the development of the new poetry. Certainly the broader creative influence of the early twentieth-century Russian avant-garde cannot be overemphasized. Finally, the revolution, with its emphasis on the child's role in society, provided unprecedented opportunities for the publication of children's literature. Unfortunately, revolution was soon followed by increasing repression—first came the pedologists, intent on uprooting fantasy in children's literature, then the Stalinist dogma that effectively destroyed all creativity for another two decades. But with the "thaw" the strong motivating impulse of the 1920s helped effect a poetic revival despite the enforced pause of many years. The qualities that make the works of Chukovskii, Marshak, and Kharms so successful with children have reappeared in the best contemporary poetry of the post-Stalin era. The older poets served as both vital inspiration and yardstick for the "thaw" generation and will continue to do so for generations to come. That fact is the true measure of the greatness of the vanguard of Russian children's poets.

ON CHUKOVSKII'S "THE CROCODILE"

NADEZHDA KRUPSKAIA

Must this book be given to small children? A crocodile . . . Children have seen him in pictures, or even at the zoo. They know very little about him. We have so few books that describe the life of animals. At the same time children are terribly interested in the life of animals. Not horses, sheep, frogs, etc., but precisely those animals they have not seen and about whose lives they wish to know. That is a tremendous deficiency of our children's literature. But from "The Crocodile" children learn nothing about what they would like to learn. Instead of a story about the life of a crocodile, they will hear incredible balderdash about him.

Children, however, need not be given exclusively "positive" knowledge; they should also be given things for amusement: animals dressed as people are funny. It is funny to see a crocodile smoking a cigar and riding on an airplane. It is funny to see a little crocodile lying in bed, to see a lady crocodile in a ribbon and night shirt, to see an elephant in a hat, etc. It is also funny that the crocodile has a first name and patronymic, that the rhinoceros caught his horn on the threshold, and that the jackal played the piano. All of this amuses children, makes them happy. That is fine.

But along with amusement they are given something else. The people are depicted. The people roar, are angry, drag others to the police; the people are cowards, they tremble, they scream from fear. ("And the people [crowd] are chasing him, yelling and screaming . . ."; "The people got angry and called and screamed: 'Hey, hold him and tie him up! Quickly take him to the police station!'" "Everybody is trembling from fear, everyone is squealing from fear . . .")

To this picture are added peasants with "bowl-style" haircuts, who thank Vania with chocolate for his feat. This is already by no means an innocent, but an extremely malicious depiction, which perhaps a child cannot fully understand, but it penetrates his consciousness. The second part of "The Crocodile" depicts the bourgeois domestic conditions of the crocodile family: in connection with this the laughter arising from the fact that the crocodile swallowed a napkin out of fear hides the banality that is depicted and trains children not to notice it. The people reward Vania for valor, the crocodile gives presents to his countrymen and they embrace and kiss him in exchange. Into a child's brain creeps the idea that "they pay for good deeds, they buy sympathy."

The crocodile kisses the feet of the hippopotamus-tsar. He bares his soul before the tsar. The author puts into the crocodile's mouth an inspired speech, a parody of Nekrasov. . . . That parody of Nekrasov is not accidental. Chukovskii was editing a new edition of Nekrasov and provided it with his article "The Life of Nekrasov." Although this article is interspersed with praise of Nekrasov, it is penetrated through and through by a vividly expressed hatred of Nekrasov. Describing what Nekrasov observed in childhood, he notes: "When he was very young, he understood little of what he saw, and was a very ordinary landowner's son." The author further overemphasizes Nekrasov's noble origin: " . . . in essence, Nekrasov was a nobleman, the son of a landowner, the same kind of gentleman as Herzen, Turgenev, Ogarёv".

[There follow five similar paragraphs decrying Chukovskii's treatment of Nekrasov.]

Well fine. Let us return to "The Crocodile." From the above it is clear why this parody on Nekrasov is so strident in a children's book. Chukovskii was so carried away while writing a parody of Nekrasov that he forgot he was writing for little children . . . . The plot continues thus: under the influence of the devourer of children, the bourgeois crocodile who smokes cigars and strolls down Nevsky Prospect, the beasts go to free their brother-beasts languishing in cages. Everyone runs away from them out fear, but they are conquered by the hero Vania Vasil'chikov. However, the beasts had taken Lialia as a hostage, and so in order to free her, Vania frees the beasts: "I am giving freedom / to your people, / I am giving them freedom!"

What is the meaning of all this nonsense? What kind of political significance does it have? It clearly has some kind. But it is so carefully masked, that it is rather difficult to guess what it is. Or is it a simple collection of words? But it is not at all such an innocent collection. A hero who gives freedom to the people in order to redeem Lialia is a bourgeois touch that will not go past a child unnoticed. To teach a child to say all kinds of nonsense, to read all kinds of trash, may even be nice in bourgeois families, but it has nothing in common with the kind of upbringing we want to give our young generation. Such jabber shows disrespect toward the child. First he is deceived with gingerbread—the merry, innocent rhythms and comic images—and incidentally he is made to swallow some kind of dregs that will not pass without leaving a trace.

I think we must not give our children "The Crocodile," not because it is a fairy tale, but because it is bourgeois dregs.
(1928)

CHAPTER 1. KORNEI CHUKOVSKII AND HIS POETICS

1. The most complete biographical outline is by M.P. Sashkol'skaia, "Letopis zhizni i tvorchestva," in *Zhizn' i tvorchestvo Korneia Chukovskogo*, ed. Valentin Berestov (Moscow: Detskaia literature, 1978), 197–246. See also Miron Petrovskii, *Kniga o Kornee Chukovskom* (Moscow: Sovetskii pisatel', 1966). For a more general survey in English see Lauren G. Leighton, "Homage to Kornei Chukovsky," *Russian Review* 31 (1972): 38–48.

2. Mikhail Slonimskii, "Za mnogo let," *Vospominaniia o Kornee Chukovskom*, ed. K.I. Lozovskaia, Z.S. Papernyi, and E.Ts. Chukovskaia (Moscow: Sovetskii pisatel', 1977), 82.

3. He returned to England two more times, once on a peace mission with a delegation of Russian writers and journalists in 1916, and many years later for an honorary degree from Oxford University in 1962.

4. Chukovskii, "Priznaniia starogo skazochnika," *Literaturnaia Rossiia*, 23 Jan. 1970, p. 13. For a translation see "Confessions of an Old Story-teller," *Horn Book* 46 (1970): 577–91; 47 (1971): 28–39.

5. Significantly, by this time he was beginning to rear what grew into a large family. His eldest child Nikolai was born in 1904, followed by Lidiia in 1907, Boris in 1909, and Mariia, affectionately called Mura, in 1920.

6. Chukovskii, "Detskie zhurnaly," *Rech'*, 23 Dec. 1907, p. 4.

7. Chukovskii, "O detskom iazyke," *Rech'*, 14 Dec. 1909, p. 3.

8. I was able to see this volume in the Rare Books Room of the Lenin Library in Moscow.

9. Chukovskii, "Moia rabota i zhizn'," *Detskaia literatura*, no. 22 (1937): 40.

10. Chukovskii, "Ob ètikh skazkakh," *Sobranie sochinenii v shesti tomakh*, I (Moscow: Khudozhestvennaia literatura, 1965), 165.

11. Petrovskii, *Kniga o Kornee Chukovskom*, 127–28.

12. Ibid., 190–92; Chukovskii, "O sebe," *Sobranie sochinenii*, I, 10.

13. See Barry Scherr, "Notes on Literary Life in Petrograd, 1918–1922: A Tale of Three Houses," *Slavic Review* 36 (1977): 256–67.

14. Chukovskii, "Ob ètikh skazkakh," 166.

15. Ibid., 165–69; Petrovskii, *Kniga o Kornee Chukovskom*, 193.

16. Chukovskii, "Ob ètikh skazkakh," 169. Chukovskii's defense of topsy-turvy rhymes originally appeared as an article: "Lepye nelepitsy," *Russkii sovremennik*, no. 4 (1924): 178–93. In 1928 he included this in *Malen'kie deti*, the first edition of what later became *Ot dvukh do piati*. "People in cases" is an allusion to Chekhov's story "Man in a Case," which has as its hero a sycophantic petty bureaucrat, via an article by Gor'kii in defense of Marshak against the pedologists. (See ch. 5, n. 30) For a discussion of pedology (the study of the child) in the early Soviet period, see Raymond A. Bauer, *The New Man in Soviet Psychology* (Cambridge, Mass.: Harvard Univ. Press, 1952), 49–66.

17. For more on the pedological controversy, see Lidiia Chukovskaia, *V. laboratorii redaktora*, 2nd ed. (Moscow: Iskusstvo, 1963), 234–39.

18. Much of the debate appeared on the pages of the periodical *Kniga-detiam* in 1928. See also K. Sverdlova, "O 'Chukovshchine,'" *Krasnaia pechat'*, no. 9–10 (1928): 92–94.

19. Nadezhda Krupskaia, "O 'Krokodile' K. Chukovskogo," *Pravda*, 1 Feb. 1928, p. 5. This also appeared in *Kniga—detiam*, no. 2 (1928): 13–16.

20. Chukovskii, "K sporam o detskoi literature," *Literaturnaia gazeta*, 30 Dec. 1929, p. 2.

21. This is available in English: *The Silver Crest, My Russian Boyhood*, trans. Beatrice Stillman (New York: Holt, Rinehart and Winston, 1976).

22. Earlier he had translated Kipling (*Just So Stories* and *Rikki-Tikki-Tavi*, 1923), Lofting (*Doctor Dolittle*, 1925), and Raspail (*Munchausen*, 1928). Then he turned to Defoe (*Robinson Crusoe*, 1935) and Twain (*Tom Sawyer*, 1935; *The Prince and the Pauper*, 1936).

23. This attack was part of Stalin's renewed vigilance after a certain amount of cultural relaxation during the war. See P. Iudin, "Poshlaia i vrednaia strapnia K. Chukovskogo," *Pravda*, 1 Mar. 1944, p. 3.

24. Chukovskii would be deeply grieved to know the fate of his beloved library. In 1978 there was a mysterious fire, which most seriously damaged the shelves holding autographed editions. Without informing the Chukovskii family, the authorities removed all the books to storage. Visible damage to the exterior was repaired, but no steps were taken to restore the interior and to reopen the library to the public. This sad situation is a part of the apparently futile struggle against the Soviet bureaucracy being waged by the family to preserve the Chukovskii dacha in Peredelkino as a literary museum in memory of their famous father and grandfather. The Pasternak family is involved in a similar struggle over their dacha, only a few minutes' walk down the road from Chukovskii's. See *New York Times*, 23 Jan. 1982, p. 2.

25. See Marina Chukovskaia, "V zhizni i v trude," 168; Petrovskii, "Chitatel'," 379–80; and Margarita Aliger, "Dolgie progulki," 267–68; all in *Vospominaniia o Kornee Chukovskom*.

26. Cited in Vladimir Zaitsev, "Kornei Chukovskii i deti," *Doshkol'noe vospitanie*, no. 7 (1971): 55. See also the childhood reminiscences of Lidiia

Chukovskaia: "Na morskom beregu," *Sem'ia i shkola*, no. 9 (1972): 44–48; 10 (1972): 46–47; "Pamiati detstva (Glava iz knigi)," *Novyi zhurnal*, no. 128 (1977): 7–22.

27. Evgenii Shvarts, "Nekomnatnyi chelovek," *Neva*, no. 3 (1957): 203.

28. Throughout his life Chukovskii contributed frequent articles not only on children's language but on the subject of children in general. Only three significant gaps appear: the time of World War I and the revolution, the years of RAPP rule, and the latter period of Stalinism.

29. "Detskie zhurnaly," 3. This slogan echoes the attitude expressed by Lev Tolstoi when he opened his school for peasant children. See "Komu u kogo uchit'sia pisat', krest'ianskim rebiatam u nas ili nam u krest'ianskikh rebiat?" *Polnoe sobranie sochinenii*, VIII (Moscow: Khudozhestvennaia literatura, 1936), 301–24.

30. For this study I have primarily used *Malen'kie deti* (Moscow: Krasnaia gazeta, 1928) and *Ot dvukh do piati*, in *Sobranie sochinenii*, I, 333–725. References to the latter will be identified by page number following the quotation. For an abridged English version, see *From Two to Five*, trans. Miriam Morton (Berkeley: Univ. of California Press, 1963; rev. 1968). It should be noted that Chukovskii was sufficiently dissatisfied with Morton's translation to criticize her publicly. See *New Yorker* 42 (21 Jan. 1967): 81–84. Her response in self-defense followed shortly. See *New Yorker* 42 (18 Apr. 1967): 166–71. Chukovskii was upset primarily because Morton did not incorporate in subsequent editions the corrections he had asked her to make. She claimed she never received his list.

31. *Ot dvukh do piati*, 5th ed. (Leningrad: Khudozhestvennaia literatura, 1935), 5.

32. Chukovskii read widely in the area of child psychology, including works by James Sully, Frederick Tracy, and G.S. Hall. (See *Malen'kie deti*, 78) His interest in children's stages of development suggests the work of Jean Piaget, who began his lifelong observation of children in the early 1920s. Chukovskii's category "from two to five" comes close to Piaget's "pre-operational stage" (two to seven years). There is no evidence that Chukovskii was familiar with Piaget's theories, which only began to appear in Russian translation in the early 1960s.

33. *Malen'kie deti*, 12.

34. *Ibid.*, 37–38, 47.

35. Susanna Millar, *The Psychology of Play* (Baltimore: Penguin, 1968), 248.

36. *Malen'kie deti*, 38.

37. *Ibid.*, 38.

38. *Ibid.*, 63.

39. *Ibid.*, 42. For a recent discussion of binary meters, with reference to children's preference for trochees, see Daniel Laferrière, "Iambic vs. Trochaic: The Case of Russian," *International Review of Slavic Linguistics* 4 (1979): 81–136.

40. *Malen'kie deti,* 39.

41. See Iona and Peter Opie, *The Oxford Dictionary of Nursery Rhymes* (Oxford: Clarendon Press, 1951), 12–15.

42. Viktor Shklovskii, "Zaumnyi iazyk i poèziia," *Sborniki po teorii poèticheskogo iazyka,* I (Petrograd: Tip. Z. Sokolinskogo, 1916), 6–7.

43. John Holt, *How Children Learn* (New York: Pitman, 1967), 54.

44. Chukovskii's source for this was mothers' diaries. See *Malen'kie deti,* 58.

45. *Ibid.,* 68.

46. *Ibid.,* 57.

47. Iurii Tynianiov, "Iliustratsii," *Arkhaisty i novatory* (1929; rpt. Munich: Wilhelm Fink, 1967), 509. For an interesting discussion of illustration in children's books see "Questions to an Artist Who Is Also an Author (A conversation between Maurice Sendak and Virginia Haviland)," *Quarterly Journal of the Library of Congress* 28 (1971): 263–80.

48. Theodore Roethke, *On the Poet and his Craft,* ed. Ralph J. Mills, Jr. (Seattle: Univ. of Washington Press, 1965), 77.

49. Vladimir Maiakovskii, "Kak delat' stikhi," *Polnoe Sobranie sochinenii v trinadtsati tomakh,* XII (Moscow: Khudozhestvennia literatura, 1959), 106.

50. Holt, *How Children Learn,* 28. Modern developmental psycholinguistic theory has established children's tendency to emphasize the ends of words. In "Cognitive Prerequisites for the Development of Grammar," *Studies of Child Language Development,* ed. Charles Ferguson and Dan I. Slobin (New York: Holt, Rinehart and Winston, 1973), Slobin designates children's first operating principle: "Pay attention to the ends of words" (191).

51. Paul Hazard, *Books, Children and Men,* trans. Marguerite Mitchell (Boston: Horn Book, 1944), 81.

52. An apt example came from my daughter at 16 months of age. Before she knew how to use verbs as such, she used the word "go" as a noun referring to any motor vehicle.

53. Kenneth Koch, *Wishes, Lies and Dreams* (New York: Random, 1974), 2.

54. Samuil Marshak, "Dom, uvenchannyi globusom," *Sobranie sochinenii v vos'mi tomakh,* VII (Moscow: Khudozhestvennaia literatura, 1971), 568.

55. Chukovskii, "Priznaniia starogo skazochnika," 13.

56. Marshak, "O bol'shoi literature dlia malen'kikh," *Sobranie sochinenii,* VI, 208.

57. Stanislav Rassadin, *Tak nachinaiut zhit' stikhom (Kniga o poèzii dlia detei)* (Moscow: Detskaia literatura, 1967), 147.

58. For an application of these functions to Russian literature, see Hugh McLean, "The Development of Modern Russian Literature," *Slavic Review* 21 (1962): 389–410.

59. Frank and Theresa Caplan, *The Power of Play* (Garden City, N.Y.:

Anchor Press, 1974), 123. For a recent, lucid book on play in the lives of children, see Catherine Garvey, *Play* (Cambridge: Harvard Univ. Press, 1977). In ch. 5 ("Play with Language"), which begins with reference to Chukovskii, the author classifies social play with language into three types: spontaneous rhyming and word play, play with fantasy and nonsense, and play with speech acts and discourse conventions, all of which are found in Chukovskii's *skazki*. On sound play, see also Elinor O. Keenan, "Conversational Competence in Children," *Journal of Child Language* 1 (1974): 171.

60. Maksim Gor'kii, "Chelovek, ushi kotorogo zatknuty vatoi," *Pravda*, 19 Jan. 1930, p. 3.

61. Marc Soriano, "From Tales of Warning to Formulettes: The Oral Tradition in French children's Literature," *Yale French Studies* 43 (1969): 42–43.

62. Nikolai Chekhov, *Detskaia literatura* (Moscow: Pol'za, 1909), 152.

CHAPTER 2. CHILDREN'S FOLKLORE

1. This topic is treated today both in general works on the Russian oral tradition and in histories of children's literature. See, for example, *Russkoe narodnoe tvorchestvo*, ed. Petr Bogatyrëv et al. (Moscow: Vysshaia shkola, 1966), 292–302; *Russkaia detskaia literatura*, ed. F.I. Setin (Moscow: Prosveshchenie, 1972), 16–34.

2. See, for example, *Detskaia kukla ili izbrannye basni, skazki, povesti i proch. sluzhashchiia dlia pol'zy i uveseleniia detei* (St. Petersburg, 1788).

3. Ol'ga Kapitsa, *Detskii fol'klor* (Leningrad: Priboi, 1928), 13. *Uchitel'*, a journal for teachers and parents, appeared twice a month from 1861 to 1870, in the period of "great reforms."

4. Lev Tolstoi, "Iasno-polianskaia shkola za noiabr' i dekabr' mesiatsy," *Polnoe sobranie sochinenii*, VIII, 60.

5. Cited in Kapitsa, *Detskii fol'klor*, 13.

6. For a recent selection of Dal's work for children with illustrations by V.K. Konashevich, see *Starik godovik. Skazki, zagadki, poslovitsy, igry*, ed. Ivan Khalturin (Moscow: Detskaia literatura, 1979).

7. P.A. Bessonov, *Detskie pesni* (Moscow: Morozov, 1868). Kapitsa gives due credit to the groundwork laid by Bessonov in her survey of early collectors in *Detskii fol'klor* (14–15), and in a separate tribute, "Pervyi sbornik detskogo fol'klora," *Detskii byt i fol'klor* (Leningrad: Izdatel'stvo gosudarstvennogo russkogo geograficheskogo obshchestva, 1930), 11–12. Of the modern poets, Samuil Marshak was especially appreciative of Bessonov's good taste, which he found lacking in the erudite transcriptions of Shein. See "Dve besedy S. Ia. Marshaka s L.K. Chukovskoi," *Sobranie sochinenii*, VII, 588.

8. N.V. Novikov, "P.V. Shein kak sostavitel' sbornika *Russkie narodnye pesni* in *Russkii fol'klor: Issledovaniia i materialy*, V (1960): 395.

9. Shein first published his transcriptions in *Chteniia obshchestva istorii i drevnostei rossiiskikh Moskovskogo universiteta*, 1868. With additional material they appeared as a separate book, *Russkie narodnye pesni*, 1870.

Before his death the Academy of Sciences published a further expanded edition, *Velikoruss v svoikh pesniakh, obriadakh, verovaniiakh, skazkakh, legendakh i t. p.* (St. Petersburg, 1898). See Kapitsa, *Detskii fol'klor,* 17–19; and Novikov, "Shein kak sostavitel'," esp. 403–4.

10. Among the best-known local collections is Aleksandr Mozharovskii, *Iz zhizni krest'ianskikh detei Kazanskoi gubernii. Potekhi, zabavy, ostroty, prozvishcha, stishki i pesni* (Kazan: Tipografiia G.M.Vecheslava, 1882). Of collections devoted to a specific genre, outstanding is E.A. Pokrovskii, *Detskie igry* (Moscow, 1887).

11. V.P. Anikin, *Russkie narodnye poslovitsy, pogovorki, zagadki i detskii fol'klor* (Moscow: Uchpedgiz, 1957), 123.

12. The best introduction to Vinogradov's work is his survey article posthumously published by A.N. Martynova, "Detskii fol'klor," *Iz istorii russkoi fol'kloristiki,* ed. A.A. Gorelov (Leningrad: Nauka, 1978), 158–88.

13. For an outline of her accomplishments, see G. Vinogradov, "O.I. Kapitsa," *Sovetskii fol'klor,* no. 7 (1940): 235–39.

14. Vinogradov, "Detskii fol'klor," 166–67.

15. Cited in Vinogradov, "O.I. Kapitsa," 238.

16. One conclusion he drew from listening to children's language was that they "learn the language from the people." He cites frequent examples of children's lexical and grammatical constructions which, although they appear to be incorrect or nonexistent in modern Russian, he has identified as archaisms or dialecticisms. Children's manipulation of semantics and morphology occurs within the tradition of the language they have heard from birth. "In an attempt to imitate adults, children create words that do not seem out of keeping with the language" (*Ot dvukh do piati,* 345). Chukovskii provides many examples of children's literalism, which he compares to "folk etymology." From my own experience I can add one he would have appreciated. At age two my daughter used the word "wipecloth" for washcloth.

17. Neither the work of Kapitsa nor Vinogradov has been republished.

18. Shein, *Detskie pesni,* in *Chteniia obshchestva istorii,* 5.

19. Shein, *Velikoruss v svoikh pesniakh,* 6. Unless otherwise noted, all examples come from either the 1868 or 1895 edition of Shein's collection and will be identified by year of publication and page.

20. One typical recurring line—"Prianiki pekutsia" (Gingerbread is baking)—inspired a collection of folk rhymes magnificently illustrated by Tat'iana Mavrina, an artist who has done much to develop contemporary interest in Russian folk culture. See her children's book *Prianiki pekutsia, kotu v lapy ne daiutsia* (Moscow: Malysh, 1966). See also Vladimir Kostin, *Tat'iana Alekseevna Mavrina* (Moscow: Sovetskii khudoznik, 1966).

21. *Raduga: skazki, pesenki, poteshki,* ed. L. Ia. Libet (Moscow: Detskaia literatura, 1976), 22–24. With illustrations by Iurii Vasnetsov, this volume is a most handsome collection of children's folklore.

22. *Russkoe narodnoe poèticheskoe tvorchestvo,* ed. N.I. Kravtsov (Moscow: Prosveshchenie, 1971), 362.

23. *Khrestomatiia po detskoi literature,* ed. O.V. Alekseeva and V.I. Sillander, 2nd ed. (Moscow: Gosuchpedgiz, 1954), 11.

24. Kapitsa, *Detskii fol'klor,* 178.

25. This statistic is from Vinogradov, "Detskii fol'klor," 178. Kapitsa's figure is "from 4 to 10," *Detskii fol'klor,* 192. My own computations, based on Shein's 1868 edition, give an average of 13 lines. In Shein there are 48 texts over 12 lines long, and of them only 18 contain more than 20 lines.

26. Kapitsa, *Detskii fol'klor,* 193.

27. Kapitsa, (*ibid.,* 193) says 4 to 6 syllables per line predominate. Vinogradov ("Detskii fol'klor," 180) gives three ranges: from 3 to 5, 4 to 7, 6 to 8.

28. Vinogradov, "Detskii fol'klor," 180.

29. Ibid., 181.

30. From the time my daughter began to enjoy being read to, sometime before her first birthday, her favorite book for over a year was a large-format illustrated collection of nursery rhymes.

31. In 1870 the famous collector of folktales A.N. Afanas'ev published *Russkie detskie skazki.* Although his book was not reprinted until 1890, in the succeeding ten years it went through eighteen editions, demonstrating a marked interest in folktales for children at the turn of the twentieth century. See N.N. Kononov, "Detskaia literatura 60-kh godov XIX stoletiia," *Russkaia detskaia literatura,* 139.

32. I have selected versions reworked for children, since those are the ones they hear most: *Russkie narodnye skazki* (Moscow: Detskaia literatura, 1960).

33. Chukovskii, *Ot dvukh do piati,* 552.

34. Bruno Bettelheim, *The Uses of Enchantment: The Meaning and Importance of Fairy Tales* (New York: Vintage, 1977), 5.

## CHAPTER 3. PREREVOLUTIONARY POETRY

1. See Philippe Ariès, *Centuries of Childhood: A Social History of Family Life* (New York: Vintage, 1962).

2. Nikolai Chekhov, *Detskaia literatura* (Moscow: Pol'za 1909), 34–35. In this first survey of Russian children's literature, Chekhov treats a diversity of areas with much understanding. He continued his work on the history of children's literature into the 1920s. See *Materialy po istorii russkoi detskoi literatury (1750–1855),* ed. A.K. Pokrovskaia and N.V. Chekhov, 2 vols. (Moscow: Institut metodov vneshkol'noi raboty otdel detskogo chteniia, 1927).

3. Among those I had an opportunity to examine are: *Detskii vestnik* (1915), *Zvezdochka* (1842–63), *Podsnezhnik* (1858–62), *Detskoe chtenie* (1869–90), *Zadushevnoe slovo* (1877–1917), *Rodnik* (1882–1909).

4. E.P. Privalova, "I.A. Krylov," *Russkaia detskaia literatura,* 76–77; see also *Materialy po istorii russkoi detskoi literatury,* 59.

5. According to the Lenin Library catalogue, Krylov's fables have been appearing regularly in children's editions since 1892.

6. One of the most beautiful recent editions of "Tsar Saltan," for example, has good quality reproductions of Ivan Bilibin's charming art nouveau illustrations. It is available in English prose translation from Progress Publishers in Moscow. The most fanciful contemporary illustrations are by T. Mavrina. Editions illustrated by her include: *Skazka o zolotom petushke* (Moscow: Malysh, 1971), and *Skazka o mërtvoi tsarevne i o semi bogatyriakh* (Moscow: Sovetskaia Rossiia, 1972).

7. Marshak devoted two articles to Pushkin: "O Pushkine, o detiakh i o detskoi literature," *Sobranie sochinenii*, VI, 385–91; "Zametki o skazkakh Pushkina," in ibid., VII, 7–17. Although Chukovskii has no separate article on Pushkin, there are numerous references to him in *Ot dvukh do piati.*

8. N.V. Izmailov, "Primechaniia," in V.A. Zhukovskii, *Sobranie sochinenii*, III (Moscow-Leningrad: Khudozhestvennaia literatura, 1960), 538.

9. A daughter was born in 1842, a son in 1845. I.M. Semenko, "Primechaniia," in Zhukovskii, *Sobranie sochinenii*, II, 470.

10. See, for example, "Ptichka," *Khrestomatiia dlia malen'kikh detei,* ed. L.N. Eliseeva (Moscow: Prosveshchenie, 1972), 112.

11. Some scholars suggest Pushkin rewrote the first four lines, but Azadovskii finds that improbable. He considers it more likely that Pushkin simply made some corrections. It is also said Pushkin intended to publish an edition with colored pictures. His desire was realized in part by the appearance of *lubok* (chapbook) editions in the countryside, preceding the first complete edition in 1856. See M. Azadovskii's introduction to *Konëk-gorbunok, Stikhotvoreniia* (Leningrad: Sovetskii pisatel', 1961).

12. A.P. Babushkina, *Istoriia russkoi detskoi literatury* (Moscow: Gosuchpedgiz, 1948), 307.

13. Usually noted in the history of children's poetry is the work of Aleksei Pleshcheev (1825–1893), who addressed a number of poems to children. Most of them were written in the 1870s and appeared together in a special section of the 1887 edition of his work. A few years later he published *Dedushkiny pesni* (1891), where he also included poems not originally intended for children. See "Primechaniia," in A. Pleshcheev, *Izbrannoe* (Moscow: Khudozhestvennaia literatura, 1960), 654. As Marshak justifiably stated, "What Pleshcheev wrote was literary philanthropy, crumbs from the literary table of adults." ("O nasledstve i nasledstvennosti v detskoi literature," *Sobranie sochinenii*, VII, 296.)

14. For a discussion of Carroll in Russian translation, see Simon Karlinsky, "Anya in Wonderland: Nabokov's Russified Lewis Carroll," *Triquarterly,* no. 17 (Winter 1970): 310–15. The best Russian version is Boris Zakhoder, *Prikliucheniia Alisy v Strane chudes,* 3rd ed. (Moscow: Detskaia literatura, 1977). Lear has appeared in Marshak's translation; see *Sobranie sochinenii,* III, 705–30.

15. Viktor Shkovskii, *Staroe i novoe (Kniga statei o detskoi literature)* (Moscow: Detskaia literatura, 1966), 11.

16. A basic dissatisfaction with Russian children's literature at the turn of the century is expressed throughout Chukovskii's and Marshak's numerous essays on the subject. Tynianov's spirited protest is voiced in his article "Kornei Chukovskii," *Detskaia literatura,* no. 4 (1939): 24–26.

17. E.S. Litvin, "Obshchaia kharakteristika detskoi literatury kontsa XIX–nachala XX veka," in *Russkaia detskaia literatura,* ed. Setin, 289–90.

18. Marshak, "O nasledstve," 297. See also "Shchedryi talant," *Sobranie sochinenii,* VI, 364.

19. Shklovskii, *Staroe i novoe,* 11.

20. "Questions to an Artist Who is Also an Author," 274–75.

21. Aleksandr Blok, *Zapisnye knizhki* (Moscow: Khudozhestvennaia literatura, 1965), 269–70. He was invited to review the book by his friend Poliksena Solov'ëva.

22. Marshak, "Shchedryi talant," 364; "O nasledstve," 295. Pleshcheev is identified in n. 13 above.

23. Chukovskii, *Materiam o detskikh zhurnalakh* (St. Petersburg: Russkaia skoropechatnia, 1911), 18. "Created legend" is the title of a novel by the symbolist Fëdor Sologub.

24. The poems can be found in the following: Konstantin Bal'mont, *Stikhotvoreniia* (Leningrad: Sovetskii pisatel', 1969); Aleksandr Blok, *Sobranie sochinenii,* V. (Moscow-Leningrad: Khudozhestvenaia literatura, 1960).

25. Chukovskii, *Materiam o detskikh zhurnalakh,* 34–35.

26. Tynianov, "Kornei Chukovskii," 24; Marshak, "O bol'shoi literature dlia malen'kikh," VI, 209.

27. Walter de la Mare, *Songs of Childhood* (1902; rpt. New York: Dover, 1968).

28. For further biographical details, see L.A. Spiridonova (Evstigneeva), *Russkaia satiricheskaia literatura nachala XX veka* (Moscow: Nauka, 1977), 170–78.

29. Chukovskii, "Sasha Chërnyi," *Sobranie sochinenii,* II, 386.

30. The collections are *Zhar-ptitsa,* ed. K. Chukovskii and A. Benois (St. Petersburg: Shipovnik, 1912); and *Golubaia knizhka* (St. Petersburg: Izdanie Popovoi, n.d.), a project inspired by Gor'kii. *Tuk-tuk!* (Moscow: Sytin, 1913) contains twelve poems, eight of which were published previously.

31. See Sasha Chërnyi, *Detskii ostrov* (1921; rpt. Paris: Lev, 1980).

32. Chukovskii, "Sasha Chërnyi," 394.

33. *Ibid.,* 374.

34. Chërnyi, *Stikhotvoreniia* (Leningrad: Sovetskii pisatel', 1960), 238.

35. Soviet critics of children's poetry tend to underplay or ignore Chërnyi's role. As an émigré he fell into disfavor by the end of the 1920s. It is surprising, therefore, to find a flattering, if brief, mention of him in the 1930s: Boris Begak, "Vesëlaia knizhka," *Detskaia literatura,* no. 5 (1935): 12. The fact of his death may have made it easier to write about him. More

recently a small edition of his poems for children appeared: *Chto komu nravitsia* (Moscow: Detskaia literatura, 1976).

36. Chërnyi, *Stikhotvoreniia,* 499. Further references will be identified in the text.

### CHAPTER 4. CHUKOVSKII'S *SKAZKI*

1. Chukovskii, "Priznaniia starogo skazochnika," 13.

2. Ibid.

3. Ibid. All these men were important collectors of the oral tradition in 19th-century Russia. Ivan Snegirëv (1793–1868) specialized in proverbs, Pëtr Kireevskii (1808–1856) collected folk songs, Pavel Rybnikov (1831–1885) and Aleksandr Gil'ferding (1831–1872) are known for their transcriptions of epic songs, while Elpidifor Barsov (1836–1917) included in his research the theme of earlier Russian history as reflected in folklore. See ch. 2 for mention of the specifically child-oriented work of Afanas'ev and Shein.

4. Chukovskii, "Futuristy," *Sobranie sochinenii,* VI, 210.

5. Aleksei Kruchënykh, *Sobstvennye rasskazy, stikhi, i pesni detei* (Moscow: tip. Cit, 1923).

6. Vladimir Markov, *Russian Futurism: A History* (Berkeley: Univ. of California Press, 1968), 16–22. See also Vera Kalina-Levine, "Through the Eyes of the Child: The Artistic Vision of Elena Guro," *Slavic and East European Journal* 25 (1981): 30–43.

7. See Nikolai Stepanov, *Velimir Khlebnikov, Zhizn' i tvorchestvo* (Moscow: Sovetskii pisatel, 1975).

8. Chukovskii, "Maiakovskii," *Sobranie sochinenii,* II, 351.

9. Chukovskii, "Futuristy," 232.

10. Iurii Tynianov, "O Khlebnikove," *Arkhaisty i novatory,* 586.

11. Stepanov, *Khlebnikov,* 90.

12. Ibid., 49, 211.

13. Ibid., 68.

14. Petrovskii, "Glubina postizheniia," *V mire knig,* no. 8 (1977): 84.

15. *Ot dvukh do piati,* 639.

16. Stepanov, *Khlebnikov,* 72.

17. See, for example, Markov, *The Longer Poems of Velimir Khlebnikov* (Berkeley: Univ. of California Press, 1962), 30.

18. Stepanov, *Khlebnikov,* 115.

19. Tynianov, "Kornei Chukovskii," 25.

20. Chukovskii, "Telefon," *Sobranie sochinenii,* I, 199. Unless otherwise identified, subsequent quotations from the poetry are from this volume and will be designated by page (and title when necessary) following the quotation.

21. From Re-Mi on, illustrators of Chukovskii's *skazki* have often included caricatures of the author in their work. See Vladimir Glotser, "On 'Velikii umyval'nik, znamenityi moidodyr'," in *Zhizn' i tvorchestvo Korneia Chukovskogo,* 44–54.

22. These three lines are quoted by Petrovskii, *Kniga o Kornee Chukovskom,* 23. I could not locate the poem but found one that begins in a suspiciously similar manner ("Ėkzoticheskie triolety").

> Zhil-byl zelënyi krokodil,
> Arshina, ètak, na chetyre.
> On byl v rastsvete iunykh sil,
> I po kharakteru on byl
> Pozhalui, samyi milyi v mire.
> Zelënyi ètot krokodil
> Arshina, ètak, na chetyre.

N. Agnivtsev, *Stikhotvoreniia* (San Paulo: Kniga, 1960), 39. Perhaps Petrovskii was quoting from memory. Agnivtsev emigrated soon after the revolution but returned to the Soviet Union within a few years. In the second half of the 1920s he published a considerable quantity of second-rate children's poetry.

23. Rassadin, *Tak nachinaiut zhit' stikhom,* 30.

24. Ibid.

25. Cited in Petrovskii, *Kniga O Kornee Chukovskom,* 125–26.

26. See Chukovskii on Severianin's interpretation of children in "Futuristy," 210–11.

27. Petrovskii, *Kniga o Kornee Chukovskom,* 216. For an expression of Chukovskii's attitude toward literary parody, see his letter to Gor'kii (1930), " 'Ia liubliu Leningrad liubov'iu pisatel'a ...,' " *Zvezda,* no. 8 (1972): 199.

28. Rassadin, *Tak nachinaiut zhit' stikhom,* 33.

29. Both Rassadin and Petrovskii make this same point. The poem is cited by Petrovskii, *Kniga o Kornee Chukovskom,* 217.

30. First published in Kharkov in a lithographed edition of 50. See "Primechaniia," V.V. Khlebnikov, *Sobranie sochinenii,* I (1928; rpt. Munchen: Wilhelm Fink Verlag, 1968), 315.

31. Khlebnikov, *Sobranie sochinenii,* 189.

32. Ibid., 188.

33. Ibid., 184.

34. Several images in Maiakovskii's works find echoes in Chukovskii's *skazki.* The revolt of objects in "Moidodyr" recalls a similar revolt at the end of Act I of *Vladimir Maiakovskii, Tragediia* (1914). Fedora's reconciliation with her kitchen utensils in "Fedorino gore" is not unlike that between the things and the unclean ones in the last act of *Misteriia-buff* (1918).

35. *Ot dvukh do piati,* 724.

36. "Priznaniia starogo skazochnika," 30 Jan. 1970, pp. 13, 16; *Ot dvukh do piati,* 724–25.

37. See P.A. Rudnev, "Opyt opisaniia i semanticheskoi interpretatsii polimetricheskoi struktury A. Bloka 'Dvenadtsat',' " *Trudy po russkoi i slavianskoi filologii,* XVIII (Tartu: Uchënye zapiski Tartuskogo gosudarstvennogo universiteta, 1971), 195–221.

38. V.E. Kholshevnikov, "Pereboi ritma," *Russkaia sovetskaia poèziia i stikhovedenie* (Materialy mezhvuzovskoi konferentsii) (Moscow: Ministerstvo prosveshcheniia RSFSR, 1969), 173–84.

39. Kholshevnikov wisely warns of the impossibility of such generalizations (ibid., 178).

40. The rhythm and sounds of Chukovskii's lines strongly echo a poetic fragment by Khlebnikov: "Tam, gde zhili sviristeli, / Gde kachalis' tikho eli, / Gde shumeli zvonko eli, / Pro-leteli, uleteli / Staia lëgkikh / Vremirei." *Sobranie sochinenii* II, 276).

41. René Wellek and Austin Warren, *Theory of Literature*, 3rd ed. (New York: Harcourt, Brace & World, 1961), 158.

42. Simon Karlinsky, *Marina Tsvetaeva: Her Life and Art* (Berkeley: Univ. of California Press, 1966), 147. *Iavlennost'* is a difficult word to translate due to its semantic complexity. Besides "displayfulness," it also conveys the sense of "openness," "appearance," and "occurence," all of which are contained in Tsvetaeva's statement. I am indebted to Hugh McLean for his adroit translation of Tsvetaeva's comment.

43. Instances of the crocodile's swallowing things are found in "Tarakanishche," "Moidodyr," "Barmalei," and "Kradenoe solntse."

44. *Ot dvukh do piati*, 707.

45. Vladimir Leibson, "Poètika skazok Chukovskogo," *Detskaia literatura. 1960 god* (Moscow: Detgiz, 1961), 132.

46. Osip Brik, "Zvukovye povtory," *Poètika* (Petrograd, 1919). Rpt. in *Two Essays on Poetic Language*, Michigan Slavic Materials, No. 5 (Ann Arbor: Dept. of Slavic Languages and Literatures, 1964), 1–45.

47. *Ot dvukh do piati*, 712–14.

48. Ibid., 712.

49. According to several native Russians, Aibolit is the only one of these names that children understand literally. Moidodyr (wash until there are holes) is usually taken as a proper name rather than three meaningful words. Mukha-tsokotukha is onomatopoetic, from the verb *tsokotat'* (to speak nonstop). Barmalei is said to come from a street name in Leningrad; see Lev Uspenskii, *Zametki starogo peterburzhtsa* (Leningrad: Lenizdat, 1970), 462–63. The second part of Akula karakula may be seen as a playful combination of *akula* (shark) and *karakatitsa* (cuttlefish), or possibly as a contamination from *karaul* (guard).

50. Listening to my daughter at age three, I was surprised to see how frequently she made imaginative comparisons with the word "like."

51. It is likely Chukovskii's use of wild African animals was influenced by his familiarity with Kipling's *Just So Stories*, which originally appeared in English in 1902. "Limpopo," of course, comes from Kipling. Another possible literary source for exotic animals could have been the poetry of Nikolai Gumilëv, whose collections of 1908 and 1910 included such poems as "Nosorog," "Kenguru," and "Popugai."

52. Vera Smirnova, *O detiakh i dlia detei* (Moscow: Detskaia literatura, 1967), 29–30.

53. Petrovskii, *Kniga o Kornee Chukovskom*, 252.

54. See ch. 5 in Chukovskii's *Masterstvo Nekrasova*, in *Sobranie sochinenii*, IV, 680–721. For a thought-provoking study of the "adult content" of Chukovskii's skazki, see E.M. Neëlov, "Perestupaia vozrastnye granitsy," *Problemy detskoi literatury* (Petrozavodsk: Petrozavodskii gosudarstvennyi universitet, 1976), 53–72.

55. Chukovskii, *Chudo-derevo i drugie skazki* (Moscow: Detskaia literatura, 1971), 117–18.

56. Kaverin, "Ia—dobryi lev," *Zhizn' i tvorchestvo Korneia Chukovskogo*, 104. Kaverin reminds the reader that such lines as the following, from "Telefon" and "Tarakanishche," respectively, have become common expressions: "Esli mogu, pomogu"; "Okh, nelëgkaia èto rabota— / iz bolota tashchit' begemota!"

CHAPTER 5. SAMUIL MARSHAK

1. Samuil Marshak, "Dom, uvenchannyi globusom," *Sobranie sochinenii*, VII, 55–56.

2. Chukovskii, *Vysokoe iskusstvo*, in *Sobranie sochinenii*, III, 455–57.

3. Ibid., 464.

4. Marshak, "Dve besedy S.Ia. Marshaka s L.K. Chukovskoi," *Sobranie sochinenii*, VII, 577.

5. I learned this and many other details of Marshak's life during an interview in Moscow in March 1972 with his late son Immanuil, his literary executor, who since then published in preliminary form the first part of his father's biography: "Ot detstva k detiam. Glavy iz biograficheskoi knigi," in *Zhizn' i tvorchestvo Marshaka (Marshak i detskaia literatura)*, ed. B. Galanov, I. Marshak, and M. Petrovskii (Moscow: Detskaia literatura, 1975), 347–486.

6. Marshak, *V nachale zhizni*, in *Sobranie sochineii*, VI, 84. In this short book of childhood reminiscences Marshak describes his experiences until his stay with Gor'kii's family in Yalta. It is available in English: *At Life's Beginning: Some Pages of Reminiscences*, trans. Katherine Hunter Blair (London: Golancz, 1964).

7. Ibid., 85.

8. Ibid., 142–50.

9. Ibid., 173–80.

10. Marshak, "Ot detstva k detiam," 402, 407; Iu. Ia. Marshak-Fainberg, "Chastitsa vremeni," "Ia dumal, chuvstoval, ia zhil . . ." (*Vospominaniia o S. Ia. Marshake*), ed. B.E. Galanov, I.S. Marshak, and Z.S. Papernyi (Moscow: Sovetskii pisatel', 1971). 29.

11. Marshak, "O sebe," *Sobranie sochinenii*, I, 5.

12. Ibid., 9.

13. Marshak, Letter to A.M. Gor'kii (9 Mar. 1927), *Sobranie sochinenii*, III, 94.

14. A. Viktorova, "V Petrozavodskoi detskoi kolonii," *"Ia dumal, chuvstvoval, ia zhil . . .,"* 125.

15. Marshak, Letter to E.P. Peshkova (20 Nov. 1915), *Sobranie sochinenii,* VIII, 85.

16. Soon Marshak was again rearing his own family. His first son, Immanuil, was born in 1917; the second, Iakov, in 1925.

17. Viktorova, "V Petrozavodskoi detskoi kolonii," 127.

18. See A. Bogdanova, "Detskii gorodok," *"Ia dumal, chuvstvoval, ia zhil . . .,"* 128–47.

19. See *Teatr dlia detei* (Krasnodar, 1922).

20. For a history of the theater, see *Leningradskii teatr iunykh zritelei,* ed. S. Druzhinina and N. Mervol'f (Leningrad: Iskusstvo, 1972).

21. See E. Privalova, "U istokov," 158–61, and E. Bereskaia, "Krestnyi otets," 149, both in *"Ia dumal, chuvstvoval, ia zhil . . . ."*

22. The play was published only posthumously. Marshak did not actively revive his interest in children's theater until World War II. In the early 1940s he wrote a first version of *Umnye veshchi,* which he was reworking for the Malyi Theater in Moscow at the time of his death. The Malyi first performed it in 1965. In 1943 he wrote *Dvenadtsat' mesiatsev,* which was produced by Moscow's TIuZ in 1947, the Moscow Art Theater in 1948, and won a Stalin Prize in 1951. See I.A. Notkina, "Primechaniia," in Marshak, *Sobranie sochinenii,* II, 587–91.

23. The nursery rhymes were the first truly children's poems he translated. In 1914–1916 he had begun publishing his versions of William Blake, including some of the *Songs of Innocence* and *Songs of Experience,* which are sometimes considered in the context of children's poetry although they were written from a distinctly adult point of view. Marshak's other translations of children's poetry include poems by Wilhelm Busch, Lewis Carroll, A.A. Milne, Edward Lear, and Gianni Rodari.

24. Annotated reprints of the original editions of several of Marshak's picture books from the 1920s appeared a half-century later in two reprint series in Leningrad (Khudozhnik RSFSR) and Moscow (Sovetskii khudozhnik).

25. Marshak, "Dve besedy," 577.

26. See, for example, D. Kal'm, "Kuda nos ego vedët . . . ," *Literaturnaia gazeta,* 16 Dec. 1929, p. 2.

27. Isai Rakhtanov, *Rasskazy po pamiati* (Moscow: Detskaia literatura, 1971), 9, 15; see also Lidiia Chukovskaia, *V laboratorii redaktora,* 219–334.

28. Marshak, Letter to Gor'kii (9 Mar. 1927), *Sobranie Sochinenii,* III, 94.

29. *Ezh,* an acronym for *Ezhemesiachnyi zhurnal* (monthly magazine), a periodical for primary school children, came into existence in 1928 and survived until 1935; *Chizh,* or *Chrezvychainyi interesnyi zhurnal* (extraordinarily interesting magazine), for preschool children, appeared from 1930 to 1938.

30. Unfortunately, Marshak himself did not survive the era without

some capitulation. In 1930, at the height of the proletarian campaign against the *skazka*, he decided to look for new material. Thinking his work in children's literature was effectively over, he went to the Krasnodar region to write about a collective farm. Then Gor'kii published two articles in *Pravda* defending imagination in children's literature, with special reference to Marshak. Gor'kii's intervention temporarily helped secure Marshak's professional survival. See "Chelovek, ushi kotorogo zatknuty vatoi," *Pravda* (19 Jan. 1930), p. 3, and "O bezotvetstvennykh liudiakh i o detskoi knige nashikh dnei," *Pravda* (16 Mar. 1930), p. 2.

31. Marshak, Letter to Razova (26 Apr. 1962), *Sobranie sochinenii,* VIII, 422.

32. Marshak, "O bol'shoi literature dlia malen'kikh," *Sobranie sochinenii,* VI, 208.

33. For a fuller description of those bleak events, see L. Chukovskaia, *V. laboratorii redaktora,* 321–23.

34. Marshak, *Vospitanie slovom,* in *Sobranie sochinenii,* VII, 275.

35. Chukovskii, *Vysokoe iskusstvo,* in *Sobranie sochinenii,* III, 463.

36. Petrovskii, "V nachale bylo slovo narodnoe," *Doshkol'noe vospitanie,* no. 1 (1965): 111.

37. Marshak, Letter to I.M. Dol'nikov (27 Apr. 1955), *Sobranie sochinenii,* VIII, 281.

38. Chukovskii, *Vysokoe iskusstvo,* 463.

39. Marshak, *Sobranie sochinenii,* II, 85. The next four rhymes are from this volume and will be identified by page following the citation.

40. For the original edition Marshak used drawings by Cecil Oldin. See Letter to Matafonov (7 May 1963), *Sobranie sochinenii,* VIII, 471–72.

41. Marshak, *Sobranie sochinenii,* I, 47. Unless otherwise indicated, all subsequent poems are from this volume and will be designated by page following the citation.

42. See "Primechaniia," in Marshak, *Sobranie sochinenii,* VII, 621.

43. Marshak, Letter to Razova (20 Apr. 1962), *Sobranie sochinenii,* VIII, 418.

44. According to L. Panteleev, along with Pushkin and Blake, Khlebnikov was one of Marshak's favorite poets. See "O Marshake," *Novyi mir,* no. 10 (1966): 145.

45. See "Primechaniia," in Marshak, *Sobranie sochinenii,* I, 508–509.

46. Letter to Razova, 421.

47. Chukovskii, "Marshak," *Novyi mir,* no. 11 (1962): 224.

48. N. Vengrov, "S. Ia. Marshak," *Istoriia russkoi sovetskoi literatury,* III (Moscow: Nauka, 1968), 395.

49. Marshak, "Dve besedy," 585. Chukovskii confirms Marshak's love of children's imperious willfulness in *Vysokoe iskusstvo,* 456.

50., Dina B. Crockett, "Marshak's Children's Verses through a Computer," *Slavic and East European Journal* 13 (1969): 84.

51. When "Mister Tvister" first appeared in *Ezh,* Marshak was criticized and forced to remove the conspiracy of hotel clerks against a

foreign tourist, a change to which he was never reconciled. See Marshak, Letter to D.M. Balashov (24 Jan. 1963), *Sobranie sochinenii*, VIII, 460–61.

52. Aleksandr Tvardovskii, "O poèzii Marshaka," *Novyi mir*, no. 2 (1968): 235–42. Not only are some of his children's poems considered to be among his best, there are also unifying links between his work for children and for adults, especially in his last period of creativity (1941–1964).

### CHAPTER 6. THE OBERIU POETS

1. For further details of the Oberiu children's "collective," see I. Rakhtanov, *Rasskazy po pamiati* (Moscow: Detskaia literatura, 1971), 109–44; Igor' Bakhterev, "Kogda my byli molodymi," *Vospoinaniia o Zabolotskom*, ed. E.V. Zabolotskaia and A.V. Makedonov (Moscow: Sovetskii pisatel', 1977), 55–85. See also Gertrude König, "Eine Kinderlyrik der Gruppe OBERIU," *Wiener Slawistischer Almanach* 1 (1978): 57–78.

2. For a short survey of his life and works, see Irina H. Corten, "Evgeny Lvovich Shvarts: A Biographical Sketch," *Russian Literature Triquarterly*, no. 16 (1979): 223–43.

3. Nikolai Chukovskii, in *My znali Evgeniia Shvartsa* (Leningrad-Moscow: Iskusstvo, 1966), 25.

4. Ibid., 28.

5. Mikhail Slonimskii, in *My znali Evgeniia Shvartsa*, 18.

6. Ibid.

7. Evgenii Shvarts, "Stranitsy dnevnika," *Redaktor i kniga* (Moscow: Iskusstvo, 1963), 250. Such rhymed prose as Shvarts's is called *raëshnik*; rhymes, usually paired, occur at the end of lines.

8. Chukovskii, in *My znali Evgeniia Shvartsa*, 29.

9. Ibid., 31.

10. For more on Oleinikov, see A. Dymshits, "Poèt Nikolai Oleinikov," *Problemy i portrety* (Moscow: Sovremennik, 1972), 290–301.

11. George Gibian, *Russia's Lost Literature of the Absurd* (Ithaca, N.Y.: Cornell Univ. Press, 1971), 10, 13.

12. Marshak, "Dve besedy," VII, 586.

13. I. Bakhterev and A. Razumovskii, "O Nikolae Oleinikove," *Den' poèzii* (Leningrad: Sovetskii pisatel', 1964), 154.

14. A. Makedonov, *Nikolai Zabolotskii* (Leningrad: Sovetskii pisatel', 1968), 15.

15. See, for example, Rakhtanov, *Rasskazy po pamiati*, 123; Bakhterev, "Kogda my byli molodymi," 58.

16. "The Oberiu Manifesto," in Gibian, *Russia's Lost Literature*, 195.

17. Andrei M. Turkov, *N. Zabolotskii* (Moscow: Khudozhestvennaia literatura, 1966), 23.

18. Gibian, *Russia's Lost Literature*, 12.

19. According to Camilla Gray, "immediately after the Revolution, some charming children's books, ranking among the first typographical

experiments of modern design and layout were produced by Russian abstract artists, among whom was El Lissitsky." See *The Russian Experiment in Art: 1863–1922* (London: Thames and Hudson, 1962), 189. As late as 1929, Vladimir Tatlin illustrated Kharms's story "Vo pervykh i vo vtorykh" (Gibian, *Russia's Lost Literature*, 24).

20. Gibian, *Russia's Lost Literature*, 9.

21. Ibid., 6, 24.

22. Daniil Kharms, *Igra* (Moscow: Detskii mir, 1962); *Chto èto bylo?* (Moscow: Malysh, 1967); *12 povarov* (Moscow: Malysh, 1972). See also the afterword in *Chto èto bylo?* by N. Khalatov, "Ego zvali—Daniil Kharms," n.p.; and M. Petrovskii, "Vozvrashchenie Daniila Kharmsa" (review of *Chto èto bylo?*), *Novyi mir*, no. 8 (1968): 258–60.

23. Gibian, *Russia's Lost Literature*, 3–4, 10.

24. See, for example, *Kogda ia vyrastu bol'shoi* (Moscow, 1960); *Dozhdik, dozhdik!* (Moscow: Detskii mir, 1962); *Sny* (Moscow, 1966).

25. Evgenii Binevich, " 'Vdokhovennyi mal'chishka,' " *O literature dlia detei*, XVI (Leningrad: Detskaia literatura, 1972), 153.

26. Makedonov, *Zabolotskii*, 10.

27. Zabolotskii, "Aftobiografiia," in *Stikhotvoreniia* (Washington: Inter-Language Literary Associates, 1965), 2.

28. Makedonov, *Zabolotskii*, 15.

29. Zabolotskii, "Aftobiografiia," 2.

30. Evgenii Shvarts, *Rasskaz staroi balalaiki* (Leningrad-Moscow: Gosizdat, 1925), 3.

31. Evgenii Shvarts, *Shariki* (Leningrad: Raduga, 1926), n.p.

32. Evgenii Shvarts, *Voina Petrushki i Stëpki Rastrëpki* (Leningrad: Raduga, 1925), 20.

33. Evgenii Shvarts, *Stop! Pravila ulichnogo dvizheniia znai, kak tablitsu umnozheniia* (Moscow: Molodaia gvardiia), n.p.

34. Evegenii Shvarts, *Vasia Shelaev* (Moscow: Molodaia gvardiia), n.p.

35. Evgenii Shvarts, *Rynok* (Leningrad: Raduga, 1926), n.p.

36. Evgenii Shvarts, *Kto bystrei?* (Moscow: Gosizdat, 1928), n.p.

37. Evgenii Shvarts, *Priatki* (Leningrad: Raduga, 1927), n.p.

38. A good example of Pakhomov's constructivist style are his illustrations to Shvarts's *Lager'* (Leningrad: Gosizdat, 1925). His shift a few years later toward a more conservative style can be seen in his illustrations to Evgenii Shvarts, *Vedro* (Leningrad: Gosizdat, 1929).

39. For Western editions of Kharms's work, see *Izbrannoe*, ed. George Gibian (Wurzburg: Jal-verlag, 1974), and *Sobranie proizvedenii*, ed. Mikhail Meilakh and Vladimir Erl', 2 vols. (Bremen: K-Presse, 1978).

40. Makedonov, *Zabolotskii*, 162.

41. V. Trenin, "O smeshnoi poèzii," *Detskaia literatura*, no. 9 (1939): 23.

42. Kharms, *Teatr* (Moscow: Gosizdat, 1928), n.p.

43. For an insightful discussion of Kharms as a children's writer, see Boris Begak, "Ozornoi talant," *Doshkol' noe vospitanie*, no. 11 (1968): 122–27.

44. *Ot dvukh do piati*, 719.

45. Kharms, *Chto èto bylo?*, n.p.

46. Marshak, "Dve besedy," 586.

47. Kharms, *Chto èto bylo?*

48. Kharms, *Igra,* n. p.

49. Kharms, *Chto èto bylo?*

50. Ibid. The name Toporyshkin that Kharms created is a good example of his verbal imagination. It is a playful hybrid, combining *topor* (ax) and *toropyshkin* (someone in a hurry). Both those concepts in turn are developed in the poem.

51. Khalatov, "Ego zvali—Daniil Kharms."

52. Kharms, *Chto èto bylo?*

53. Ibid.

54. Millar, *The Psychology of Play,* 139–40. Millar's formulation is based on the theory of Jean Piaget.

55. Kharms, *Chto èto bylo?* For a study of his unpublished children's works, see A.A. Aleksandrov, "Materialy D.I. Kharmsa v rukopisnom otdele Pushkinskogo doma," *Ezhegodnik rukopisnogo otdela Pushkinskogo doma na 1978 god* (Leningrad: Nauka, 1980), 64–79.

56. Iurii Vladimirov, "Baraban," quoted by E. Binevich, " 'Vdokhnovennyi mal'chishka,' " 152–53.

57. Vladimirov, *Ninochkiny pokupki* (Leningrad: Krasnaia gazeta, 1928), n. p.

58. Vladimirov, *Orkestr* (Leningrad: Raduga, 1929), n. p.

59. Vladimirov, *Evsei* (Moscow: Gosizdat, 1930), n. p.

60. See "Oberiu Manifesto," in Gibian, *Russia's Lost Literature,* 196.

61. Aleksandr Vvedenskii, *Mnogo zverei* (Leningrad: Gosizdat, 1928), n. p.

62. Vvedenskii, *Leto* (Moscow-Leningrad: Detizdat, 1941).

63. Vvedenskii, *Stikhi* (Moscow-Leningrad: Detizdat, 1940), 3–4.

64. Vvedenskii, *Volodia Ermakov* (Moscow: Detgiz, 1935), 13.

65. For some discussion of this interrelationship, see Makedonov, *Zabolotskii,* 173–78; Inna Rostovtseva, *Nikolai Zabolotskii* (Moscow: Sovetskaia Rossiia, 1976), 26–29; V. Kaverin, "Schast'e talanta," *Vospominaniia o Zabolotskom,* 116–18.

66. E. Putilova, "N.A. Zabolotskii—detiam," *O literature dlia detei,* XVI (Leningrad: Detskaia literatura, 1972), 126–27.

67. Zabolotskii, *Stikhotvoreniia,* 353–54. All subsequent quotations from this volume will be designated by page number in the text.

68. Recently there appeared a well-illustrated edition of *Kak myshi s kotom voevali* (Leningrad: Detskaia literatura, 1980). One hopes there will be more.

## CHAPTER 7. VLADIMIR MAIAKOVSKII AND OTHERS

1. In his excellent book on Maiakovskii, Edward J. Brown does not mention the poetry written for children; see *Mayakovsky: A Poet in the Revo-*

*lution* (Princeton, N.J.: Princeton Univ. Press, 1973). This is in contrast to Clarence Brown, who in his book *Mandelstam* (Cambridge: Cambridge Univ. Press, 1973), at least notes that Mandel'shtam wrote some children's poems, which deserve separate study.

2. "On a Generation that Squandered Its Poets," trans. E.J. Brown, *Major Soviet Writers* (New York: Oxford Univ. Press, 1973), 20–21.

3. *The Symbolic System of Majakovskij* (The Hague: Mouton, 1964), 119.

4. M. Petrovskii, " 'Sdelal Diadia Maiakovskii . . . ,' " *Detskaia literatura 1973* (Moscow: Detskaia literatura, 1973), 24–29.

5. Vasilii Katanian, *Maiakovskii: Literaturnaia khronika* (Moscow: Khudozhestvennaia literatura, 1961), 48.

6. Ibid., 447.

7. Vladimir Maiakovskii, *Polnoe sobranie sochinenii*, II (Moscow: Khudozhestvennaia literatura, 1955), 8. The imagery of this poem suggests possible echoes of Elena Guro's *Nebesnye verbliuzhata* (1914), a work Maiakovskii is said to have praised highly. See N. Khardzhiev, "Zametki o Maiakovskom," *Literaturnoe nasledstvo* 65 (1958): 406.

8. Katanian, *Maiakovskii*, 110.

9. S. Maev, "Maiakovskii i sovetskaia detskaia literatura," *Zvezda*, no. 5 (1952): 152.

10. Katanian, *Maiakovskii*, 192.

11. Ibid., 228.

12. Maiakovskii, *Polnoe sobranie sochinenii*, X, 218, 220. Subsequent quotations from the children's poetry in this volume will be designated simply by page number following the citations.

13. See Ia. A. Satunovskii, "Ritmy schitalki v stikhakh Maiakovskogo," *Russkaia rech'*, no. 4 (Jul.–Aug. 1968): 21–31.

14. E.J. Brown, *Mayakovsky*, 19.

15. Maiakovskii, *Polnoe sobranie sochinenii*, I, 27.

16. Vladimir Leibson, "Zhanrovye i stilisticheskie osobennosti stikhotvorenii Maiakovskogo dlia detei," *Voprosy sovetskoi literatury* (Moscow: Moskovskii gosudarstvennyi pedagogicheskii institut, 1961), 219.

17. He also introduces some neologisms similar to those created by children: *zliunia, shchenik;* others parallel folk usage: *kartoshkin* (*ibid.*, 218). See also Asya Humesky, *Majakovskii and His Neologisms* (New York: Rausen, 1964). Chukovskii remarked upon Maiakovskii's use of *shchen* (from *shchenok*), a common child creation (*Ot dvukh do piati*, 346).

18. Miron Levin, "Maiakovskii i deti," *Detskaia literatura*, no. 4 (1939): 11.

19. Vladimir Azov, "Kotoryi lopnul," *Zhar-ptica*, 43–46. Petrovskii points out that the image of bursting has antecedents in Maiakovskii's own poetry. In "150,000,000" Ivan bursts, creating a pile of Ivans; and in "Rasskaz pro to, kak kuma o Vrangele tokovala bez vsiakogo uma," a woman bursts from overeating. Maiakovskii made real the then-current

slogan "NEP obozhrëtsia, lopnet" (NEP will gorge itself and burst). See "Sdelal Diadia Maiakovskii," 50–53.

20. Tvardovskii, "O poèzii Marshaka," 238.

21. Rakhtanov, *Rasskazy po pamiati*, 61.

22. S.A. Kovalenko, "Primechaniia," in *Polnoe sobranie sochinenii*, X, 370.

23. Petrovskii takes issue with the usual reading of this poem as simply cognitive, finding it playful in a sophisticated manner. In his opinion, Maiakovskii here, as in his adult work, turned current newspaper clichés into visual metaphors, with lighthouse, storm, and ship representing the Communist International, the revolution, and the state. Petrovskii also points out that "Maiak" was one of the poet's youthful nicknames; he was fond of it and used it in his poetry (42–45).

24. Maiakovskii, "Iz besedy s sotrudnikom gazety *Èpokha*," in *Polnoe sobranie sochinenii*, XIII, 234.

25. Katanian, *Maiakovskii*, 487.

26. Leibson, "Zhanrovye osobennosti," 222.

27. Ibid., 225. Unfortunately, this was changed in later editions.

28. Katanian, *Maiakovskii*, 465.

29. Ibid., 230.

30. Ibid., 228.

31. Maev, "Maiakovskii," 152.

32. Two of the more familiar names are that of Elizaveta Polonskaia, the only woman among the Serapion Brothers, and Nikolai Chukovskii.

33. Aleksandr Tvardovskii, "O poèzii Marshaka," 237.

34. This view is also held by Guy de Mallac in *Boris Pasternak: His Life and Art* (Norman: Univ. of Oklahoma Press,) 101.

35. Marina Tsvetaeva, "O novoi russkoi detskoi knige," *Volia Rossii* 5–6 (1931): 554.

36. Boris Pasternak, *Stikhotvoreniia i poèmy* (Moscow-Leningrad: Sovetskii pisatel', 1965), 546. Subsequent quotations from this volume will be designated by page following the citation.

37. de Mallac, *Pasternak*, 108.

38. "Primechaniia," in Pasternak, *Stikhotvoreniia i poèmy*, 700–701.

39. Osip Mandel'stam, "Zamorskie deti," *Vorobei*, no. 5 (1924): 27; "Odeial'naia strana," *Novyi Robinzon*, no. 12 1924): 17.

40. Interview with Nadezhda Mandel'shtam in Moscow, May 1972.

41. Tvardovskii, "O poèzii Marshaka," 238.

42. "Primechaniia," in Osip Mandel'shtam, *Sobranie sochinenii*, I (Washington: Inter-Language Literary Associates, 1967), 543. Subsequent quotations from this volume will be designated by page number following the quotation.

43. For some commentary on Mandel'shtam's relationship with Marshak, see Nadezhda Mandel'shtam, *Vospominaniia* (New York: Chekhov Publishing, 1970), 171.

44. Mandel'shtam, "Detskaia literatura," *Sobranie sochinenii,* III (1969), 50.

45. Mandel'shtam's poem may have been written as a parody of another poem on the same subject, which in turn is clearly imitative of Chukovskii's style. See A. Kholodov, *Chistil'shchik sapog* (Leningrad: Raduga, 1926).

46. Lidiia Chukovskaia notes that Marshak worked hard to improve Mikhalkov's poem when the young poet first brought it to him (*V laboratorii redaktora,* 264).

47. For collections of their children's poetry, see Agniia Barto, *Stikhi detiam v dvukh tomakh* (Moscow: Detskaia literatura, 1966); Sergei Mikhalkov, *Sobranie sochinenii v chetyrëkh tomakh* (Moscow: Khudozhestvennaia literatura, 1963), I–II.

48. Vladimir Prikhod'ko, "Liriky Eleny Blagininoi," *Detskaia literatura,* no. 3 (1969): 31.

49. Cited by Boris Begak, "Prazdnik sveta i tepla," *Doshkol'noe vospitanie,* no. 5 (1973): 31.

### CHAPTER 8. THE LEGACY OF THE 1920S

1. See review by V. Glotser, *Novyi mir,* no. 2 (1963): 285–86.

2. V. Iudin, "Triukh-triukh!" *Krokodil,* 10 Feb. 1963, p. 3.

3. Glotser further developed the interest of Chukovskii and the futurists, collecting children's poetry and art. See "Istoriia odnoi knizhechki," *Doshkol'noe vospitanie,* no. 2 (1972): 119–24.

4. Lev Tokmakov, Viktor Pivovarov, and Il'ia Kabakov, for example, are known for their contemporary style, while Iurii Vasnetsov and Tat'iana Mavrina excel at folk-inspired art.

5. My knowledge of the more recent developments in Russian children's poetry comes from interviews with literary figures in Moscow on four visits between 1972 and 1981.

6. Zakhoder's Russian version has appeared in an American edition: *Vinni-Pukh i vse-vse-vse* (New York: Dutton, 1967).

7. In his introduction Zakhoder reveals the inimitable imagination that gives his writing universal appeal: "'bud' moia volia, ia nazval by knizhku, naprimer, tak: 'Alënka v Voobrazilii'. Ili 'Alia v Udivliandii'. Ili 'Al'ka v Chepukhanii'. Nu uzh, na khudoi konets: 'Aliska v Raschudesii'. No stoilo mne zaiknut'sia ob ètom svoëm zhelanii, kak vse nachinali na menia strashno krichat', chtoby ia ne smel. I ia ne posmel!" *Prikliucheniia Alisy v Strane chudes,* 4. One wonders whether Zakhoder avoided the name Ania because Vladimir Nabokov's 1923 version, unavailable in the Soviet Union, is entitled *Ania v strane chudes.* (The latter is available in a reprint edition—New York: Dover, 1976).

8. Prikhod'ko, "O sovremennom skazochnike i davnei traditsii," *Doshkol'noe vospitanie,* no. 8 (1977): 47–50.

9. Prikhod'ko, " 'Ne BYL, a ostalsia!' " *Doshkol'noe vospitanie*, no. 9 (1977): 53.

10. Boris Zakhoder, *Tovarishcham detiam* (Moscow: Detskaia literatura, 1966), 195.

11. Ibid., 33–41.

12. Ibid., 77.

13. Ibid., 164.

14. Ibid., 204.

15. Chukovskii, *Sobranie sochinenii*, I, 306.

16. Mirra Ginsburg, *Oookie-Spookie* (New York: Crown, 1979), n. p.

17. His works have been reviewed in adult periodicals; see, for example, B. Sarnov, "Dlia malen'kikh i bol'shikh," *Novyi mir*, no. 12 (1957): 195–97; A. Asarkan, "Mir Vinni-Pukha," ibid., no. 8 (1961): 269–71; V. Shitova, "Tovarishcham detiam," ibid., no. 1 (1963): 283.

18. Zakhoder, *Tovarishcham detiam*, 169.

19. Prikhod'ko, " 'Ne BYL, a ostalsia!," 56.

20. Zakhoder, *Schitaliia* (Moscow: Malysh, 1979), n. p.

21. Prikhod'ko, "Dom poèta," *Detskaia literatura 1975* (Moscow: Detskaia literatura, 1975), 111.

22. Ibid., 113.

23. Èmma Moshkovskaia, *Diadia Shar* (Moscow: Detskii mir, 1962), n. p.

24. Moshkovskaia, *Ziablik sogrelsia* (Moscow: Malysh, 1967), n. p.

25. Prikhod'ko, "Dom poèta," 117.

26. Moshkovskaia, *Dom postroili dlia vsekh* (Moscow: Detskaia literatura, 1970), 52.

27. Moshkovskaia, *Ziablik sogrelsia*.

28. Ibid.

29. Moshkovskaia, *Diadia Shar*.

30. Moshkovskaia, *Zhil-byl na svete seren'kii kozlik* (Moscow: Detskaia literatura, 1971), 3.

31. Ibid., 5.

32. Ibid., 31–32.

33. Ibid., 64.

34. Cited in Prikhod'ko, "Dom poèta," 113.

35. Chukovskii, "Ob ètikh skazkax," *Sobranie sochinenii* I, 171.

36. Genrikh Sapgir, *Schitalki* (Moscow: Malysh, 1965), n. p.

37. Ibid.

38. Sapgir, *Zdravstvui* (Moscow: Malysh, 1965), 16.

39. Sapgir, *Pro Fomu i pro Erëmu* (Moscow: Detskaia literatura, 1971), 19.

40. Sapgir, *Zdravstvui*, 22–25.

41. Sapgir, *Lesa-chudesa* (Moscow: Detskaia literatura, 1967), 19–28.

42. This poem might be read as a satire of the current regime; apparently the censor chose to view it innocently.

43. Tokmakova, autobiographical sketch, *Detskaia literatura*, no. 3 (1971): 54.

44. Tokmakova, *Zërnyshko* (Moscow: Detskaia literatura, 1964), 6.

45. Tokmakova, *Gde spit rybka?* (Moscow: Detgiz, 1963), 8–9.

46. Ibid., 16.

47. Tokmakova, *Zërnyshko*, 10.

48. Tokmakova, *Gde spit rybka?*, 5.

49. Sef, *Shagaiut velikany* (Moscow: Detgiz, 1963), illustrated by Tokmakov. Pivovarov illustrated *Neobychnyi peshekhod* (1965) and *Esli ty ne verish'* (1968), both published by Detskaia literatura.

50. Sef, *Shagaiut velikany*, n. p.

51. Sef, *Esli ty ne verish'*, 1.

52. Sef, *Shagaiut velikany*.

53. Tokmakova, "Ty eshchë ne videl chuda?" *Doshkol'noe vospitanie*, no. 5 (1968): 126.

54. Sef, *Eslie ty ne verish'*, 3–4.

55. Ibid., 9.

56. Boris Begak, "Dobroe utro," *Doshkol'noe vospitanie*, no. 10 (1973): 58.

57. Berestov, *Zhavoronok* (Moscow: Detskaia literatura, 1978), 24.

58. Ibid., 76.

59. Berestov, *Zloe utro* (Moscow: Malysh, 1968), n. p.

60. Berestov, *Zhavoronok*, 80.

61. Ibid., 85.

62. Among their more recent works are: Uspenskii, *Udivetel'noe delo* (Moscow: Malysh, 1976); Levin, *Koshki-myshki* (Moscow: Malysh, 1978); Pivovarova, *Dva ochen' smelykh krolika* (Moscow: Sovetskaia Rossiia, 1975); Morits, *Poprygat'-poigrat'* (Moscow: Malysh, 1978).

63. Since 1967, when the last page of *Literaturnaia gazeta* was first dedicated to humor, there has been an occasional column entitled "detskaia komnata" (the children's room), where such poets as È. Moshkovskaia, R. Sef, and V. Levin have published satirical poems in the manner of children's verse.

# SELECTED BIBLIOGRAPHY

$M$UCH OF THE MATERIAL used for this book is not easily available, if at all, in this country. For this and other reasons, the bibliography includes only the most fundamentally important works.

## 1. BIBLIOGRAPHIES

*Sovetskie detskie pisateli: Bio-bibliograficheskii slovar' (1917–1957)*. Moscow: Detskaia literatura, 1961.

Startsev, Ivan. *Detskaia literatura (Bibliografiia, 1961–1963)*. Moscow: Detskaia literatura, 1966.

———. *Detskaia literatura (Bibliografiia, 1964–1966)*. Moscow: Detskaia literatura, 1970.

———. *Voprosy detskoi literatury i detskogo chteniia, 1918–1961 (Bibliograficheskii ukazatel' knig i statei po istorii, teorii i kritike)*. Moscow: Detskaia literatura, 1961.

———. *Voprosy detskoi literatury i detskogo chteniia, 1962–1965*. Moscow: Detskaia literatura, 1967.

## 2. THE MAJOR POETS

### Sasha Chërnyi
### 1880–1932

*Stikhotvoreniia*. Leningrad: Sovetskii pisatel', 1960.

Chukovskii, Kornei. "Sasha Chërnyi," *Sobranie sochinenii*, II. Moscow: Khudozhestvennaia literatura, 1965.

### Kornei Ivanovich Chukovskii
### (1882–1969)

*Sobranie sochinenii v shesti tomakh*. Moscow: Khudozhestvennaia literatura, 1965–69.

*From Two to Five,* trans. and ed. Miriam Morton. Rev. ed. Berkeley: University of California Press, 1968.

*The Silver Crest, My Russian Boyhood,* trans. Beatrice Stillman. New York: Holt, Rinehart and Winston, 1976.

Leighton, Lauren G. "Homage to Kornei Chukovsky." *Russian Review* 31 (1972): 38–48.

Petrovskii, Miron. *Kniga o Kornee Chukovskom.* Moscow: Sovetskii pisatel', 1966.

*Vospominaniia o Kornee Chukovskom,* ed. K.I. Lozovskaia, Z.S. Papernyi, E.Ts. Chukovskaia. Moscow: Sovetskii pisatel', 1977.

*Zhizn' i tvorchestvo Korneia Chukovskogo,* ed. Valentin Berestov. Moscow: Detskaia literatura, 1978.

## Samuil Iakovlevich Marshak
### (1887–1964)

*Sobranie sochinenii v vos'mi tomakh.* Moscow: Khudozhestvennaia literatura, 1968–72.

*At Life's Beginning: Some Pages of Reminiscences,* trans. Katherine Hunter Blair. London: Gollancz, 1964.

Galanov, Boris. *S.Ia. Marshak, Zhizn' i tvorchestvo.* 4th ed. Moscow: Detskaia literatura, 1965.

*"Ia dumal, chuvstvoval, ia zhil . . ." (Vospominaniia o S. Ia. Marshake),* ed. B.E. Galanov, I.S. Marshak, and Z.S. Papernyi. Moscow: Sovetskii pisatel', 1971.

Sarnov, Benedikt. *Samuil Marshak (Ocherk poèzii).* Moscow: Khudozhestvennaia literatura, 1968.

*Zhizn' i tvorchestvo Marshaka (Marshak i detskaia literatura),* ed. B. Galanov, I. Marshak, M. Petrovskii. Moscow: Detskaia literatura, 1975.

## Vladimir Vladimirovich Maiakovskii
### (1893–1930)

*Polnoe sobranie sochinenii v trinadtsati tomakh.* Moscow: Khudozhestvennaia literatura, 1955–61.

Petrovskii, Miron. " 'Sdelal Diadia Maiakovskii . . . .' " In *Detskaia literatura 1973.* Moscow: Detskaia literatura, 1973.

*Daniil Kharms*
(1905–1942)

*Chto èto bylo?* Moscow: Malysh, 1967.

*Igra.* Moscow: Detskii mir, 1962.

*12 povarov.* Moscow: Malysh, 1972.

Bakhterev, Igor'. "Kogda my byli molodymi," In *Vospominaniia o Zabolotskom,* ed. E.V. Zabolotskaia and A.V. Makedonov. Moscow: Sovetskii pisatel', 1977.

### 3. WORKS ON CHILDREN'S LITERATURE
### AND FOLKLORE (IN RUSSIAN)

Anikin, V.P. *Russkie narodnye poslovitsy, pogovorki, zagadki i detskii fol'klor.* Moscow: Uchpedgiz, 1957.

*Belinskii, Chernyshevskii, Dobroliubov o detskoi literature i detskom chtenii,* ed. S. Sillegodskii. Moscow: Detgiz, 1954.

Chekhov, Nikolai. *Detskaia literatura.* Moscow: Pol'za, 1909.

Gor'kii, Maksim. *O detskoi literature.* Moscow: Detskaia literatura, 1968.

Ivich, Aleksandr. *Vospitanie pokolenii (O sovetskoi literature dlia detei).* 4th ed. Moscow: Detskaia literatura, 1969.

Kapitsa, Ol'ga. *Detskii fol'klor.* Leningrad: Priboi, 1928.

*Materialy po istorii russkoi detskoi literatury (1750–1855),* ed. A.K. Pokrovskaia and N.V. Chekhov. 2 vols. Moscow: Institut metodov vneshkol'noi raboty otdel detskogo chteniia, 1927–1929.

Rakhtanov, Isai. *Rasskazy po pamiati.* Moscow: Detskaia literatura, 1971.

Rassadin, Stanislav. *Tak nachinaiut zhit' stikhom (Kniga o poèzii dlia detei).* Moscow: Detskaia literatura, 1967.

*Russkaia detskaia literatura,* ed. F.I. Setin. Moscow: Prosveshchenie, 1972.

Shklovskii, Viktor. *Staroe i novoe (Kniga statei o detskoi literature).* Moscow: Detskaia literatura, 1966.

Smirnova, Vera. *O detiakh i dlia detei.* Rev. ed. Moscow: Detskaia literatura, 1967.

*Sovetskaia detskaia literatura,* ed. V.D. Razova. Moscow: Prosveshchenie, 1978.

*Sovetskaia detskaia literatura (Sbornik statei),* ed. V.I. Bochkareva, S.T. Liubimova, I.M. Mikhailova. Moscow: Gosuchpedizat, 1958.

Vinogradov, Georgii. *Russkii detskii fol'klor.* Irkutsk: Irkutskaia sektsiia nauchnykh rabotnikov, 1930.

## 4. ADDITIONAL WORKS OF SPECIAL INTEREST
### (IN ENGLISH)

Ariès, Philippe. *Centuries of Childhood: A Social History of Family Life,* trans. Robert Baldick. New York: Vintage, 1962.

Bettelheim, Bruno. *The Uses of Enchantment: The Meaning and Importance of Fairy Tales.* New York: Vintage, 1977.

Garvey, Catherine. *Play.* Cambridge: Harvard Univ. Press, 1977.

Hazard, Paul. *Books, Children and Men,* trans. Marguerite Mitchell. Boston: Horn Book, 1944.

Holt, John. *How Children Learn.* New York: Pitman, 1967.

Hurlimann, Bettina. *Three Centuries of Children's Books in Europe,* trans, and ed. Brian W. Alderson. Cleveland: World, 1968.

Luthi, Max. *Once upon a Time: On the Nature of Fairy Tales,* trans. Lee Chadeayne and Paul Gottwald. Bloomington: Indiana Univ. Press, 1970.

Millar, Susanna. *The Psychology of Play.* Baltimore: Penguin, 1968.

Morton, Miriam. *A Harvest of Russian Children's Literature.* Berkeley: Univ. of California Press, 1970.

Opie, Iona and Peter. *The Lore and Language of Schoolchildren.* Oxford: Claredon Press, 1951.

————. *The Oxford Book of Children's Verse.* New York: Oxford Univ. Press, 1973.

————. *The Oxford Dictionary of Nursery Rhymes.* Oxford: Clarendon Press, 1952.

————. *The Oxford Nursery Rhyme Book.* London: Oxford Univ. Press, 1955.

Piaget, Jean. *The Language and Thought of the Child,* trans. Marjorie Gabain. New York: World, 1955.

————. *Play, Dreams and Imitation in Childhood,* trans. C. Gattegno and F.M. Hodgson. New York: Norton, 1962.

————, and Barbel Inhelder. *The Psychology of the Child,* trans. Helen Weaver. New York: Basic Books, 1969.

Sale, Roger. *Fairy Tales and After: From Snow White to E.B. White.* Cambridge, Mass.: Harvard Univ. Press, 1978.

Townsend, John Rowe. *Written for Children.* Harmondsworth, England: Penguin, 1965.

# INDEX

Since the names of Chukovskii, Kharms, Maiakovskii, and Marshak occur repeatedly throughout the book, this index only lists references to them in connection with specific topics and works.

239

*Russian Poetry for Children* was composed on the Variable Input Phototypesetter in ten point Trump Medieval with two-point line spacing. The book was designed by Frank O. Williams, composed by Computer Composition, Inc., printed offset by Thomson-Shore, Inc., and bound by John H. Dekker & Sons. The paper on which the book is printed carries acid-free characteristics and is designed for an effective life of at least three hundred years.

THE UNIVERSITY OF TENNESSEE PRESS : KNOXVILLE